Capitol Hill Library

JUL 14 2018

422/18

D0699393

# RISOTTO
# &
# BEYOND

# RISOTTO & BEYOND

100 Authentic Italian Rice Recipes for
Antipasti, Soups, Salads, Risotti,
One-Dish Meals, and Desserts

**JOHN COLETTA**

WITH NANCY ROSS RYAN AND MONICA KASS ROGERS

Photographs by Stephen DeVries

*RIZZOLI*
NEW YORK

New York · Paris · London · Milan

First published in the United States of America in 2018
by Rizzoli International Publications, Inc.
300 Park Avenue South
New York, NY 10010
www.rizzoliusa.com

© 2018 John Coletta

Photographs by Stephen DeVries
Photographs on pages 8, 10, 11, 13 (both), 23, 65, 116,
125, 205 by Monica Kass Rogers
Prop and Food Styling by Nathan Carrabba

Design by Jan Derevjanik

All rights reserved. No part of this publication may be
reproduced, stored in a retrieval system, or transmitted
in any form or by any means, electronic, mechanical,
photocopying, recording, or otherwise, without prior
consent of the publishers.

2018 2019 2020 2021 / 10 9 8 7 6 5 4 3 2 1

Distributed in the U.S. trade by Random House,
New York

Printed in China

ISBN-13: 978-0-8478-6236-8

Library of Congress Catalog Control Number:
201795320

# CONTENTS

---

# Acknowledgments

Without being aware of it, we all leave traces of ourselves on those who are close to us, through events, encounters, deeds, words, smiles, and contact. How can one remember to thank everyone? It is impossible.

This being said, I would like to dedicate these thoughts to the people who have accompanied me along the journey, encouraging me to evolve and helping me to grow. I acknowledge them here in chronological order.

First and foremost comes my mother, Lucia Bove, from whom I learned the sense of equilibrium and good taste.

My late father, John Coletta, who more than anyone else contributed to my cultural growth culminating in the contents of my work. My aunt, Vincenzina Bove, for whom I would need another book to document her abilities.

Then there is my wife Jenifer, who has been—and remains—my life companion. After her are our children, Olivia Foy and Christian Bernard, who, despite the too-little time I have dedicated to them, have with their growth, brought qualities to bear that have increasingly helped me to understand what is within me.

My partners at Quartino: Steve Lombardo, Hugo Ralli, Larry Shane, Stephen Lombardo III, Gregg Horan, Bob Kanzler, John Colletti, Michael Lombardo, Liz Stark, Mathew Graham, and Adam Zolno. A brilliant team of focused professionals with uncompromising standards of excellence.

I also want to recognize past and present customer-obsessed Quartino associates for their commitment, dedication, and invaluable contributions.

My wonderful friends Piero and Maria Nava Rondolino of Acquerello, who provided a platform for the realization of this book. They have revolutionized Italian rice production in Italy, along with transforming Italian excellence throughout the world.

This book is written as a tribute to the people of Italy, who have unselfishly given the world a unique perspective on food. A contribution that continues to be emulated on all socioeconomic levels. *Un abbrachio forte.*

Lisa Ekus, my dearest friend and literary agent extraordinaire, who connected all the dots, held everyone accountable, and guided this book to market in a highly professional manner. Thank you.

I was fortunate to have not one, but two top editors to work with at Rizzoli. Christopher Steighner was the initial Rizzoli editor who captured the spirit of this book and painstakingly turned over the project to Tricia Levi with a sense of purpose and focus.

I also want to recognize Nancy Ross Ryan, who meticulously uncovered and displayed

the essence of my cooking, the varying species of Italian rice, and seamlessly embraced my enthusiasm. May you rest in peace.

Monica Kass Rogers inherited the beginnings of a manuscript left behind by Nancy Ross Ryan, skillfully researched the essays, and elaborated, tested, and transformed my vision to a reality. Bravo!!

Stephen DeVries captured images of Italian rice and my cooking in ways that I have never thought possible. You are truly an artist.

Nathan Carrabba, who spent five mornings, five days, and five evenings at Quartino, in search of the perfect mouthwatering presentations. A humble genius.

I cannot, however, close before acknowledging the contribution of Alessandro Bellini, since it was he, who, having believed in this project from the start, encouraged me to write this book.

*Warmest culinary regards,*
*John Coletta*

# The Italian Way with Rice

**Drive across the Po Valley in September and you feel like you are** floating on gold. It's a saffron sensaround of ripening rice. Bright yellow grasses, bowed under the weight of the fat grains, sway, their tops level with your feet. Beneath you, rooted two to three feet below road grade, are the aquaculture rice plots that make the valley so famous.

Italy is the largest producer of rice in Europe, and 90 percent of that rice is grown here. Almost all of it is some type of *japonica*—one of the two major eco-geographical rice races—rounder-grained and creamier in texture than the other, *indica*. And there is an incredible diversity of Italian rice, two hundred kinds to be exact.

At least a dozen Italian rices are well known in Italy, but few people know about them elsewhere. In America, where we consume less than 1 percent of Italy's rice exports each year, diners may have tried Arborio and Carnaroli, but hardly anybody knows balilla from Baldo. And when it comes to preparing Italian rice, most have never ventured beyond risotto.

With this book, I hope to change that: Rice is an overlooked grain that gets very little credit. It's the easiest to digest and a great source of energy, while being gluten free, fat free, and without cholesterol or sodium. It's also incredibly versatile—one of the few healthful staples that can be used every day, in every meal category, from starters, soups, and salads to main courses and sweets.

Gathering and creating these recipes has been an organic process, starting with the Italian rice snacks and soups my mother made when I was growing up in Queens. My parents were from Italy, Dad from Rome and Mom from Molise, so my visits there with relatives, and professionally as a chef, have been frequent. I learned simple basic rice dishes at home and then, one by one, collected so many more.

I watched women who in their youth were *le mondine* (rice workers) make *panissa*, a hearty rice, bean, and sausage stew, and learned to make fried rice snacks from friends in Sicily. Seppi Renggli, the esteemed executive chef at the Four Seasons for many years, taught me to work with Black Venus rice and make elaborate timbales. Each time I returned home, I experimented with Italian rice in many more dishes on my own.

One thing I observed? Just as people in the States can be fiercely loyal to local ingredients, such is the case with Italians and their rice. Ask chef Christian Costardi which Italian rice he is most excited about using at his restaurant in Vercelli, and he'll tell you about his favorite local rice farmer who specially mills rice to create a version of Carnaroli that is exclusive to the Costardi brothers. Ask Giancarlo Perbellini, chef at one of Italy's most celebrated restaurants, Casa Perbellini, the same question in Verona, and it's all about Vialone Nano.

But no matter which region you visit, centuries-old Italian rice traditions and cultural habits run deep. I've done my best to honor the heritage of the dishes collected in this book, while at the same time adding some fresh spins on the classics. I've kept contemporary health concerns and tastes in mind to create recipes for dishes that aren't typically part of Italian meals—main-course creations, for example, that use risotto as a filling.

The six chapters in this book will take you from appetizers through desserts. There are familiar comforts, such as *arancini*, the little deep-fried rice ball antipasti, season-specific soups, surprising rice salads and one-dish meals, and a generous supply of *dolci*. Prepare one rice dish from this cookbook each week and you'll have enough for two years' worth of rice discoveries.

*Benvenuto* to the Italian way with rice!

# The History of Italian Rice

The story of Italian rice is a rich one, with its share of intrigue, uncertain parentage, famous people, social uprisings—even a smuggling Jesuit priest. But few outside of Italy know this story, or that the country is the largest rice grower in Europe, producing 1.5 million tons annually. So how did it become so?

Archaeologists and historians place the beginnings of rice domestication in Asia at eight to ten thousand years ago. Rice is a grass, belonging to the *Oryza* genus, which includes twenty wild and two cultivated rice species. Of the cultivated species, *Oryza sativa, L.*, is the mother of *japonica* and *indica* rices, the primary ecotypes grown throughout the world—*indica* in tropical regions and *japonica* in temperate climes such as those in Italy.

Rice's move westward started with Persian King Darius, who brought rice to Mesopotamia at the end of the sixth century BC. Then came Alexander the Great, who introduced rice to the Romans during his campaigns to India two centuries later. But historians aren't as clear on the details of rice's establishment in Europe. Researchers suggest that rice traveled from Persia to Egypt between the fourth and first centuries BC and then charted a route from Greece or Egypt to Spain before heading to Sicily in the eighth century AD. Others point to research that suggests rice hopped from Persia to Spain in the eighth century, traveling with the Spaniards to Italy between the thirteenth and sixteenth centuries.

Initially, rice was a luxury, used medicinally to soothe stomachs and later in sweets.

The Arabs are credited with trying to cultivate it in southern Italy. But the earliest *documented* rice cultivation in Italy dates back to 1468, in the wetlands of Tuscany near Pisa. At about the same time, rice started spreading throughout the well-watered regions of the Po River basin (Piedmont, Lombardy, Veneto, and Romagna) where 90 percent of Italy's rice is still grown today.

In about 1400, the Sforzas, lords of Milan, started reclaiming the wetlands. With advice from Leonardo da Vinci, who dedicated much of his genius to water studies (and also served

as Milan's war, arms, and engineering consultant for twenty years), the Sforzas started building large canals to help with transportation, irrigation, and flood control. These also captured the waters melting from the surrounding Alps (the glaciers of the Valle d'Aosta and Piedmont) during warm weather, and better dispersed the waters of the wetlands. The Sforzas' early experiments with the cultivation of rice showed that rice had an incredible yield compared with other types of grain. Still reeling from the ravages of the Black Death, or bubonic plague, which devastated Italy beginning in 1348, the country needed a ready solution for feeding and restoring a depleted population. In 1475, Galeazzo Maria Sforza sent a sack of rice to the Duke d'Este of Ferrara, promising that, if planted, it would yield twelve-fold. His promise delivered and rice paddies spread across the Po Valley.

For four hundred years, Nostrale—a *japonica* rice—was the only rice grown in Italy. But Nostrale was prone to disease and crops suffered. This is where the smuggling priest enters the story. On December 15, 1839, Jesuit Father Calleri, a missionary in Tong-Tao, China, secreted a parcel of forty-three varieties of Philippine rice to Italy. No one knows why Calleri sent Philippine rather than Chinese rice, but while many of the seeds he smuggled weren't suitable for Italy's climate, some did flower and proved to thrive better than the rices Italy already had. To this day, plant geneticists are conducting research to decipher the smuggled rices' genetic origins. But despite the uncertain parentage, experiments breeding those rices, plus others introduced from China

and Japan in the early nineteenth century, led to the development of the Italian rices that are grown today.

A big boost in Italy's rice production came in 1853, when Camillo Benso, conti di Cavour, rallied Vercellese farmers together to further improve on Da Vinci's canals, constructing the famed Cavour Canal irrigation system that draws water from five different rivers. But despite the rich soil and abundance of water, growing rice in Italy is climatically challenging, needing to fit within a 180-day cycle. Until the 1950s, and the beginning of farm mechanization, more than two hundred thousand workers traveled to the valley each season to make this happen. Men maintained the canals and plowed the fields with oxen. But the worst jobs fell to the women: spreading manure, and planting and weeding the rice, up to their knees in the watery fields for eight to twelve hours a day. In Italian, the phrase "to weed" is *mondare* and these women became known as *le mondine*. As working conditions worsened, *le mondine*, backed by their male counterparts, rose up to protest in 1906, striking for better treatment. Their efforts established the country's eight-hour workday, making them the first heroines of Italian women's rights.

Today, Italy's rice production is mechanized, but competition from imported rices and other challenges have reduced the number of working rice farms by 50 percent over the last twenty-five years. Those farms that remain are doing their best to preserve the customs, traditions, and quality of Italian rice, a cultural treasure.

# Varieties of Italian Rice

One of my pet peeves? Finding "risotto rice" listed in a recipe as if it were an actual variety. That's about the same as looking up a recipe for a standing rib roast and finding "red meat" specified as the main ingredient. The truth is, there are two hundred rice varieties registered in the Italian catalog of agricultural plant species. Of the seventy currently grown, at least a half dozen are great for making risotto, and many more work well in other rice dishes, soups, and salads. For the sake of consistency, quality, and availability, I recommend using *superfino* rices for most of the recipes in this book. But once you've tried those, this glossary will help you branch out to try more. If you don't know your Balilla from your Roma, here are helpful facts on some popular Italian rices to get you started. You can find most of them at Italian specialty stores or online through eataly.com.

By law, Italian rices are classified in groups based on the length of the grain in relationship to its width. (All *japonica* rices are barrel shaped.)

- *Comune* or *originario* rices have a small, round grain.

- *Semifino* rices have a medium-length, rounded grain.

- *Fino* rices have a medium to long grain, with an oval shape that is tapered at the ends.

- *Superfino* rices are the largest of the four groups, with a long grain and the fattest kernel.

All rice has two molecules that make up the starch content: amylopectin and amylose, which are arranged in stratified layers. Amylopectin is released during the cooking process and is responsible for *japonica* rice's characteristic creaminess. Amylose, on the other hand, stays put, giving rice its "bite" and texture. How much of each kind of starch molecule is contained in a particular rice determines its best use in recipes. More amylopectin makes for a creamier finished dish; more amylose, a firmer texture. For most dishes, you'll want a good balance between the two.

For best overall results and greater consistency from recipe to recipe throughout this book, I've recommended that you choose a *superfino* rice. But feel free to try semifino, *fino*, or *comune* rices to make the appetizer, salad, soup, and dessert recipes. Risottos, however, should be made with *superfino* rices, or Vialone Nano, a *semifino* rice.

**COMUNE OR ORIGINARIO:** Used for everyday cooking, in soups or desserts.

**Balilla:** The cheapest and most basic rice, Balilla is a short, round *comune* rice that cooks quickly but lacks the structure needed in a risotto dish. Other varieties of *comune* rice are Centauro, Cripto, Rubino, and Selenia.

**SEMIFINO:** Used for soups, croquettes, and rice "cakes" and—in the case of Vialone Nano—risotto.

**Maratelli:** Another popular *semifino* in Italy, Maratelli has a very high starch content and is a very soft rice.

**Rosa Marchetti:** Medium length with rounded grains, Rosa Marchetti is a good soup rice, but can also be used as an alternative to *superfino* rices for making risotto.

**Vialone Nano:** While *superfino* rices are usually the best choices for risottos, Vialone Nano is an old *semifino* Italian rice that has long been the country's choice for seafood risottos. Medium grained and round with good absorption, this rice is especially popular in the Veronese lowlands of the Veneto.

**FINO:** Used for timbales, rice balls, rice-cake appetizers, and molded rice salads.

**Sant'Andrea:** The stickiest rice on this list, Sant'Andrea is also soft in texture.

**SUPERFINO:** Used for rice salads and risottos.

**Arborio:** The most readily available and least-expensive *superfino* rice outside of Italy, Arborio is the classic go-to for risotto preparation. Arborio can absorb as much as five times its weight in liquid without losing shape.

**Baldo:** A more recent development, bred from Arborio rice, Baldo is one of the top ten rices eaten in Italy. It cooks faster than Carnaroli or Arborio, and maintains its firmness and bite.

**Carnaroli:** First bred in 1945 and still produced from the same stock, Carnaroli has been called "the king of Italian rices." It is preferred by chefs for use in risottos because of its large shape and ability to retain good texture without stickiness. At the same time, it lends a superior silky creaminess to the finished dish.

**Roma:** Another of Italy's most popular rices, Roma is also one of Italy's oldest rices. It has long, dense grains with good absorption.

# Recipe Guidelines & Equipment

In order to achieve the most authentic (and delicious) results, follow these basic guidelines when preparing the recipes in this book:

- All fruits and vegetables (except mushrooms) should be peeled, cored, seeded, and trimmed, unless skin-on is noted.

- All hard grating cheese is finely grated, unless shaved cheese or curls are noted.

- All canned tomato products are Italian. Carmelina brand is a good choice.

- All herbs are fresh.

- All olive oil is Italian DOP Extra Virgin. (For a definition of DOP, see page 22.)

- All rice must be an Italian varietal.

**CHOOSING BROTH AND STOCK:** Homemade vegetable, poultry, meat, and fish broths and stocks are preferred (for recipes, see pages 66, 101, 117, 153, 158). Good-quality, low-sodium store-bought versions and high-quality concentrates reconstituted at *half strength* are suitable. Better Than Bouillon or imported Italian organic bouillon cubes can be used if none of the above are available.

**COOKING EQUIPMENT:** Choosing the right vessels can make a world of difference in the finished quality of your risottos and soups. Size and materials matter. For simmering risotto broth, choose a 3½- or 4-quart saucepan or pot. For cooking the risotto, choose a pan deep enough to allow for stirring, but not too deep to prevent evaporation. A heavy-gauge sauté pan or skillet 10 inches in diameter and at least 3 to 4 inches deep is perfect. Pans can be made of copper-clad stainless steel, multi-ply stainless steel, or enamel-coated cast iron. Use a sturdy wooden risotto spoon (birch is best because it doesn't warp). Unlike other wooden cooking spoons, risotto spoons are made with a hole in the center to let the rice flow through.

**SOUPS:** You'll need a large 6-quart stockpot. Look for straight sides, tight-fitting lids, and heavy-gauge construction with a heavy (thick) bottom and nonreactive material. One helpful note here: A pot's thickness is measured either in mils or gauge—which can be a little confusing. Just know that the *higher* the mils, the thicker the pot (1 mil = 1/1,000th of an inch). But the *lower* the gauge, the thicker the pot (10 gauge is thicker than 22 gauge). Sturdy construction is also good: Look for pots with handles that are riveted on rather than welded or screwed in place. As far as materials go, while stainless steel doesn't react with acidic ingredients, it's a poor conductor of heat. For this reason, look for a pot that has a *multi-ply* construction: a disc of conductive metal at the bottom layered with a stainless steel interior. Or choose a copper-clad pot that is lined with stainless steel. (Copper is an excellent conductor of heat.)

DEEP-FRYING: Choose a high-smoke-point oil such as safflower, rice bran, soybean, or canola. The oil can be saved and reused for deep-frying multiple times. I prefer to use a small (3- or 4-quart-capacity) deep fryer. It maintains a steady temperature and has built-in safety features lacking in an open pot filled with oil. If you don't own a deep fryer and must use an open pot, do not overfill it—leave at least three inches of space between the top of the oil and the top of the pot.

GRATING CHEESE: Because the volume of grated cheese is subject to wide variations, depending on how finely or coarsely the cheese is grated or how much the grated cheese has settled in the measuring cup, I recommend weighing the cheese before you grate it. That way, no matter how it is grated or packed, the amount is always the same. I prefer to finely grate rather than coarsely shred hard cheeses because they meld more easily with other ingredients in a dish that way. Finely grate by hand, or use the fine-grating attachment/disc on a stand mixer or food processor. Handheld or freestanding electric graters with fine-grating drums also grate quickly and efficiently.

# An Italian Pantry

Each of the world's major cuisines incorporates special ingredients with unique textures and flavors. Italian cuisine is no exception. A short primer of some essential items includes:

**ANCHOVIES (*ACCIUGA*):** True anchovies are found only in the Mediterranean and in southern European waters. Canned in olive oil or salted, these pack powerful flavor.

**ASIAGO:** This cheese from the Veneto region is made from partly skimmed cow's milk and comes in three age-related forms. Aged less than six months, it is a mild, pale dessert cheese. Aged six months, *asiago da taglio* is stronger and saltier but can still be eaten as a table cheese. Aged twelve months or more, *stravecchio* is grainy, sharp, and suitable for grating and cooking.

***BACCALÀ* (SALTED DRIED COD):** Widely used in a variety of dishes, salt cod must be soaked for at least twenty-four hours before using. Properly soaked, its flavor is sweet, not fishy. If not available locally, it can be ordered online.

**BORLOTTI (CRANBERRY) BEANS:** Borlotti is a variety of cranberry bean bred in Italy that is used fresh and dried. Fresh borlotti beans are available in some markets in summer and fall.

**BOTTARGA (*BOTARGA*):** Cured roe of mullet or tuna. The roe sacs are salted, pressed, formed, and sun-dried to be grated, ground, or sliced to season pasta or risotto, or can be spread on bread.

**BRESAOLA:** High-quality versions of the Italian PGI version of this salted, air-dried, aged beef are produced in Lombardy and, at this writing, not exported. However, high-quality Latin American versions are available. Sliced paper thin and served as antipasto, *bresaola* is also sometimes dressed and served with arugula as a salad.

**CASTELMAGNO CHEESE:** Known since 1277, this semi-hard, half-fat cow's milk cheese with blue-green veins from Piedmont is eaten on its own and also used extensively in cooking.

**CUTTLEFISH (*SEPPIE*):** Larger than squid but related to them, ten-tentacle cuttlefish require tenderizing before cooking. They are also a source of ink.

**FIOR DI LATTE (*SEE* MOZZARELLA)**

**FONTINA:** Only cheese from Val d'Aosta in the Italian Alps is genuine fontina. Made from rich Valdostana cow's milk, it is 45 percent fat, mild, nutty, and creamy. It is eaten on its own or used in place of mozzarella because it melts smoothly.

**GORGONZOLA:** Soft, blue-veined, full-fat cow's milk cheese originally made in the first century in the town of Gorgonzola, Lombardy, it is now produced in Lombardy and Piedmont. Young Gorgonzola dolce (sweet) is mild; aged Gorgonzola piccante (spicy) is strong; however, cooking mellows the flavor so that Gorgonzola does not overwhelm even delicate dishes.

**GRANA PADANO:** A hard, part-skim, cow's milk cheese from the Po River Valley that's made like Parmigiano Reggiano but with milk from different regions. It is aged nine to sixteen months, over sixteen months, and, for the the reserve variety, over twenty months. Like Parmigiano, it's a good grating cheese.

**GUANCIALE:** Cured from the pork jowl (or cheek, *guancia*) with salt, pepper, chili, and sugar, it is hung for one month then aged an additional month. Guanciale can be used in place of pancetta to flavor a variety of cooked dishes.

**LARDO:** Very fatty pig's back bacon cured with salt, pepper, rosemary, and garlic. Lardo can be thinly sliced for antipasto, but more often it's used in cooking.

**MASCARPONE:** Rindless, rich (90 percent fat), soft cow's milk cheese from Lombardy lends its delicate, slightly tangy flavor and velvety texture to cooked sweet and savory dishes, from tiramisù and ice cream to risotto and pasta.

**MOZZARELLA:** Fresh, semisoft mozzarella is called *mozzarella di bufala* when made from the milk of the domesticated Italian water buffalo; it is produced in Campania, Lazio, Apulia, and Molise. When made from cow's milk it is called *fior di latte*, or "flower of the milk," and is made in and outside Italy. Because freshness is paramount, it is sometimes better to buy locally produced *fior di latte*, rather than imported, from a gourmet Italian market. *Mozzarella di bufala* can be ordered online but is very perishable.

**OLIVES, BLACK, DRY-CURED:** Cured by salting, which removes moisture and creates wrinkles in the skin, these Italian olives are often rubbed with oil and/or herbs before being bottled, jarred, and sold in bulk. Available year-round. Look for olives imported from Sicily.

**PANCETTA:** Like bacon from the hog's belly, pancetta is cured but not usually smoked. Can be eaten as antipasto and cooked as an ingredient.

**PARMIGIANO REGGIANO:** Perhaps Italy's most famous cheese, it has been made for at least eight centuries, from local cow's milk only, in a clearly demarcated zone between Parma, Modena, Reggio-Emilia, Bologna, and Mantua. It is made into approximately eighty-pound wheels and aged for a minimum of twelve months, but usually for eighteen to twenty-four months. Some may be aged for up to seven years. It is a hard grating cheese, and has Italy's PDO (Protected Designation of Origin).

**PECORINO ROMANO:** Sheep's milk cheese of great antiquity. It's wonderful for grating and use in cooking, with a pungent salty flavor that is better for robust dishes.

**PORCINI MUSHROOMS, FRESH AND DRIED (*CÈPES*):** These members of the *Boletus edulis* species can weigh from one ounce to a pound—as much as a tiny pig (*porcini* means "little piglet"). They are prized for their meaty texture and deeply savory flavor. Fresh porcini are in season late spring and autumn but can be hard to find. Dried are more readily available, and when rehydrated, the soaking water can be filtered and used in cooking.

**PROSCIUTTO CRUDO:** A seasoned, uncooked, salt-cured, unsmoked ham, the most famous is from Parma. Prosciutto di San Daniele is equally well-regarded but produced in smaller quantities. Sold thinly sliced for antipasto, it is also used in cooking, but is best added when the dish is about to be served, to avoid toughening.

**PROVOLONE CHEESE:** Provolone Valpadana, a semifirm cow's milk cheese originally made in southern Italy, is now made in Valpadana in the Po Valley. Dolce, aged three months, is delicate and a good melting cheese. Piccante, aged six months, is stronger, and good for grating. Both the dolce and piccante versions are sometimes smoked.

**RAPINI OR BROCCOLI RABE (*CIME DI RAPE*):** A green cruciferous vegetable from the turnip family, its leaves, buds, and stems are edible. Prized in Italy for its mildly bitter flavor.

**RICE FLOUR:** Finely milled white rice used as a thickener and stabilizer in cooking and as a coating or batter for gluten-free fried dishes. In Italy, Arborio rice flour is available; Bob's Red Mill or Koda Farms Mochiko sweet white rice flour are good alternatives. If these are unavailable, substitute plain white rice flour milled from domestic medium- or long-grain rice.

**RICOTTA:** Soft, fresh whey cheese. The leftover whey comes from cheeses made with cow's, sheep's, goat's, or sometimes water buffalo milk. *Ricotta* means "recooked." It is low in fat, high in protein, and can be eaten on its own or in a wide variety of sweet or savory dishes.

**SCAMORZA CHEESE:** Semisoft, made mostly from whole cow's milk (sometimes sheep's and/or goat's milk is added), it melts well, and is a firmer and more flavorful alternative to mozzarella. It is sometimes available smoked.

**SPECK:** Italian speck (not German speck) is made in Alto Adige from smoked, cured pig's thighs. Served thinly sliced for antipasto or used in cooking like pancetta.

**TALEGGIO:** Previously known as stracchino, genuine PDO taleggio is produced only in specified provinces of Lombardy, Veneto, and Piedmont. It is a semisoft, creamy cow's milk cheese with a fat content of almost 50 percent and an edible rind. Its strong aroma belies its milder flavor, which becomes more pungent as it ages. Eat on its own or use in cooking, especially in risotto and polenta.

**TUSCAN KALE, BLACK-LEAF KALE, *CAVALO NERO*, DINOSAUR KALE, *LACINATO KALE*:** A cabbage that develops fronds instead of heads. A fall-winter vegetable now available year-round, its bold, appealing flavor is featured in many savory Italian dishes.

---

## THE REAL THING

Too many so-called Italian products are misleadingly labeled. To ensure authenticity and quality when purchasing imported Italian ingredients, look for the following abbreviations:

**DOP/PDO** means Denominazione d'Origine Protetta (Italian) and Protected Designation of Origin (European Union).

**IGP/PGI** means Indicazione Geografica Protetta (Italian) and Protected Georgraphical Indication (European Union).

**STG/TSG** means Specialità Tradizionale Garantita (Italian) and Traditional Specialties Guaranteed (European Union). This applies to genuine traditional food products not limited to a specific geographical designation. For example, although it has "Naples" in its name, *pizza Napoletana* can be considered genuine if it's made according to tradition in a different region. The same goes for *mozzarella di bufala*.

# A Few Words about Italian Wine

There are over six hundred named grape varieties used to make wine in Italy. Within that number there are dozens of varieties that are actually the *same grape*, just listed more than once according to different local names or winemaking styles. Don't let this keep you from exploring: Pushing outside the boundaries of Pinot Grigio and Chianti will not only lead you to new and exciting flavors, but to stellar bargains from regions and varietals that are less popular or lesser known.

With his passion for and knowledge of Italy's wines, certified sommelier and wine specialist Torrence O'Haire was the perfect man to put together the wine pairing suggestions for this book. Both practical and fun, Tory's suggestions are designed to work well with Italian rice, and to expand your Italian wine horizons.

# CHAPTER ONE

# ANTIPASTI

Italy's splendid tradition of *antipasti* or "before the meal" snacks long ago cut a swath across a world culinary landscape where small plates now dominate. Crostini and bruschetta, *fritto misto*, *caponata*, *bagna cauda* . . . the panoply of *antipasto* possibilities may be warm or chilled, hot or cold, teensy bites or ample slices. All are meant to whet the appetite—to tempt it, not satiate or kill it.

The first Italian *antipasto* recipe was published in the sixteenth century. Domenico Romoli, Florentine banquet director to the stars (the pope was one of his clients), wrote a cookbook titled *La Singolar Dottrini*, including the recipe that made him famous but also saddled him with the unfortunate nickname "*il Panuto*," or "greasy bread," for the rest of his life. The recipe, the earliest recorded version of bruschetta, called for toasting bread over the fire and flavoring it with pork lardo (cured pork fat) or fresh cheese.

While that dish was a big hit, over the centuries the popularity of *antipasti* has waxed and waned. For a long season, *antipasti* moved out of the home entirely, taking up residence in restaurant and hotel kitchens. Home cooks opted, instead, for the simpler soup course.

Happily, today, home cooks are showing renewed interest in delving into the wealth of historic *antipasti* recipes that restaurants don't often feature—including those made with rice.

I've included recipes for everything from rice crostini and arancini to frittatas and stuffed vegetables. For those, in this chapter and throughout the book, I've matched each stuffing to the vegetable with which it works best, but you can certainly vary the filling-and-vegetable pairings to suit your taste. If you have a seasonal vegetable garden, it's likely you'll have an excess of one or another vegetable at any given time, so changing up the filling options will keep the bounty of your home kitchen table from feeling redundant. Also good to know: Each filling recipe makes more than you'll need for one recipe's worth of vegetable stuffing. This allows for variation in the size of the vegetables chosen for stuffing, and for each cook's preference on how amply to stuff. Making extra is also, as they say in Italy, *Uccidendo due piccioni con una fava,* "killing two birds with one stone." When I have extra filling, I like to use it in a frittata or in a dip or as a spread. One precaution: If a filling contains uncooked eggs, be sure to use leftovers in a cooked application.

**PREVIOUS SPREAD:** Zucchini Blossoms Filled with Rice, Fresh Peas, and Mint (see recipe, page 55)

**OPPOSITE:** Until the 1950s, more than two hundred thousand workers traveled to the Po Valley to work the rice fields seasonally. The women, *le mondine*, lived in dormitories adjacent to the fields.

# Rice Crostini with Fresh Ricotta and Oregano

### CROSTINI DI RISO CON RICOTTA FRESCA E ORIGANO

Italy's famous crostini, or "little toasts," can be made with rice or polenta as the base instead of bread. These have a texture similar to firm maki sushi, but minus the vinegar tang, and with a nice buttery flavor instead. They use sweet white rice flour as a binder, closest to the finely milled Arborio rice flour more typically used in Italy. MAKES 24 CROSTINI; SERVES 6 TO 8

**WINE PAIRING:** Chilled Vermentino di Sardegna. Its fresh acidity and lemon-pear flavors go well with the earthiness of the oregano.

3 tablespoons sweet white rice flour (see page 22)

1¼ cups Arborio *superfino* rice

4 tablespoons (½ stick) unsalted butter, cubed

1½ teaspoons finely ground sea salt, plus more as needed

1 cup fresh ricotta

Extra virgin olive oil, for drizzling

1 bunch oregano, leaves only (about ½ cup lightly packed)

Finely ground black pepper

Pour 3 cups water into a medium heavy-gauge saucepan or pot. Whisk in the rice four, making sure there are no lumps. Add the rice, butter, and salt. Heat to a gentle boil over medium heat; reduce the heat to very low, stirring occasionally to prevent sticking, until the rice has absorbed the water and is cooked through and sticky, about 30 minutes.

Line a 9 x 13-inch baking dish with parchment paper, leaving a four-inch overhang on all sides. Press the cooked rice into the parchment-lined dish, smoothing to make level. Fold the parchment paper over to cover the rice, using additional parchment paper as needed. Cover the baking dish with plastic wrap and refrigerate until the rice cake is quite firm, at least 3 hours.

To assemble the crostini, discard the plastic wrap and any extra parchment paper. Uncover the rice crostini and spread the rice cake with the ricotta. Using a sharp knife dipped in cold water to prevent sticking, divide the cake into 24 squares. These will be slightly flexible. Drizzle the crostini with olive oil, sprinkle with fresh oregano leaves, and season with pepper and salt. Transfer to a large platter and serve.

# Rice Crostini with Prosciutto Cotto

### CROSTINI DI RISO AL PROSCIUTTO COTTO

Most Americans are familiar with prosciutto *crudo* (see page 20), the cured Italian ham so popular on salumi and charcuterie boards. But fewer know prosciutto *cotto*, which is cooked rather than cured and has a pleasant mild and savory flavor. At Quartino's, we shave our house-made *cotto* ham into paper-thin shards and serve it with bread. Here, rice crostini are topped with twirled rosettes of the *cotto*. Purchase prosciutto *cotto* from a good Italian grocer or order it online. MAKES 24 CROSTINI; SERVES 6 TO 8

**WINE PAIRING:** A citrusy, minerally Soave Classico pairs well with the *cotto* ham and fresh parsley.

3 tablespoons sweet white rice flour (see page 22)

1¼ cups Arborio *superfino* rice

4 tablespoons (½ stick) unsalted butter, cubed

1½ teaspoons finely ground sea salt

1 bunch Italian flat-leaf parsley, leaves only, torn to make 1 loosely packed cup and minced

3½ ounces prosciutto *cotto*, sliced paper thin

Pour 3 cups water into a medium heavy-gauge saucepan or pot. Whisk in the rice four, making sure there are no lumps. Add the rice, butter, and salt. Heat to a gentle boil over medium heat; reduce the heat to very low, stirring occasionally to prevent sticking, until the rice has absorbed the water and is cooked through and sticky, about 30 minutes.

Line a 9 x 13-inch baking dish with parchment paper, leaving a four-inch overhang on all sides. Press the cooked rice into the parchment-lined dish, smoothing to make level. Fold the parchment paper over to cover the rice, using additional parchment paper as needed. Cover the baking dish with plastic wrap and refrigerate until the rice cake is quite firm, at least 3 hours.

To assemble the crostini, discard the plastic wrap and any extra parchment paper. Uncover the rice crostini and, using a sharp knife dipped in cold water to prevent sticking, divide the cake into 24 squares. These will be slightly flexible. Put the minced parsley in a shallow dish. Dip the top of each square into the minced parsley. Transfer to a serving tray.

Divide the prosciutto *cotto* into 24 portions. Using a small fork, twirl each portion into a loose circle, or use tongs to gather each portion into a loose bunch. Top each crostini with *cotto*. Serve immediately.

# Arancini with Fresh Mozzarella and Italian Parsley

## ARANCINI DI RISO CON FIOR DI LATTE E PREZZEMOLO

Ever since the invading Arabs brought rice to Sicily, the region has been known for *arancini*, or "little oranges." Named for the shape and color these diminutive rice balls take on when deep-fried, *arancini* can be filled with meat sauce, cheese, mushrooms—even pistachios or roasted eggplant. The choice of which Italian rice to use is up to you: *Arancini* made with Arborio rice have a stickier texture while Carnaroli rice preserves the texture of the separate rice grains. I like to serve these with a spicy *arrabbiata sugo* dipping sauce. MAKES 16 *ARANCINI*; SERVES 4

**WINE PAIRING:** When the deep fryer comes out, it's time to reach for something sparkling. Add to that the milk-sweet, creamy cheese and fiery dipping sauce used here and your best bet will be "dry" or "extra dry" Prosecco Superiore.

3 cups Arborio or Carnaroli *superfino* rice

4 tablespoons (½ stick) unsalted butter, cubed

2 teaspoons finely ground sea salt

3 large eggs, well beaten

¼ cup sweet white rice flour (see page 22)

1 small bunch Italian flat-leaf parsley, leaves only, coarsely chopped and lightly packed to make ½ cup

2½ ounces Parmigiano Reggiano or Grana Padano, finely grated to make 1 cup

1 pound *fior di latte* (fresh cow's milk mozzarella in liquid; see page 20) drained and cut into ¼-inch cubes

**FOR DEEP-FRYING**

3 large eggs, well beaten

2 cups fine dry Italian, panko, or gluten-free breadcrumbs

4 to 5 cups high-smoke-point oil (safflower, rice bran, soybean, or canola)

*Salsa All'Arrabbiata* (recipe follows), for serving

Pour 5½ cups water into a medium heavy-gauge saucepan or pot and stir in the rice, butter, and salt. Heat to boiling over medium heat; reduce the heat to low. Simmer briskly, uncovered and without stirring, until the rice has absorbed the water, about 30 minutes. Remove the pot from the heat. Stir in the eggs, rice flour, parsley, and Parmigiano.

Line a 9 x 13-inch baking dish with parchment paper. Transfer the cooked rice to the parchment-lined dish, smoothing to make level. Bring the rice to room temperature. (To finish the recipe the next day, cover the rice with parchment paper and the baking dish with plastic wrap; refrigerate. Bring the rice to room temperature before continuing with the recipe.)

Assemble and fry the *arancini*: Using a sharp knife dipped in cold water, score and cut the rice cake into 16 equal pieces. Place one portion of rice in your hand and shape it into a cone;

fill with 3 cubes of mozzarella. Close the rice over the cheese and squeeze to shape it into a ball. Place on parchment paper. Repeat until all the *arancini* are formed.

Place two large bowls on a work surface. Place the eggs in one and the breadcrumbs in the other. Immerse a rice ball in the egg; move it to the bowl of breadcrumbs and dredge until well coated. Place the breaded ball on the parchment paper. Repeat until all the rice balls are breaded.

Pour the oil into a small electric fryer (amount specified by fryer model) or a heavy-gauge pot, ensuring that the oil reaches no higher than 3 inches from the top of the pot. Preheat the oil to 350°F. Carefully transfer 3 or 4 of the balls into the hot oil, being careful not to crowd them. Fry until golden brown, 4 to 6 minutes. Test one to ensure doneness, adjusting frying time as needed. Proceed with the remainder.

Blot the fried *arancini* on paper toweling. Place on a platter and serve with spicy *salsa all' arrabbiata* sauce.

Variation: To make traditional Sicilian *arancini*, use the recipe above, but add 1 teaspoon saffron threads to the rice mixture. Fold in the eggs and rice flour, but omit the parsley and Parmigiano Reggiano. Cook, cool, and cut the rice cake as directed. When ready to shape into balls, fill each with about 1 tablespoon of ragu and two small cubes of provolone or buffalo mozzarella (instead of the fresh cow's milk mozzarella; see page 20). Bread and fry according to the recipe directions.

# Salsa All'Arrabbiata

MAKES ABOUT 2 CUPS SAUCE

¼ cup extra virgin olive oil

1 whole clove garlic

1 teaspoon roughly chopped red chili pepper

1 (14.28-ounce) can Italian whole peeled tomatoes in puree

1 cup boiling water

Finely ground sea salt and white pepper

1 tablespoon roughly chopped Italian flat-leaf parsley leaves

Pour the olive oil into a medium heavy-gauge saucepan or pot over medium heat and, 1 minute later, add the garlic clove. Reduce the heat to low and sauté the garlic clove until slightly almond colored. Add the red chili; simmer for 5 minutes.

Discard the garlic clove. Add the tomatoes. Using a potato masher or slotted spoon, crush the tomatoes until pulverized. Pour in the boiling water; season with salt and white pepper and simmer for 10 minutes. The sauce is ready when the *salsa all'arrabbiata* coats the back of a spoon. Stir in the parsley leaves and serve with the arancini.

# Roman Rice Balls "on the Phone"

## SUPPLI AL TELEFONO

The title conjures whimsical images of coquettish *crocchettes* talking on the telephone, but the name is really about the cheesy filling: When pulled apart, the fresh buffalo mozzarella in these deep-fried morsels stretches into long strings like telephone wires. Among the most popular of all regional *arancini*, these *suppli* are made with rice that's been cooked in a tomato ragu made with beef sirloin and enriched with chicken liver. An Italianization of the French word for "surprise," *suppli* taste best hot out of the fryer. Great party fare, this recipe makes enough for a crowd. Note: Start soaking the porcini mushrooms the night before you want to make this recipe. MAKES 40 *CROCCHETTES*; SERVES 10

**WINE PAIRING:** A few producers in the Piedmont region of Italy are making sparkling Barbera wines—deep ruby red, bone dry, and medium weight. These offer electric acidity, sour red berry fruit, and an alluring violet-cedar aroma that goes well with these *crocchettes*.

¾ ounce (22 grams) dried porcini mushrooms, brushed free of any dust or sand to make 1 loosely packed, mounded cup; once soaked and chopped, the mushrooms will measure ¾ cup

2 tablespoons extra virgin olive oil

4 tablespoons (½ stick) unsalted butter, cubed

1 small white or yellow onion, finely chopped to make 1 cup

6 ounces finely ground beef sirloin

3 ounces chicken livers, finely chopped

½ cup dry Italian white wine

1 cup bottled Italian tomato puree (*passata*)

Finely ground sea salt and black pepper

3 cups Arborio *superfino* rice

2½ ounces Grana Padano, finely grated to make 1 cup

3 large eggs, well beaten

¼ cup sweet rice flour (see page 22)

1 pound fresh buffalo mozzarella in liquid (see page 20), drained and cut into ¼-inch cubes

### FOR DEEP-FRYING

4 large eggs, beaten

3 cups dry Italian, panko, or gluten-free breadcumbs

4 to 5 cups high-smoke-point oil (safflower, rice bran, soybean, or canola)

To rehydrate the porcini, cover them with warm water in a medium bowl, placing a small plate on top to keep the mushrooms submerged for at least 1 hour—several hours is better; overnight is best. When the porcini are soft and pliant, strain through a coffee filter into a medium bowl, saving 1 cup of the mushroom-soaking water to use when cooking the rice. Pat the mushrooms dry; mince them and set aside.

In a medium heavy-gauge sauté pan or skillet at least 3 inches deep, heat the olive oil and 2 tablespoons of the butter over low heat until the butter melts. Add the onion and cook, stirring, until soft and translucent but not browned. Add the beef and cook, stirring, until evenly browned. Add the chicken livers and chopped porcini mushrooms, sautéing for 5 minutes more. Add the wine and tomato puree; season with salt and pepper. Cook, stirring occasionally, until the sauce is thick enough to coat the back of a spoon.

Stir in the rice. Add 4¼ cups water, plus the reserved 1 cup mushroom-soaking water. Cook, stirring, until the rice is *al dente* and the liquid has been absorbed, about 30 minutes.

Remove the pot from the heat. Add the remaining 2 tablespoons butter and the grated Grana Padano cheese. Stir in the beaten eggs and the rice flour, mixing well.

Line a 9 x 13-inch baking dish with parchment paper. Transfer the cooked rice to the parchment-lined dish, smoothing to make level. Bring the rice to room temperature. (To finish the recipe the next day, cover the rice with parchment paper, wrap the baking dish in plastic wrap, and refrigerate. Bring the rice to room temperature before continuing with the recipe.)

Assemble and fry the *supplì*: Using a sharp knife dipped in cold water, to prevent sticking, score and cut the cakes into 40 pieces total. Wet the palms of your hands.

Place one square of rice in your hand and shape it into a circle. Place 3 or 4 mozzarella cubes in the center. Close the rice around the cheese and squeeze it into a compact oval. Place on a piece of parchment paper. Repeat until all 40 *supplì* are formed.

Put two large bowls on your work surface. Put the beaten eggs in one bowl and the bread-crumbs in the other. Immerse a *supplì* in the egg; move it to the bowl of breadcrumbs and dredge until well coated. Place on the parchment paper. Repeat until all the *supplì* are breaded.

Pour the oil into a small electric fryer (amount specified by fryer model) or a heavy-gauge pot, ensuring that the oil reaches no higher than 3 inches from the top of the pot. Preheat the oil to 350°F. Carefully transfer 3 or 4 *supplì* into the hot oil, being careful not to crowd them. Fry until golden brown, 4 to 6 minutes. Test one to ensure doneness, adjusting frying time as needed. Proceed with the remaining rice, mozzarella, and breading.

Transfer the fried *supplì* to paper towels to blot the oil. Move to a serving platter. Serve hot.

# Rice Croquettes with Four Cheeses

### CROCCHETTE DI RISO AI QUATTRO FORMAGGI

The flavor of these crisp-outside, gooey-inside *crocchettes* is complex, commingling two well-aged cow's milk cheeses (Parmigiano Reggiano and Grana Padano) with a tangy-sharp sheep's milk cheese (Pecorino Romano) and featuring a little ooze of mild, fresh cow's milk mozzarella at the center. Hot out of the fryer, the center will be nearly molten. At room temperature? A bit firmer. I serve these plain or, for a more contemporary twist, with a mild marinara sauce. *24 CROQUETTES*; SERVES 6 TO 8

**WINE PAIRING:** Rich, creamy, cheesy foods need something to help scrub the palate. A bright, young, coarsely tannic Rosso di Montalcino is a good choice.

3 cups Arborio *superfino* rice

4 tablespoons (½ stick) unsalted butter, cubed

2 teaspoons finely ground sea salt

3 large eggs, well beaten

3 tablespoons sweet white rice flour (see page 22)

½ ounce Grana Padano, finely grated to make ¼ cup

½ ounce Pecorino Romano, finely grated to make ¼ cup

1½ ounces Parmigiano Reggiano, finely grated to make a rounded ½ cup

1 pound *fior di latte* (fresh cow's milk mozzarella in liquid; see page 20) drained and cut into ¼-inch dice

FOR DEEP-FRYING

3 large eggs, well beaten

2 cups fine dry Italian, panko, or gluten-free breadcrumbs

4 to 5 cups high-smoke-point oil (safflower, rice bran, soybean, or canola)

Salsa Marinara (recipe follows), for serving

In a medium heavy-gauge saucepan or pot, combine 5¼ cups water, the rice, butter, and salt. Heat to boiling over medium heat; reduce the heat to low and simmer, uncovered and without stirring, until the rice has absorbed the water, about 30 minutes. Remove the pot from the heat. Stir in the beaten eggs, the rice flour, and the three grated cheeses.

Line a 9 x 13-inch baking dish with parchment paper. Transfer the cooked rice to the parchment-lined dish, smoothing to make level. Bring the rice to room temperature. (To finish the recipe the next day, cover the rice with parchment paper, wrap the baking dish in plastic wrap, and refrigerate. Bring the rice to room temperature before continuing with the recipe.)

Assemble and fry the *crocchettes*: Using a sharp knife dipped in cold water to prevent sticking, score and cut the rice cake into 24 squares. Wet the palms of your hands with cold water.

Place one square of rice in your hand and shape it into a circle. Place 3 or 4 mozzarella cubes in the center. Close the rice around the cheese and shape it into a compact oval. Place on a piece of parchment paper. Repeat until all 24 *crocchettes* are formed.

Put two large bowls on your work surface. Put the beaten eggs in one bowl and the breadcrumbs in the other. Immerse a *crocchette* in the egg; move it to the bowl of breadcrumbs and dredge until well coated. Place on the parchment paper. Repeat until all the *crocchettes* are breaded.

Pour the oil into a small electric fryer (amount specified by fryer model) or a heavy-gauge pot, ensuring that it reaches no more than 3 inches from the top of the pot. Preheat the oil to 350°F. Carefully transfer 3 or 4 *crocchettes* into the hot oil, being careful not to crowd them. Fry until golden brown, 4 to 6 minutes. Test one to ensure doneness, adjusting frying time as needed. Proceed with the remainder.

Transfer the *crocchettes* to paper towels to blot the oil. Move to a serving platter. Serve hot or at room temperature with *salsa marinara*.

# Salsa Marinara

### MAKES ABOUT 2 CUPS SAUCE

¼ cup extra virgin olive oil

1 clove garlic, thinly sliced on the bias

1 (14.28-ounce) can Italian whole peeled tomatoes in puree

1 sprig oregano, leaves only, roughly chopped to make 1 tablespoon

1 cup boiling water

Finely ground sea salt and white pepper

Pour the olive oil into a medium heavy-gauge saucepan or pot over medium heat. One minute later, stir in the garlic. Reduce the heat to low; sauté the garlic slices until tender and translucent but not browned.

Pour in the tomatoes. Using a potato masher or slotted spoon, crush the tomatoes until pulverized. Add the oregano and boiling water; season with salt and pepper and simmer for 10 minutes, until the sauce coats the back of a spoon.

# Rice Croquettes with Tomato and Basil

## CROCCHETTE DI RISO AL POMODORO E BASILICO

The bright flavors of tomato paste and fresh basil, enriched with tangy sheep's milk Pecorino Romano, give these deep-fried *crocchettes* a special appeal. MAKES 24 *CROQUETTES*; SERVES 6

**WINE PAIRING:** A Sicilian unoaked (or barely oaked) Carricante (Planeta makes several lovely options) would be great here—a fabulous alternative to light, unoaked Chardonnay.

3 cups Arborio *superfino* rice

4 tablespoons (½ stick) unsalted butter, cubed

2 teaspoons finely ground sea salt

3 tablespoons tomato paste, preferably Carmelina brand

1 small bunch fresh basil, leaves only, hand torn or coarsely chopped to make ½ loosely packed cup

3 large eggs, well beaten

3 tablespoons sweet white rice flour (see page 22)

Just over ½ ounce Pecorino Romano, finely grated to make ⅓ cup

**FOR DEEP-FRYING**

3 large eggs, well beaten

2 cups fine dry Italian, panko, or gluten-free breadcrumbs

4 to 5 cups high-smoke-point oil (safflower, rice bran, soybean, or canola)

In a medium heavy-gauge saucepan or pot, combine 5¼ cups water, the rice, butter, and salt. Heat to boiling over medium heat; reduce the heat and simmer, uncovered and without stirring, until the rice has absorbed the water, about 30 minutes. Remove the pot from the heat. Stir in the tomato paste, basil, beaten eggs, rice flour, and cheese.

Line a 9 x 13-inch baking dish with parchment paper. Transfer the cooked rice to the parchment-lined dish, smoothing to make level. Bring the rice to room temperature. (To finish the recipe the next day, cover the rice with parchment paper and the baking dish with plastic wrap; refrigerate. Bring the rice to room temperature before continuing with the recipe.)

Assemble and fry the *crocchettes*: Using a sharp knife dipped in cold water, score and cut the rice cake into 24 squares. Wet the palms of your hands with cold water. Place one square of rice in your hand and shape it into an oval. Put it on a piece of parchment paper. Repeat until all the *crocchettes* are formed.

Place two large bowls on your work surface, the eggs in one bowl, breadcrumbs in the other. Immerse a *crocchette* in the egg, then dredge in crumbs until well coated. Place on the parchment paper. Repeat until all the *crocchettes* are breaded.

Pour the oil into a small electric fryer (amount specified by fryer model) or a heavy-gauge pot, ensuring that the oil reaches no more than 3 inches from the top of the pot. Preheat the oil to 350°F. Carefully transfer 3 or 4 *crocchettes* into the hot oil. Fry until golden brown, 4 to 6 minutes. Test one to ensure doneness, adjusting frying time as needed. Proceed with the remaining *crocchettes*. Drain the fried *crocchettes* on paper toweling. Serve.

# Rice Croquettes with Arugula and Pancetta

## CROCCHETTE DI RISO CON RUCOLA E PANCETTA

The popular pairing of spinach and bacon in the States is echoed in Italy with arugula and pancetta. The peppery taste of this spicy green plays perfect counterpoint to the richness of the pork. MAKES 20 *CROQUETTES*; SERVES 5

**WINE PAIRING:** A peachy, lean Pinot Grigio from Alto Adige, a cold-climate region in the far northeast, is perfect here: no frills, no fruit bombs, just clean, light, fresh.

2½ cups Arborio or Carnaroli *superfino* rice

2 ounces finely chopped pancetta

1 small bunch arugula, hand torn or coarsely chopped to make 1 lightly packed cup

4 tablespoons (½ stick) unsalted butter, cubed

2 teaspoons finely ground sea salt

3 large eggs, well beaten

¼ cup sweet rice flour (see page 22)

Just over ½ ounce Pecorino Romano, finely grated to make ⅓ cup

FOR DEEP-FRYING

3 large eggs, well beaten

2 cups fine dry Italian, panko, or gluten-free breadcrumbs

4 to 5 cups high-smoke-point oil (safflower, rice bran, soybean, or canola)

In a medium heavy-gauge saucepan or pot, combine 5¼ cups water, the rice, pancetta, arugula, butter, and salt. Heat to boiling over medium-high heat; reduce the heat to maintain a simmer and cook, uncovered and without stirring, until the rice has absorbed the water, about 30 minutes. Remove the pot from the heat. Stir in the beaten eggs, rice flour, and cheese.

Line a 9 x 13-inch baking dish with parchment paper. Transfer the cooked rice to the parchment-lined dish, smoothing to make level. Bring the rice to room temperature. (To finish the recipe the next day, cover the rice with parchment paper and the baking dish with plastic wrap; refrigerate. Bring the rice to room temperature before continuing.)

Assemble and fry the *crocchettes*: Run a spatula around the edges of the pan; invert the pan over a cutting board to dislodge the rice cake. Using a sharp knife dipped in cold water, score and cut the rice cake into 20 squares.

Put two large bowls on your work surface, with eggs in one and the breadcrumbs in the other. Wet the palms of your hands with cold water. Scoop one portion of rice into your hand and form a small oval shape. Immerse the *crocchette* in the egg, then dredge in crumbs until well coated. Place on parchment paper. Repeat until all the *crocchettes* are formed and breaded.

Pour the oil into a small electric fryer (amount specified by fryer model) or a heavy-gauge pot, ensuring that the oil reaches no more than 3 inches from the top of pot. Preheat the oil to 350°F. Carefully transfer 3 or 4 *crocchettes* into the hot oil, being careful not to crowd them. Fry until golden brown, 4 to 6 minutes. Test one to ensure doneness, adjusting the frying time as needed. Drain the *crocchettes* on paper towels. Serve with marinara sauce (page 37).

# Rice Frittata with Sun-Dried Tomatoes, Leeks, and Onions

**FRITTATA DI RISO CON POMODORI SECCHI, PORRI E CIPOLLE**

Traveling throughout Italy during summers past, I have always enjoyed the cheerful, polka-dotty vision of bright red tomatoes spread on mats to dry in the sun. Although most sun-dried tomatoes today are processed in a more mechanized fashion, I still love that drying tomatoes concentrates the sweetness and flavor of the fruit and preserves vitamins and minerals. When you shop, look for bright, tender sun-dried tomatoes, and avoid those that are hard or overly dark-hued. MAKES 12 APPETIZER SERVINGS OR 6 MAIN-COURSE SERVINGS

**WINE PAIRING:** Gaglioppo is a rough-and-ready grape from the deep south of Italy that produces wines with wild muscle. Explore the wine region of Ciro for reds made with this grape that are earthy and tannic with the flavors of roasted tomato and dried orange.

1¼ cups Arborio *superfino* rice

4 tablespoons (½ stick) unsalted butter, cubed

1½ teaspoons finely ground kosher or sea salt

10 large eggs, well beaten

¼ cup finely chopped sun-dried tomatoes

1 leek, white portion only, carefully washed of any grit or dirt, finely chopped, and blanched to make ⅓ cup

1 small white or yellow onion, thinly sliced and sautéed to make ⅓ cup cooked

1¼ ounces Parmigiano Reggiano or Grana Padano, finely grated to make ½ cup

Finely ground black pepper

Extra virgin olive oil

In a medium heavy-gauge saucepan or pot, combine 2⅔ cups water, the rice, butter, and salt. Heat to boiling over medium heat. Reduce the heat to maintain a simmer and cook, uncovered and without stirring, until the rice has absorbed the water, about 30 minutes. Remove the pot from the heat and let cool to room temperature; stir.

In a large bowl, mix together the eggs, tomatoes, leek, onion, and cheese. Season with pepper. Stir in the cooled rice. Set aside to rest for 30 minutes.

Set the oven rack to the center position and preheat the oven to 375°F. Coat a 12-inch oven-safe nonstick skillet with olive oil. Add the rice-egg mixture, leveling the top with a spatula. Bake until the frittata is firm and golden, 30 to 35 minutes. Transfer the skillet from the oven to a cooling rack. Rest for 2 minutes. Run a thin spatula around the edges of the pan. Unmold onto a serving platter. Slice and serve hot or at room temperature.

# Rice Frittata with Spinach and Parmigiano Reggiano

### FRITTATA DI RISO CON SPINACI E PARMIGIANO REGGIANO

Whipped up with texturally enhancing rice, colorful spinach, and flavorful Parmigiano, this frittata makes a tasty, fork-tender appetizer that can also serve as a light brunch or luncheon dish. **MAKES 12 APPETIZER SERVINGS OR 6 MAIN-COURSE SERVINGS**

**WINE PAIRING:** With floral, rosy aromas, richness, and intrigue, a dry, white Tuscan Viognier is just the thing here.

1¼ cups Arborio *superfino* rice

4 tablespoons (½ stick) unsalted butter, cubed

1½ teaspoons finely ground sea salt

1½ tablespoons extra virgin olive oil, plus more for pan

3 cups lightly packed fresh spinach leaves

10 large eggs, well beaten

Just under 3 ounces Parmigiano Reggiano or Grana Padano, finely grated to make 1⅓ cups

Finely ground black pepper

Extra virgin olive oil

In a medium heavy-gauge saucepan or pot, combine 2⅔ cups water, the rice, butter, and salt. Heat to boiling over medium heat. Reduce the heat to maintain a simmer and cook, uncovered and without stirring, until the rice has absorbed the water, about 30 minutes. Remove the pot from the heat and cool to room temperature; stir.

In a 12-inch oven-safe nonstick skillet, heat the oil over medium-high heat. Stir the spinach until it releases liquid and is cooked. Transfer the spinach to a large bowl. Wipe out the skillet and reuse to bake the frittata.

Whisk the eggs, cheese, and pepper into the bowl of spinach. Stir in the cooked rice and set aside to rest for 30 minutes.

Set the oven rack to the center position and preheat the oven to 375°F. Coat the skillet with olive oil. Add the rice-egg mixture, leveling the top with a spatula. Bake until the frittata is cooked through, firm to the touch, and golden, 30 to 35 minutes. Transfer the skillet from the oven to a cooling rack. Rest for 2 minutes. Run a thin spatula around the edges of the pan. Unmold onto a serving platter. Slice and serve hot or at room temperature.

# Rice Frittata with Fresh Mushrooms

## FRITTATA DI RISO AI FUNGHI

When autumn comes to Italy, baskets of mushrooms sprout like mushrooms themselves along the market paths. The combination of mushrooms with eggs has been a forever-favorite. Adding the texture of rice makes this classic duo a tempting trio. Choose white or brown mushrooms—whatever fresh seasonal variety your local forager brings to market.

**MAKES 12 APPETIZER SERVINGS OR 6 MAIN-COURSE SERVINGS**

**WINE PAIRING:** Wines made from the Arneis grape have the elegant essence of almond, wet stone, and forest floor and show off the earthy sweetness of fresh mushrooms with absolute panache. Look for a rich Arneis from the region of Roero in Piedmont.

1¼ cups Arborio *superfino* rice

4 tablespoons (½ stick) unsalted butter, cubed

1½ teaspoons finely ground sea salt

3 cups fresh mushrooms of choice

1½ tablespoons extra virgin olive oil, plus more as needed

10 large eggs, well beaten

1 small bunch flat-leaf Italian parsley, leaves only, chopped to make 2 tablespoons

1¼ ounces Parmigiano Reggiano or Grana Padano, finely grated to make ½ cup

Finely ground black pepper

In a medium heavy-gauge saucepan or pot, combine 2⅔ cups water, the rice, butter, and salt. Heat to boiling over high heat. Reduce the heat to maintain a simmer and cook, uncovered and without stirring, until the rice has absorbed the water, about 30 minutes. Once the rice is cooked, remove the pot from the heat and let cool to room temperature; stir.

While the rice is cooking, remove the stems from the mushrooms; save to use for making stock another time. Slice the mushroom caps in half; thinly slice the halves. Set aside.

In a 12-inch oven-safe nonstick skillet, heat the oil over medium-high heat. Lower the heat, add the mushrooms and sauté, stirring occasionally, until the mushrooms have released their juices and the juices have evaporated. Transfer the mushrooms to a large bowl. Wipe out the skillet to reuse for the frittata.

Whisk the beaten eggs, parsley, and cheese into the bowl of mushrooms. Season with pepper. Stir in the reserved rice. Set aside to rest for 30 minutes.

Set the oven rack to the center position and preheat the oven to 375°F. Coat the skillet with olive oil. Add the rice-egg mixture, leveling the top with a spatula. Bake until firm and golden, 30 minutes. Transfer the skillet from the oven to a cooling rack. Rest for 2 minutes. Run a thin spatula around the edges of the pan. Unmold onto a serving platter. Slice and serve hot or at room temperature.

# Rice Frittata with Scamorza Cheese, Potatoes, and Rosemary

## FRITTATA DI RISO CON SCAMORZA, PATATE E ROSMARINO

While any waxy (red-skinned) or floury (russet) potato will work, I like the flavor and texture of Yukon Gold potatoes in this recipe. They play well with Scamorza, a cheese that looks and melts like mozzarella but has a more dominant flavor. Originally from Puglia, in southern Italy, Scamorza is usually made from cow's milk. Its creaminess and pungency are even sexier when enhanced with the fresh fragrance and piney flavor of rosemary. MAKES 12 APPETIZER SERVINGS OR 6 MAIN-COURSE SERVINGS

**WINE PAIRING:** Rosemary begs for Tuscan reds. Look for a Morellino di Scansano—a Sangiovese-based wine made in a particularly juicy style. The black-cherry spice of the wine is great with the deep fragrance of the herbs and cheese.

1¼ cups Arborio *superfino* rice

4 tablespoons (½ stick) unsalted butter, cubed

1½ teaspoons finely ground sea salt

10 large eggs, well beaten

1 medium-sized Yukon Gold potato, baked, peeled, and shredded to make 1 cup

1¼ ounces Scamorza cheese (see page 22), grated to make ½ cup

1¼ ounces Parmigiano Reggiano or Grana Padano, finely grated to make ½ cup

Finely ground black pepper

Extra virgin olive oil

3 tablespoons fresh rosemary needles

In a medium heavy-gauge saucepan or pot, combine 2⅔ cups water, the rice, butter, and salt. Heat to boiling over medium heat. Reduce the heat to maintain a simmer and cook, uncovered and without stirring, until the rice has absorbed the water, about 30 minutes. Remove the pot from the heat and let cool to room temperature; stir.

Whisk together the eggs, potato, Scamorza, and Parmigiano in a large bowl. Season with pepper. Stir in the cooled rice. Set aside for 30 minutes.

Set the oven rack to the center position and preheat the oven to 375°F. Coat a 12-inch oven-safe nonstick skillet with olive oil. Add the egg-rice mixture, leveling the top with a spatula. Sprinkle the rosemary needles over all. Bake until firm and golden, 30 to 35 minutes. Transfer the skillet from the oven to a cooling rack. Rest for 2 minutes. Run a thin spatula around the edges of the pan. Unmold onto a serving platter. Slice and serve hot or at room temperature.

# Sweet Pepper and Rice Roll-ups with Borlotti Beans and Sage

**INVOLTINI DI PEPERONI CON RISO DI FAGIOLI BORLOTTI E SALVIA**

Come summer, figuring out what to do with the beautiful backyard garden bounty inspires all manner of stuffed-vegetable dishes. This recipe for stuffed peppers is among my favorites. We make them by the hundreds at Quartino, serving them warm or chilled. The peppers can be oven-roasted or blanched in boiling water before they are skinned. Roasted peppers are sweet and soft; blanched peppers are crisp and piquant. At the restaurant, we pipe the filling into the peppers with a large pastry tube; at home, I use a spoon or butter knife. MAKES 40 ROLLS; SERVES 8 TO 10

**WINE PAIRING:** When serving roasted peppers, reach for wine made with the bold Aglianico grape with its scorched-earth, burnt-herb, roasted-meat flavors. Look to Campagna for Aglianico made in an expert style; Bisceglia Gudarrà is a great introductory producer.

1⅓ cups Arborio *superfino* rice

4 tablespoons (½ stick) unsalted butter, cubed

1½ teaspoons finely ground sea salt

1 tablespoon extra virgin olive oil, plus more as needed

1 small white or yellow onion, finely chopped to make ¾ cup

20 red, yellow, and orange bell peppers (a mixture is best)

4 large eggs, well beaten

Finely grated zest of 2 lemons

1 small bunch fresh sage, finely chopped to make 2 tablespoons

1 cup cooked, drained borlotti beans (see page 19), from ⅓ cup dried beans, or canned, rinsed and drained

3 tablespoons sweet rice flour (see page 22)

1¼ ounces Parmigiano Reggiano or Grana Padano, finely grated to make ½ cup

Finely ground black pepper

In a medium heavy-gauge saucepan or pot, combine 3 cups water, the rice, butter, and salt. Heat to boiling over high heat. Reduce the heat to maintain a simmer and cook, uncovered and without stirring, until the rice has absorbed the water, about 30 minutes. Remove the pot from the heat; let cool.

Heat the olive oil in a small heavy-gauge skillet over medium heat. Add the onion and sauté, stirring frequently, until it is translucent and limp but not browned. Remove the skillet from the heat; let cool.

Core each bell pepper with a paring knife, discarding the fiber and seeds and cutting as little of the top away as possible. Cut each pepper in half lengthwise.

Either roast the peppers (sweeter and softer) or blanch them (crisper and more piquant) as follows. To roast the bell peppers: Preheat the oven to 375°F. Line two large sheet pans with parchment paper. Arrange the pepper halves, cut side down, on the trays. Brush the tops with olive oil. Roast until the tops of the peppers are browned, about 20 minutes. Remove the pans from the oven and cover with kitchen towels; let the peppers cool. Using the towels, rub off and discard as much of the peppers' skin as comes off easily.

To blanch peppers: Fill a large pot three-fourths full of lightly salted water. Heat to boiling over high heat. Add the pepper halves in batches and simmer until just pliable, about 8 minutes. Using tongs, remove the peppers to paper towel–lined large sheet pans to cool. Discard the skins.

In a large bowl, stir together the eggs, lemon zest, sage, sautéed onion, beans, rice flour, and cheese. Season with black pepper. Gently fold in the reserved rice, being careful to keep the beans intact.

To finish, preheat the oven to 375°F. Line the two large sheet pans with fresh parchment paper. Spread a pepper open in the palm of one hand. Using a spoon or butter knife, cover the pepper with just enough of the rice filling (about 2 tablespoons) so that the pepper can be folded around the filling to form a compact packet or "roll." Place the filled pepper seam side down on a prepared sheet pan. Repeat until all the peppers are filled.

Using a pastry brush dipped in olive oil, lightly brush the tops of the rolls. Bake until the rice is heated through and the tops of the rolls are lightly browned, 30 to 35 minutes.

Transfer the rolls to large serving platters. Serve warm or at room temperature. Leftovers may be covered and refrigerated.

# Zucchini Rolls Filled with Rice and Walnuts

## ROTOLINI DI ZUCCHINE AL RISO E NOCI

Because these rolls are so popular at Quartino, my experience tells me you may wish to buy a few extra zucchini to make extra servings. Choose firm, medium-sized zucchini at least seven inches long and one and a half to two inches wide. Toast the walnuts in a dry skillet over medium heat, stirring until fragrant. MAKES 20 ZUCCHINI ROLLS; SERVES 4 OR 5

**WINE PAIRING:** Catarratto, a Sicilian native, produces delicate, highly acidic whites from the slopes of Mount Etna. Find an Etna Bianco here for a white of such freshness it might rival your favorite dry Riesling from Alsace.

1⅓ cups Arborio *superfino* rice

4 tablespoons (½ stick) unsalted butter, cubed

1½ teaspoons finely ground sea salt, plus more as needed

4 large eggs, well beaten

Finely grated zest of 2 lemons

1 small bunch fresh oregano, leaves only, finely chopped to make 3 tablespoons

1 small white or yellow onion, finely chopped and sautéed to make ½ cup cooked

1 cup chopped toasted walnuts (see recipe introduction)

3 tablespoons sweet white rice flour (see page 22)

1¼ ounces Parmigiano Reggiano or Grana Padano, finely grated to make ½ cup

Finely ground black pepper

4 medium zucchini (see recipe introduction), sliced lengthwise into twenty ¼-inch-thick planks

Extra virgin olive oil

In a medium heavy-gauge saucepan or pot, combine 3 cups water, the rice, butter, and salt. Heat to boiling over medium heat. Reduce the heat to maintain a simmer and cook, uncovered and without stirring, until the rice has absorbed the water, about 30 minutes. Remove the pot from the heat. Transfer the rice to a shallow baking dish; cool the rice to room temperature.

In a large bowl, whisk together the eggs, lemon zest, oregano, onion, walnuts, rice flour, and cheese. Season with pepper and stir in the rice. Set aside for 10 minutes.

While the rice filling is resting, preheat the oven to 375°F. Place the zucchini planks on a parchment paper–lined large sheet pan. Using a pastry brush, coat the tops and bottoms of the zucchini planks very lightly with olive oil. Sprinkle the tops with a small amount of salt. Bake until the zucchini is pliable and just starting to take on a golden color, about 15 minutes. Remove the pan from the oven and cool the zucchini to room temperature. Keep the oven on.

Use a small spoon or butter knife to evenly spread about 3 tablespoons of the rice filling lengthwise on each zucchini plank. Roll up tightly. Place the rolls, seam side down, on the same parchment paper–lined pan you used to bake the zucchini.

Lightly brush the rolls with olive oil. Bake until the filling is cooked through and the rolls are lightly browned, about 30 minutes. Transfer to a serving platter. Serve.

# Eggplant Parmesan Bundles Filled with Rice and Fennel

## INVOLTINI DI MELANZANE AL RISO E FINOCCHIO

In the minds of many diners, using "eggplant" and "Italian" in the same sentence can mean only one thing: eggplant parmesan, a Neapolitan specialty. Unfortunately, a lot of poorly executed eggplant parmesan has been served up at restaurants, which has put many people off the dish. It's my hope that our version of the classic sets things right. I like to brush eggplant slices with oil and bake them until pliable, then stuff them with a savory fennel-rice filling before baking a second time. You can leave the peel on, or take it off. And since the filling portion of the recipe is ample to allow for variation in the size of the eggplant, I recommend buying and preparing extra eggplant: My experience suggests your diners will eat *all* of the extras. MAKES 20 BUNDLES; SERVES 4 OR 5

**WINE PAIRING:** Choose a Nero d'Avola, an indigenous Sicilian grape with characteristics that fall somewhere between the smoothness of Merlot and the zing of Syrah. Eminently drinkable, Nero d'Avola's sweet, earthy fruit will blend beautifully with the sweetness of the fennel and eggplant.

1 large eggplant, peeled or unpeeled, sliced into twenty ⅓-inch-thick rounds

Kosher or coarse sea salt

1⅓ cups Arborio *superfino* rice

4 tablespoons (½ stick) unsalted butter, cubed

1½ teaspoons finely ground sea salt

2 large eggs, well beaten

Fennel fronds from the top of 1 fennel bulb, minced to make 3 tablespoons

1 fennel bulb, core discarded, finely chopped and sautéed to make 1 cup cooked

½ small white or yellow onion, finely chopped and sautéed to make ¼ cup cooked

3 tablespoons sweet white rice flour (see page 22)

1¼ ounces Parmigiano Reggiano, finely grated to make ½ cup

Extra virgin olive oil

Finely ground black pepper

Layer a large sheet pan with several thicknesses of paper toweling. Very lightly salt the eggplant slices on both sides and place in a single layer on the toweling. Cover with more toweling and place a second large sheet pan on top. Weight the pan using several equally distributed 28-ounce cans of tomatoes or other cans of food of a similar weight.

In a medium heavy-gauge saucepan or pot, combine 3 cups water, the rice, butter, and salt. Heat to boiling over medium heat. Reduce the heat to maintain a simmer and cook, uncovered and without stirring, until the rice has absorbed the water, about 30 minutes. Remove the pot from the heat; let cool.

In a large bowl, whisk together the eggs, fennel fronds, sautéed fennel bulb, and onion, rice flour, and cheese. Season with pepper and stir in the cooled rice. Set aside for 10 minutes.

To bake and fill the eggplant slices, preheat the oven to 375°F. Remove the can weights and top large sheet pan from the eggplant slices. Clean the pan and line with parchment paper. Set aside. Remove and discard the paper toweling surrounding the eggplant slices on the other pan. Move the salted eggplant slices onto the freshly papered pan. Lightly brush them on both sides with extra virgin olive oil. Bake until soft, pliable, and lightly browned, about 25 minutes. Let cool.

Place 1 tablespoon of the filling on one-half of an eggplant round. Fold the unfilled half over the filled half to cover the filling, creating a half-moon shape. Repeat until all the eggplant slices are filled.

Sprinkle each eggplant bundle with freshly ground black pepper and bake until the eggplant is cooked through and golden on top, about 20 minutes. Serve warm or at room temperature.

# Kale Bundles Filled with Rice and Sausage

## INVOLTINI DI CAVALO NERO AL RISO E SALSICCIA

*Cavalo nero*, or black leaf kale, goes by many names—Tuscan kale, dinosaur kale, and lacinato kale among them. Mineral rich, boldly flavored, and filled with vitamins K, A, C, B, and E, kale is low-calorie but very filling. Although primarily a cold-weather dish in Italy, kale's year-round availability makes this a dish you can eat whenever your kale craving strikes. MAKES 30 BUNDLES; SERVES 6

WINE PAIRING: Nebbiolo works well with savory, rich flavors like those in this dish. The famed grape of Barolo, Nebbiolo is used to produce inexpensive, light wines in Valtellina and the surrounding areas, packing plenty of acid and tannin in a charming rose-scented package.

1⅓ cups Arborio *superfino* rice

4 tablespoons (½ stick) butter, cubed

1½ teaspoons finely ground sea salt, plus more as needed

2 large eggs, well beaten

1 small bunch fresh sage leaves, finely chopped to make 3 tablespoons

½ small white or yellow onion, finely chopped and sautéed to make ¼ cup cooked

1 large link fresh Italian pork sausage, cooked and finely chopped to make 1 cup (see notes)

3 tablespoons sweet white rice flour (see page 22)

1¼ ounces Parmigiano Reggiano or Grana Padano, finely grated to make ½ cup

Finely ground black pepper

30 Tuscan kale leaves, each about 8 inches long, blanched and stemmed (see notes)

Extra virgin olive oil

In a medium heavy-gauge saucepan or pot, combine 3 cups water, the rice, butter, and salt. Heat to boiling over medium heat. Reduce the heat to maintain a simmer and cook, uncovered and without stirring, until the rice has absorbed the water, about 30 minutes. Remove the pot from the heat. Transfer the rice to a shallow baking dish; cool to room temperature.

While the rice is cooling, whisk together the eggs, sage, onion, sausage, rice flour, and cheese in a large bowl. Season with pepper and stir in the cooled rice.

Preheat the oven to 375°F. Line a large sheet pan with parchment paper.

To fill each bundle, spread a kale leaf open on your work surface. Slightly overlap the edges of the leaf to patch the gap where you removed the stem. Spoon 1 to 2 tablespoons of the rice filling near the base of the leaf; tightly roll the leaf toward the tip, tucking as you go to enclose the filling. Place the roll seam side down on the sheet pan. Repeat until all the leaves are filled and rolled. Brush the rolls lightly with olive oil; very lightly sprinkle with salt and pepper.

Bake until the filling is cooked through, about 25 minutes. Serve warm or at room temperature.

**NOTES:**

- Selecting and preparing the sausage: Depending on your taste preference, you can use either sweet or hot Italian pork sausage. To prepare, remove the sausage from the casing and crumble in a medium-sized nonstick skillet. Cook over medium heat, breaking up any clumps with a wooden spatula as the sausage cooks. When fully cooked, drain off the excess fat. Transfer the sausage crumbles to a cutting board and chop even more finely.

- To blanch and trim the kale: Heat a large pot of lightly salted water until boiling. Immerse the leaves in the boiling water until they are limp, about 7 minutes. Drain and rinse the cooked leaves under cold running water. Pat dry. When cool enough to handle, trim away the center rib of each leaf, but do not cut the leaves in half. Reserve on paper toweling.

# Oven-Roasted Italian Plum Tomatoes Filled with Rice and Savoy Cabbage

## POMODORI RIPIENI DI RISO CON LA VERZA AL FORNO

At Quartino's, we favor a small *pomodorini*, or "little tomato," that's a bit bigger than a cherry or grape tomato but smaller than a "regular" vine-ripened tomato. Since these are not always available, I have adapted this classic rice-stuffed tomato recipe for the home kitchen by specifying Roma or plum tomatoes, which are meaty and perfectly shaped for filling.

MAKES 20 PIECES; SERVES 4 OR 5

**WINE PAIRING:** Choose a lightweight, sour-cherry red from Valpolicella. But avoid anything that says "*ripasso*" on the label, as that indicates a wine made in a richer style. (Raisiny, earthy flavors would get in the way here.)

1⅓ cups Arborio *superfino* rice

4 tablespoons (½ stick) unsalted butter, cubed

1½ teaspoons finely ground sea salt, plus more as needed

4 large eggs, well beaten

Finely grated zest of 2 lemons

½ small white or yellow onion, finely chopped and sautéed to make ¼ cup

¼ head of savoy cabbage, chopped and sautéed to make 1 cup

3 tablespoons sweet rice flour (see page 22)

1¼ ounces Parmigiano Reggiano or Grana Padano, finely grated to make ½ cup

Finely ground black pepper

10 small Italian plum or Roma tomatoes

In a medium heavy-gauge saucepan or pot, combine 3 cups water, the rice, butter, and salt. Heat to boiling over medium heat. Reduce the heat to maintain a simmer and cook, uncovered and without stirring, until the rice has absorbed the water, about 30 minutes. Remove the pot from the heat; let cool.

While the rice cools, whisk together the eggs, lemon zest, onion, cabbage, rice flour, and cheese in a large bowl. Stir in the cooled rice. Season with pepper. Set aside for 10 minutes.

To prepare the tomatoes for stuffing, carefully core the tomatoes with a sharp knife. Cut them in half horizontally; scoop out and discard the seeds and pulp. (You can also save the pulp to make a fresh salsa later.) Cover a large sheet pan with parchment paper. Arrange the tomato halves, cut side up, on the parchment paper. (If the tomato halves won't stand, level them by cutting a flat sliver off the bottoms.)

Preheat the oven to 375°F. Using a small spoon, stuff each tomato half firmly with the rice filling, mounding the top. Bake in the center of the oven until the tomatoes are heated through and the tops are golden, about 30 minutes. Serve warm or at room temperature.

# Zucchini Blossoms Filled with Rice, Fresh Peas, and Mint

### FIORI DI ZUCCA FARCITI AL RISO, PISELLI E MENTA

Zucchini squash is native to Italy, where, oddly enough, diners prefer the flower over the squash itself. In the States, both the flowers and squash are plentiful in farmers markets and home gardens throughout the summer. Zucchini blossoms can be ordered online throughout the year. You can either bake the blossoms, as directed here, or fry them (see page 58).

MAKES 30 STUFFED BLOSSOMS; SERVES 5 OR 6 • PHOTOGRAPH ON PAGE 24

**WINE PAIRING:** Look for a Verdicchio from Le Marche, ideally from the Castelli di Jesi region. These light, bright wines boast delicate flavors of lemon and green pea—a charming foil for this appetizer.

1⅓ cups Arborio *superfino* rice

4 tablespoons (½ stick) unsalted butter, cubed

1½ teaspoons finely ground sea salt, plus more as needed

4 large eggs, well beaten

Finely grated zest of 2 lemons

1 bunch fresh mint, leaves only, finely chopped to make ¼ cup

½ small white or yellow onion, finely chopped and sautéed to make ¼ cup cooked

1 cup cooked fresh garden peas (English), at room temperature (see note)

3 tablespoons sweet white rice flour (see page 22)

2½ ounces Parmigiano Reggiano or Grana Padano, finely grated to make 1 cup

30 fresh zucchini blossoms, stems removed

Extra virgin olive oil

Finely ground black pepper

In a medium heavy-gauge saucepan or pot, combine 3 cups water, the rice, butter, and salt. Heat to boiling over medium heat. Reduce the heat to maintain a simmer and cook, uncovered and without stirring, until the rice has absorbed the water, about 30 minutes. Remove from the heat; let cool.

While the rice is cooling, stir together the eggs, lemon zest, mint, onion, peas, rice flour, and cheese in a large bowl. Stir in the cooled rice. Set aside for 10 minutes.

To fill the blossoms see "How to Prepare Zucchini Blossoms for Stuffing," page 58; pack them firmly. Place the stuffed blossoms on a parchment paper–lined large sheet pan.

To bake the blossoms, preheat the oven to 375°F. Brush the filled zucchini blossoms lightly with olive oil, and sprinkle very lightly with salt and pepper. Bake until the filling is cooked through and the blossoms are lightly browned, about 20 minutes. Serve warm or at room temperature.

**NOTE:** To cook fresh peas, shell and then blanch them in lightly salted boiling water until they are just tender, but not soft. Rinse under cold water and pat dry with paper towels.

# Zucchini Blossoms Filled with Rice, Radicchio, and Gorgonzola

## FIORI DI ZUCCA FARCITI AL RISO, RADICCHIO E GORGONZOLA

The combination of lemon zest, radicchio, and Gorgonzola dolce cheese enhances the sweetness of the flower quite well. Gorgonzola, Italy's famous blue cheese, comes two ways: dolce, the younger, sweeter, creamier version, and piccante, aged Gorgonzola, which is more assertively flavored. I usually make this with the dolce version, but either variety works. You can bake or fry the blossoms—your choice. MAKES 30 STUFFED BLOSSOMS; SERVES 5 OR 6

**WINE PAIRING:** This is a rare, great opportunity to show off a wine with a bit of sweetness. Brachetto d'Acqui are bubbly, floral, raspberry-flavored charmers from the far north of Italy. Unapologetically sweet, the best of them have enough acid to keep the sweetness in balance.

1⅓ cups Arborio *superfino* rice

4 tablespoons (½ stick) unsalted butter, cubed

1½ teaspoons finely ground sea salt, plus more as needed

4 large eggs, well beaten

Finely grated zest of 2 lemons

½ small white or yellow onion, finely chopped and sautéed to make ¼ cup cooked

1 small head radicchio, finely chopped and sautéed to make 1 cup cooked (see notes)

2 ounces Gorgonzola dolce or piccante (½ cup), whipped (see notes)

3 tablespoons sweet white rice flour (see page 22)

1¼ ounces Parmigiano Reggiano or Grana Padano, finely grated to make ½ cup

30 fresh zucchini blossoms

Extra virgin olive oil

Finely ground black pepper

In a medium heavy-gauge saucepan or pot, combine 3 cups water, the rice, butter, and salt. Heat to boiling over medium heat. Reduce the heat to maintain a simmer and cook, uncovered and without stirring, until the rice has absorbed the water, about 30 minutes. Remove the pot from the heat; let cool.

Stir together the eggs, lemon zest, onion, radicchio, Gorgonzola, rice flour, and Parmigiano Reggiano in a large bowl. Mix in the cooled rice. Set aside for 10 minutes.

To fill the blossoms see "How to Prepare Zucchini Blossoms for Stuffing," page 58; pack them firmly. Place the filled blossoms on a parchment paper–lined large sheet pan.

To bake the blossoms, preheat the oven to 375°F. Brush the filled zucchini blossoms lightly with olive oil, and sprinkle very lightly with salt and pepper. Bake until the filling is cooked through and the blossoms are lightly browned, about 20 minutes. Serve warm or at room temperature.

*(continued)*

**NOTES:**

- To sauté radicchio: **Clean and separate the leaves. Finely chop and sauté in a small skillet with 1 tablespoon olive oil over medium heat, stirring frequently, until soft and translucent but not browned. Radicchio has a high water content and shrinks considerably during cooking.**
- To whip Gorgonzola: **Place the cheese in a large, shallow bowl and mash with a fork. Add 1 tablespoon olive oil and, using a small whisk, whip until smooth and creamy.**

Variation for Deep Frying: If you prefer to deep-fat fry the stuffed blossoms, pour high-smoke-point oil into a small deep fryer (amount specified by fryer model) or 4 to 5 cups in a heavy-gauge pot, ensuring that the oil reaches no higher than 3 inches from the top of the pot. Preheat the oil to 375°F. In a shallow bowl, whisk together 6 tablespoons rice flour with ¾ cup water. Using a pastry brush, brush the blossoms on all sides with the batter and place them on a parchment paper–lined large sheet pan. Fry the blossoms, 4 or 5 at a time, in the deep fryer until cooked through, golden brown, and crisp, about 4 minutes. Using tongs, remove the fully cooked blossoms to several layers of paper toweling to drain. Serve warm.

## How to Prepare Zucchini Blossoms for Stuffing

PRETTY AS THEY ARE TASTY, ZUCCHINI BLOSSOMS ARE A SUMMERTIME TREAT. IN ORDER TO BE USED for recipes, the flowers must be picked at night, when the blossoms are closed. I like to purchase the blossoms at farmers markets when they are in season, but you can also pluck them from your home garden or find them at better grocery stores. When you are ready to fill the blossoms, set them on your work surface, petals pointing away. (The petals of the blossom will be closed at the end.) Hold the stem end of a flower and shake to loosen the petals. Next, insert your index finger into the blossom, locate the pistil (female flower) or stamen (male flower), and remove it by prying it loose from the base; discard.

To fill the blossoms, you can do as chefs do and place the filling into a pastry tube fitted with a plain nozzle, then squeeze the filling into the base of each blossom. If you don't have a pastry tube, use an espresso or demitasse spoon with the smallest bowl you can find and a slender handle. (A ¼-teaspoon measuring spoon will work.) Use the spoon to deposit the filling into the bulb of each blossom, packing it firmly and repeating until the blossom is filled. Gently twist the petals to close.

# Rice Tart with Prosciutto

### TORTINO DI RISO AL PROSCIUTTO CRUDO

At Quartino, we regularly bake this handsome tart in 12-inch straight-sided tart pans. But an 11-inch nonstick skillet works fine as well, because it gives the *tortino* some height. Another option is to use a 10-inch straight-sided cake pan. Trimming a piece of parchment paper to fit in the bottom of the skillet or pan helps the tart to release more easily. Use thinly sliced prosciutto with an oblong (not round) shape. If possible, have the butcher slice extra-long pieces for you. **MAKES 12 APPETIZER SERVINGS OR 6 TO 8 MAIN-COURSE SERVINGS**

**WINE PAIRING:** When the texture of your dish is smooth and soft, look for textural structure in the wine. Serve an "Extra Dry" Prosecco Superiore for fizz, freshness, and a touch of aromatic fruit.

1¼ cups Arborio *superfino* rice

4 tablespoons (½ stick) unsalted butter, cubed

½ teaspoon finely ground sea salt

4 large eggs, well beaten

Finely grated zest of 2 lemons

1 teaspoon freshly grated nutmeg

½ small white or yellow onion, finely chopped and sautéed to make ¼ cup cooked

1 tablespoon sweet rice flour (see page 22)

1¼ ounces Parmigiano Reggiano or Grana Padano, finely grated to make ½ cup

Finely ground black pepper

Extra virgin olive oil

4 ounces oblong-shaped prosciutto, sliced paper thin

In a medium heavy-gauge saucepan or pot, combine 3 cups water, the rice, butter, and salt. Heat to boiling over medium heat. Reduce the heat to maintain a simmer and cook, uncovered and without stirring, until the rice has absorbed the water, about 30 minutes. Remove the saucepan from the heat; let cool.

Whisk together the eggs, lemon zest, nutmeg, onion, rice flour, and cheese in a large bowl. Season with pepper and stir in the rice. Set aside for 10 minutes.

Set the oven rack to the center position and preheat the oven to 350°F. Coat the bottom and sides of an 11-inch oven-safe nonstick skillet or a 10-inch straight-sided cake pan with olive oil. Line the bottom with parchment paper cut to fit. Carefully line the bottom and sides of the pan with prosciutto slices, making sure the slices drape over the outside edge by at least 2 inches.

Transfer the rice mixture to the prosciutto-lined pan, leveling the top with a spatula. Fold the prosciutto overhang over the rice to cover as much of the surface of the tart as possible. Cover any exposed tart with extra prosciutto. Bake until firm but moist, about 30 minutes. Cool on a rack for 10 minutes. Invert onto a platter. Discard the parchment paper, and slice. Serve hot or at room temperature.

# Not Your Average Codfish: *Baccalà!*

*BACCALÀ* IS THE ITALIAN WORD FOR CODFISH THAT HAS BEEN DRIED AND SALTED USING A 500-YEAR-old preservation technique that keeps all of the nutrients intact. Although pungent in its dried form, once soaked in milk or water for use in a recipe, salt cod becomes plump, moist, and firm with a delicate flavor that is not at all "fishy." Traditional in the cuisines of France, Spain, Italy, Portugal, and Greece, as well Scandinavia and the Caribbean, *baccalà* recipes over the centuries have taken on the flavors indigenous to each culture. In Italy, *baccalà* is fried, boiled, grilled, and used in sauces and in salads.

To re-create these dishes in the States, salt cod can be purchased at gourmet supermarkets and Italian delis, or ordered online. (If you're lucky, you'll find an Italian deli willing to soak the salt cod for you on Fridays!) In years past, the best cod came from Labrador, but at this writing, Norway and Canada have the most plentiful, reliable supplies. Buy boneless, skinless fillets ½ to 1 inch thick. Rinse off the surface salt under cold running water. Place the fillets in a 2- to 3-inch-deep container, cover with water (or milk—my preference), and refrigerate for twenty-four hours. Every six hours, drain the liquid and cover the fish again with fresh water or milk. After soaking, be sure to check the fillet for any bones. Although salt cod is marketed as "boneless," some stray bone fragments may remain. Remove them and discard them using kitchen tweezers.

# Rice Tart with Salted Cod

## TORTINO DI RISO CON IL BACCALÀ

The combination of rice and salt cod reminds me of the classic French *brandade de morue*—mashed potatoes and salt cod. Simple, homey, and comforting, salt cod adds a full but delicate flavor and a nice, firm texture to the accompanying starch. MAKES 12 APPETIZER SERVINGS OR 6 TO 8 MAIN-COURSE SERVINGS

WINE PAIRING: *Baccalà* demands that you avoid tannins in the wine. Steer, instead, toward the smooth, bright, and fruity with an assertive Friulano, a white from the far northeast of Italy.

1¼ cups Arborio *superfino* rice

4 tablespoons (½ stick) unsalted butter, cubed

1½ teaspoons finely ground sea salt

4 large eggs, well beaten

Finely grated zest of 3 lemons

1 teaspoon freshly grated nutmeg

½ small white or yellow onion, finely chopped and sautéed to make ¼ cup cooked

4 ounces salt cod (*baccalà*), soaked in milk overnight, drained, and finely chopped (see "Not Your Average Codfish," opposite page)

3 tablespoons sweet white rice flour (see page 22), plus more for dusting the pan

Extra virgin olive oil

Freshly ground black pepper

In a medium heavy-gauge saucepan or pot, combine 3 cups water, the rice, butter, and salt. Heat to boiling over medium heat. Reduce the heat to maintain a simmer and cook, uncovered and without stirring, until the rice has absorbed the water, about 30 minutes. Remove the saucepan from the heat; let cool.

Whisk together the eggs, lemon zest, nutmeg, onion, *baccalà*, and rice flour in a large bowl. Stir in the cooled rice. Set aside for 10 minutes.

Set the oven rack to the center position and preheat the oven to 350°F. Coat the bottom and sides of an 11-inch oven-safe nonstick sauté pan or a 10-inch cake pan with straight sides with olive oil. Dust the oiled pan lightly with rice flour. Line the bottom of the pan with parchment paper cut to fit.

Spread the rice-*baccalà* mixture in the pan, leveling the top with a spatula. Bake until the tart is cooked through but moist, about 30 minutes. Let cool on a rack for 10 minutes. Invert onto a platter. Discard the parchment paper, and slice. Serve hot or at room temperature.

# CHAPTER TWO

# RICE SOUPS

MINESTRE DI RISO

Linguists tell us the word *zuppa* came from the Franks who lived in Gaul after the Romans. The term eventually came to mean "bread soaked in broth." Belly-filling, menu-stretching bread soups—such as Tuscany's famous *ribollita* and *papa al pomodoro*—have endured. And, with the establishment of Italy's prolific rice-growing regions, soups made with rice instead of bread or pasta also took hold, each with a distinct, regional stamp. There are hearty rice soups for fall and winter, bright vegetable-rice soups for spring, and refreshing chilled rice soups for hot summer days.

For the very best soup, make your broth or stock from scratch and be sure to use a nonreactive heavy-gauge pot with a thick bottom, straight sides, and a tight-fitting lid (see page 17). Most of the recipes in this chapter call for vegetable broth, so I have included a scratch recipe. But if you prefer a meatier stock, I have included recipes for white, brown, chicken, shrimp, and fish broths and stocks in the risotto chapter as well. If you are pressed for time, low-sodium store-bought broths can be used (see page 16).

For rice soups, I prefer to use a *superfino* rice, such as Carnaroli or Arborio. Baldo is also a good choice.

And one note on wine: When pairing wine with soup, pay attention to the "textural effects" that wine can add; otherwise, the endless barrage of liquid can dull the senses. High levels of acid, tannin, and occasionally alcohol add texture to wine. A good soup-wine pairing plays with at least one—and sometimes several—of those traits.

PREVIOUS SPREAD: Chilled Rice Soup with Cherry Tomatoes and Basil *(pages 68–69)*.

OPPOSITE: Rustic pots on display at Colombara rice farm.

# Vegetable Broth

MAKES 8 CUPS

1 carrot, coarsely chopped to make 1 cup

1 small stalk celery, coarsely chopped to make 1 cup

1 small white or yellow onion, coarsely chopped to make 1 cup

1 bay leaf, preferably fresh

8 whole peppercorns (1 teaspoon)

In a heavy-gauge stockpot over medium heat, combine the carrot, celery, onion, bay leaf, and peppercorns and stir. Add 12 cups water, increase the heat to high, and bring to a boil. Reduce the heat to maintain a simmer and cook for 2½ to 3 hours. Strain the broth through a fine-mesh sieve into a large bowl, reserving the cooked vegetables for another use. Cool the broth to room temperature. Refrigerate, covered, until ready to use.

# Spring Vegetable Soup with Rice

## MINESTRONE DI RISO ALLA PRIMAVERA

This soup takes us to the hillsides of southern Italy by pairing spring vegetables harvested in that region with the smoky richness of aged provolone cheese. If fresh cranberry beans (borlotti) are not available, substitute fresh tongues-of-fire beans or fresh cannellini beans (both shelling beans). If those aren't available either, substitute drained and rinsed canned borlotti beans. **MAKES 8 TO 10 FIRST-COURSE SERVINGS OR 4 TO 6 MAIN-COURSE SERVINGS**

**WINE PAIRING:** For this soup, choose a light Soave Classico, with bright lemony acidity and a clean mineral backbone. The acid will keep your guests' mouths watering and show off the lovely light-green flavors of the spring vegetables.

2 tablespoons extra virgin olive oil, plus more for drizzling

2 tablespoons finely chopped pancetta, including the fat

½ stalk celery, chopped to make ½ cup

½ small white or yellow onion, chopped to make ½ cup

5 fresh green beans, trimmed and cut into 1-inch lengths to make ½ cup

½ small head Belgian endive, chopped to make ½ cup

½ cup shelled fresh garden peas (English peas or sweet peas—not sugar snap; or frozen peas, thawed)

½ cup fresh borlotti (cranberry) beans

2 bay leaves, preferably fresh

½ teaspoon finely ground sea salt, plus more as needed

1 teaspoon finely ground white pepper, plus more as needed

8 cups vegetable broth (opposite page)

2 tablespoons tomato paste, preferably Carmelina brand

½ cup Arborio *superfino* rice

4 ounces provolone cheese, finely grated to make 1 cup

In a heavy-gauge stockpot over low heat, combine the olive oil and pancetta, cooking and stirring until the pancetta becomes soft and translucent but not browned.

Stir in the celery, onion, green beans, endive, peas, borlotti beans, bay leaves, salt, and pepper. Increase the heat to medium and continue to cook, stirring frequently, until the vegetables begin to soften but are not browned.

Add the vegetable broth and tomato paste. Increase the heat to medium-high and bring to a boil, stirring occasionally. Immediately reduce the heat to maintain a simmer and cook, covered, until the vegetables are soft and tender, about 45 minutes. Stir in the rice, cover the pot, and simmer for another 25 minutes, until the rice is soft and tender.

Remove the pot from the heat; discard the bay leaves. Adjust the seasoning, adding more salt and pepper as needed. Portion the soup into individual serving bowls. Lightly drizzle each serving with olive oil; place a pitcher containing additional olive oil on the table so that guests can add more. Serve with the grated provolone on the side.

# Chilled Rice Soup with Cherry Tomatoes and Basil

## ZUPPA FREDDA DI RISO CON POMODORINI E BASILICO

This soup is a refreshing summer showcase for garden-grown or farmers-market tomatoes. Since it's served chilled, you need to make it the day before you plan to serve it. For the basil, I like the Italian *Genovese* variety, with its uniform leaves, attractive clusters, and exceptional depth of flavor, also available at farmers markets. MAKES 8 TO 10 FIRST-COURSE SERVINGS OR 4 TO 6 MAIN-COURSE SERVINGS • PHOTOGRAPH ON PAGE 62

**WINE PAIRING:** An extra-dry chilled Prosecco with shimmering fizz and freshness will show off the bright flavors of this soup.

1 tablespoon unsalted butter

2 tablespoons extra virgin olive oil

2 tablespoons finely chopped prosciutto fat (see note)

½ medium white or yellow onion, finely chopped to make ⅔ cup

1 stalk celery, finely chopped to make ⅔ cup

2 bay leaves, preferably fresh

1 teaspoon finely ground sea salt

1 teaspoon finely ground white pepper

1 cup Arborio *superfino* rice

Just over ½ ounce Grana Padano or Parmigiano Reggiano, finely grated to make ¼ cup

3 cups halved thin-skinned cherry tomatoes or blanched, peeled, and chopped plum or Roma tomatoes

1 bunch basil, leaves only, roughly chopped to make 6 tablespoons

FOR FINISHING

Finely ground sea salt and white pepper

1 cup cold vegetable broth (page 66), or as needed

2 cups quartered thin-skinned cherry tomatoes

1 bunch basil, leaves only, roughly chopped to make 6 tablespoons, plus ¼ cup chiffonade of basil leaves or small clusters of Genovese basil, for garnish

¼ cup extra virgin olive oil, plus more for drizzling

Finely grated zest of 2 lemons

Place the butter, olive oil, and prosciutto fat in a heavy-gauge stockpot over low heat, stirring until the butter melts and the fat becomes soft and translucent but not browned.

Add the onion, celery, bay leaves, salt, and pepper. Increase the heat to medium and continue to cook, stirring frequently, until the vegetables begin to soften but are not browned.

Add 6 cups water and heat to boiling, stirring occasionally. Immediately reduce the heat to maintain a simmer and cook, covered, until the vegetables are soft and tender, about 45 minutes. Stir in the rice, cover the pot, and continue to simmer for another 25 to 30 minutes, until the rice kernels are tender.

Prepare an ice-water bath in your sink. You will need this to cool the pot.

Remove the pot from the heat. Discard the bay leaves and stir in the cheese, tomatoes, and chopped basil. Transfer the pot to the ice-water bath and cool the soup to slightly below room temperature. Transfer to an airtight container and refrigerate overnight.

**FINISH THE SOUP:** The following day, taste the soup for seasoning, adding more salt and pepper if needed. If the soup has become too thick, thin it to the desired consistency with the cold vegetable broth.

In a small bowl, combine the cherry tomatoes, chopped basil leaves, olive oil, and lemon zest. Season with salt and pepper.

Ladle the soup into individual serving bowls. Drizzle each portion with olive oil; top with the tomato-basil garnish and the basil chiffonade.

**NOTE:** If prosciutto fat is unavailable, substitute an additional 1 tablespoon unsalted butter and 1 tablespoon extra virgin olive oil. Be careful not to burn.

# Chilled Rice Soup with Fava Beans and Fresh Mint

**ZUPPA FREDDA DI RISO CON LE FAVE E MENTA**

Fava beans, very popular in Italy, star in this summertime soup, along with fresh mint and lemon. Favas tend to develop more starchiness as summer progresses, so get them early in the season. They can also get really big—avoid the really big bean pods and choose small 3- to 4-inch-long pods with the enclosed beans about 1 inch long each. I like spearmint with favas, but please experiment with your local mint species to get the balance of flavor and fragrance you like best. Because it's served chilled, you must prepare this soup the day before you plan to serve it. **MAKES 8 TO 10 FIRST-COURSE SERVINGS OR 4 TO 6 MAIN-COURSE SERVINGS**

**WINE PAIRING:** "Green" flavors (i.e., fresh favas, mint, celery) go very well with a Verdicchio from Le Marche. Choose a young and lightweight one for harmonious flavors of lime, pear, and fresh lettuce!

1 tablespoon unsalted butter

2 tablespoons extra virgin olive oil

2 tablespoons finely chopped prosciutto fat (see note, page 69)

½ medium white or yellow onion, finely chopped to make ⅔ cup

1 stalk celery, chopped to make ⅔ cup

2 bay leaves, preferably fresh

1 teaspoon finely ground sea salt

1 teaspoon finely ground white pepper

⅔ cup Arborio *superfino* rice

Just over ½ ounce Grana Padano or Parmigiano Reggiano, finely grated to make ¼ cup

2 cups fresh fava bean pods, shelled, beans blanched and peeled to make ½ cup fava beans, or ½ cup fresh peeled and steamed refrigerated fava beans (see "Preparing Fresh Favas," page 72)

1 small bunch mint, leaves only, roughly chopped to make 3 tablespoons

FOR FINISHING

1 cup cold vegetable broth (page 66), as needed

3 cups fresh fava bean pods, shelled, beans blanched and peeled to make about ⅔ cup fava beans, or ⅔ cup fresh peeled and steamed refrigerated fava beans (see "Preparing Fresh Favas," page 72)

2 tablespoons extra virgin olive oil, plus more for drizzling

Finely grated zest of 2 lemons

Finely ground sea salt and white pepper

¼ cup loosely packed fresh mint leaves, for garnish

Thin curls lemon zest, for garnish (optional)

Put the butter, olive oil, and prosciutto fat in a heavy-gauge stockpot over low heat, stirring until the butter melts and the fat becomes soft and translucent but not browned.

Add the onion, celery, bay leaves, salt, and pepper to the pot. Increase the heat to medium and continue to cook, stirring, until the vegetables begin to soften but are not browned.

Add 6 cups water and increase the heat to bring to a boil, stirring occasionally. Immediately lower the heat to maintain a simmer and cook, covered, until the vegetables are soft and tender, about 45 minutes. Stir in the rice, cover the pot, and continue to simmer for another 25 to 30 minutes, until the rice is tender.

Prepare an ice-water bath in your sink. You will need to cool the pot.

Remove the soup from the heat and stir in the cheese, fava beans, and chopped mint. Transfer the pot to an ice-water bath and let the soup cool to slightly below room temperature. Transfer to an airtight container and refrigerate overnight.

**FINISH THE SOUP:** The following day, check the consistency of the soup. If it has become too thick, thin it to the desired consistency with the cold vegetable broth.

In a small bowl, mix the fava beans, olive oil, and lemon zest. Season with salt and pepper.

To serve, ladle the soup into individual soup bowls. Lightly drizzle each serving with olive oil. Top with the fava bean–lemon zest garnish and sprinkle with the mint leaves and thin curls of lemon, if using.

## Preparing Fresh Favas: It's Worth It!

UNLIKE OTHER BEANS, FRESH FAVAS MUST NOT ONLY BE SHELLED AND BLANCHED, BUT PEELED, TOO. (Only tiny young favas may be prepared without peeling.) Here's how: Blanch the shelled beans in boiling water to loosen the skins. Shock them in cold water. When cool enough to handle, remove the peel from each bean. (You can also freeze the shelled favas overnight before peeling. The thawed beans will peel easily.) At least one brand of peeled and steamed refrigerated fava beans is available: Look for Melissa's, sold in 8.8-ounce (250g) packages.

# Rice Soup with Beans and Broccoli Rabe

## MINESTRA DI RISO CON LE FAGIOLI E CIME DI RAPA

In Puglia, dried fava and cannellini beans are often paired with assertive broccoli rabe, a green cruciferous vegetable with edible leaves, buds, and stems and an assertive flavor. Here they join chickpeas. *Ceci neri*, a unique large black chickpea grown only in Puglia, is the pea of choice. If unavailable, substitute Italian white chickpeas (the *Kabuli* type grown in the Mediterranean) rather than those grown in India. Canned white chickpeas, cannellini, and fava beans may be substituted, but if using, add at the end of the recipe.

MAKES 8 TO 10 FIRST-COURSE SERVINGS OR 4 TO 6 MAIN-COURSE SERVINGS

**WINE PAIRING:** Puglian Primitivo is a relative of red Zinfandel that grows well in the southern Italian heat. The sweet raspberry-jam fruitiness will help balance the pungent broccoli rabe.

2 tablespoons extra virgin olive oil, plus more for drizzling

2 tablespoons finely chopped pancetta, both lean and fat parts

½ stalk celery, chopped to make ½ cup

½ small white or yellow onion, chopped to make ½ cup

8 sun-dried tomatoes, chopped to make ½ cup

1 small bunch broccoli rabe, leaves, stems, and buds chopped to make 2 cups

2 bay leaves, preferably fresh

½ teaspoon finely ground white pepper, plus more as needed

⅓ cup dried cannellini beans, quick-soaked (see "Quick-Soak Method," page 83), or drained, rinsed canned beans

⅓ cup dried fava beans, quick-soaked

⅓ cup dried black Apulian chickpeas or white Italian chickpeas, quick-soaked

8 cups vegetable broth (page 66)

½ cup Arborio *superfino* rice

Finely ground sea salt

3¾ ounces Pecorino Romano, finely grated to make 1½ cups

Put the olive oil and pancetta in a heavy-gauge stockpot over low heat, stirring until the pancetta becomes soft and translucent but not browned.

Add the celery, onion, tomatoes, broccoli rabe, bay leaves, and pepper. Increase the heat to medium and cook, stirring occasionally, until the vegetables begin to soften but are not browned.

Add the pre-soaked cannellini beans, fava beans, chickpeas, and vegetable broth. (If using canned beans, do not add until the end of the recipe.) Increase the heat, stirring occasionally, until the soup comes to a boil. Reduce the heat to maintain a simmer, and cook, covered, for 1½ hours. Stir in the rice, cover the pot, and continue to simmer for another 25 to 30 minutes, until the rice is tender.

Remove the soup from the heat; discard the bay leaves. Adjust the seasoning with salt and pepper. Ladle the soup into shallow bowls. Drizzle with olive oil. Serve with the grated cheese on the side.

# Chilled Rice Soup with Speck and Fennel

## ZUPPA FREDDA DI RISO ALLO SPECK E FINOCCHIO

This soup is from Trentino, a province located in far northern Italy, where all parts of the fennel—bulb, branches, and fronds—are prized for their sweet, anise-like flavor. Look for small, young fennel with tight bulbs, firm but not woody stems, and fresh fronds. In this recipe, the speck, a type of prosciutto, is Italian (not German) from Alto Adige. It adds a layer of refined salt and pork to the soup, complementing the licorice-like flavor of the fennel. Because it's served chilled, you must prepare this soup the day before you plan to serve it.

**MAKES 8 TO 10 FIRST-COURSE SERVINGS OR 4 TO 6 MAIN-COURSE SERVINGS**

**WINE PAIRING:** Choose a chillable red wine—either a perfumy, lightweight Grignolino with tannic, raspberry-pie juiciness, or a sparkling, ruby-red Barbera with ripping acidity and a bittersweet cranberry profile.

1 tablespoon unsalted butter

2 tablespoons extra virgin olive oil

2 tablespoons finely chopped Italian speck fat, meat reserved for finishing

1 large fennel bulb, chopped to make 2 cups, stems and fronds reserved for finishing

2 bay leaves, preferably fresh

1 teaspoon finely ground sea salt

1 teaspoon finely ground white pepper

⅔ cup Arborio *superfino* rice

Just over ½ ounce Grana Padano or Parmigiano Reggiano, finely grated to make ¼ cup

**FOR FINISHING**

1 cup cold vegetable broth (see page 66), as needed

Reserved fennel stems from 1 fennel bulb, thinly sliced on the bias to make 1 cup

2 tablespoons extra virgin olive oil, plus more for drizzling

Finely grated zest of 4 lemons

Finely ground sea salt and white pepper

3 ounces Italian speck, cut into ¼ x 1-inch matchsticks (about ⅔ cup)

Reserved fronds from 1 fennel bulb, snipped to make ¼ cup

Put the butter, olive oil, and speck fat in a heavy-gauge stockpot over low heat, stirring until the butter melts and the fat becomes soft and translucent but not browned.

Add the fennel bulb, bay leaves, salt, and pepper and continue to cook, stirring, until the vegetables begin to soften but are not browned.

Add 6 cups water and increase the heat to bring to a boil, stirring occasionally. Immediately reduce the heat to maintain a simmer and cook covered, until the vegetables are soft and tender, about 45 minutes. Stir in the rice, cover, and simmer for another 25 to 30 minutes, until the rice is tender.

Prepare an ice-water bath in your sink. You will need this to cool the pot.

Remove the soup from the heat and stir in the cheese. Place the pot in the ice-water bath and cool to slightly below room temperature. Transfer the soup to an airtight container and refrigerate overnight.

**FINISH THE SOUP:** The following day, discard the bay leaves from the soup. If the soup has become too thick, thin to the desired consistency with cold vegetable broth.

In a small bowl, combine the fennel stems, olive oil, and lemon zest. Season with salt and pepper.

To serve, ladle the soup into individual soup bowls. Lightly drizzle each serving with olive oil. Top with the fennel–lemon zest garnish and sprinkle with the speck matchsticks and fennel fronds.

# Vegetable and Rice Minestrone with Lardo

## MINESTRONE DI RISO ALLA MILANESE

This lardo-enriched version of the ever-popular minestrone is nice in both spring and summer, when vegetables are at their peak flavor. Lardo is made by threading strips of fatback with rosemary and other herbs and spices, and then curing the fat. I always prepare this soup one day prior to serving; refrigerate it overnight, and then gently reheat it to serve. As the soup rests, the already-full flavors blossom even more, and an extraordinary aroma develops.

MAKES 8 TO 10 FIRST-COURSE SERVINGS OR 4 TO 6 MAIN-COURSE SERVINGS

**WINE PAIRING:** The high acidity and tannins of a zingy Nebbiolo-based wine from Valtellina work wonders here. Keep the wine just below room temperature. (Put it in the fridge 30 minutes before you serve it).

2 tablespoons extra virgin olive oil, plus more for drizzling

2 tablespoons finely chopped lardo (see notes)

1 or 2 garlic cloves, thinly sliced on the bias to make 1 tablespoon

2 cups fresh fava bean pods, shelled, beans blanched and peeled to make ½ cup fava beans, or ½ cup fresh peeled and steamed refrigerated fava beans (see "Preparing Fresh Favas," page 72)

½ cup fresh shelled garden peas (English peas or sweet peas; see notes)

½ small white or yellow onion, chopped to make ½ cup

½ carrot, chopped to make ½ cup

½ stalk celery, chopped to make ½ cup

½ zucchini (skin on), chopped to make ½ cup

2 asparagus spears, woody stems and papery scales (see page 95) discarded, cut into 1-inch pieces to make ½ cup

1 cup chopped tomato (skin on)

1 bay leaf, preferably fresh

½ teaspoon finely ground sea salt, plus more as needed

½ teaspoon finely ground white pepper, plus more as needed

8 cups vegetable broth (page 66)

½ cup Arborio *superfino* rice

5 or 6 sprigs flat-leaf Italian parsley, leaves only, roughly chopped to make 2 tablespoons

1 very small bunch basil, leaves only, roughly chopped to make 2 tablespoons

3¾ ounces Parmigiano Reggiano or Grana Padano, finely grated to make 1½ cups

Put the olive oil, lardo, and garlic in a heavy-gauge stockpot over low heat, stirring until the lardo and garlic become soft and translucent but not browned.

Add the fava beans, peas, onion, carrot, celery, zucchini, asparagus, tomato, bay leaf, salt, and pepper. Increase the heat to medium and stir until the vegetables begin to soften but are not browned.

*(continued)*

Add the vegetable broth, increase the heat, and bring to a boil, stirring occasionally. Reduce the heat to maintain a simmer and cook, for 45 minutes. Stir in the rice and continue to simmer, covered, for another 25 minutes, until the rice is tender.

Remove the soup from the heat and discard the bay leaf. Season with salt and pepper. Serve immediately. Or, chill the soup in an ice-water bath in your sink to just below room temperature, then transfer to an airtight container and refrigerate until the next day. Reheat gently before serving.

Just before serving, stir in the parsley and basil. Ladle the soup into individual bowls. Lightly drizzle with olive oil. Serve with the grated cheese on the side.

**NOTES:**

• If you can, choose Lardo di Colonnata, which has PGI (Protected Geographical Indication) status, or Valle d'Aosta Lard d'Arnad, another superior form of lardo from Aosta Valley, which has a PDO (Protected Designation of Origin) status. If lardo is unavailable, substitute 2 tablespoons unsalted butter.

• If fresh peas are out of season, substitute an equal amount of best-quality frozen peas, thawed before use.

# Rice Soup with Lentils and Chickpeas

## MINESTRA DI RISO CON LENTICCHIE E CECI

Umbria is famous for pork, fava beans, black truffles, and tiny lentils from the town of Castelluccio. These lentils have a sweet, earthy flavor and hold their shape well during long cooking. If you can't find them, substitute French Le Puy lentils. Canned Italian chickpeas can be substituted for the dried, quick-soaked ones, but if you're using canned, do not add until the soup is finished. **MAKES 8 TO 10 FIRST-COURSE SERVINGS OR 4 TO 6 MAIN-COURSE SERVINGS**

**WINE PAIRING:** Umbria gives us not only delicious legumes but wine known for its intense tannic structure and blackberry jam–plum–tobacco depth: Sagrantino di Montefalco.

2 tablespoons extra virgin olive oil, plus more for drizzling

2 tablespoons finely chopped pancetta, both lean and fat parts

½ stalk celery, chopped to make ½ cup

½ small white or yellow onion, chopped to make ½ cup

1 savoy cabbage leaf, chopped to make ½ cup

2 bay leaves, preferably fresh

1 teaspoon finely ground white pepper, plus more as needed

⅓ cup Umbrian lentils from Castelluccio or French Le Puy lentils

½ cup Italian dried white chickpeas, soaked overnight in cold water or quick-soaked (see "Quick-Soak Method," page 83), and drained, or canned, rinsed chickpeas

8 cups vegetable broth (page 66)

2 tablespoons tomato paste, preferably Carmelina brand

¾ cup Arborio *superfino* rice

Finely ground sea salt

3¾ ounces Grana Padano, finely grated to make 1½ cups

Put the olive oil and pancetta in a heavy-gauge stockpot over low heat, stirring until the pancetta becomes soft and translucent but not browned.

Add the celery, onion, cabbage, bay leaves, and pepper. Increase the heat to medium and continue to cook, stirring, until the vegetables begin to soften but are not browned.

Add the lentils and soaked and drained chickpeas. (If using canned chickpeas, do not add them until the end of the recipe.) Increase the heat and add the vegetable broth and tomato paste and cook, stirring occasionally, until the soup comes to a boil. Reduce the heat to maintain a simmer and cook, covered, for 1½ hours, stirring occasionally, until the chickpeas are tender.

Stir in the rice, cover the pot, and continue to simmer for another 25 minutes, until the rice is tender.

Remove the soup from the heat and discard the bay leaves. Season with salt and pepper. Ladle the soup into shallow bowls. Drizzle with olive oil. Serve with the grated cheese on the side.

# Rice Soup with Shrimp and Leeks

## MINESTRA DI RISO CON GAMBERETTI E PORRI

A whisper of saffron makes this soup reminiscent of a golden Milanese risotto. I've specified frozen shrimp in the recipe, which are both practical and accessible. But if fresh-caught shrimp are available, by all means, use them. MAKES 8 TO 10 FIRST-COURSE SERVINGS OR 4 TO 6 MAIN-COURSE SERVINGS

**WINE PAIRING:** Wander south to Sicily for a floral, mineral-driven rosé made from Nero d'Avola. You'll find a nice balance of strawberry and hibiscus fruit with ample acid and alcohol to balance the flavors in this dish.

2 tablespoons extra virgin olive oil

2 tablespoons finely chopped pancetta, including the fat

½ stalk celery, chopped to make ½ cup

½ small white or yellow onion, chopped to make ½ cup

1 leek, white and light green parts only, carefully washed of any grit and chopped to make 1 cup

¼ teaspoon saffron threads (see "Worth More Than Its Weight in Gold," page 100)

2 bay leaves, preferably fresh

½ teaspoon finely ground sea salt, plus more as needed

½ teaspoon finely ground white pepper, plus more as needed

8 cups vegetable broth (page 66)

⅔ cup Arborio *superfino* rice

**FOR FINISHING**

2 tablespoons extra virgin olive oil, plus more for drizzling

1 leek, white and light green parts only, carefully washed of any grit and chopped to make 1 cup

Finely grated zest of 4 lemons

1 pound headless 26/30-count shrimp, peeled and deveined if fresh, or thawed if frozen

Finely ground sea salt and white pepper

Put the olive oil and pancetta in a heavy-gauge stockpot over low heat, stirring until the pancetta becomes soft and translucent but not browned.

Add the celery, onion, leek, saffron, bay leaves, salt, and pepper. Increase the heat to medium and cook, stirring, until the vegetables begin to soften but are not browned.

Add the vegetable broth, increase the heat, and bring to a boil, stirring occasionally. Reduce the heat to maintain a simmer and cook for 45 minutes. Stir in the rice and simmer, covered, for another 25 minutes, until the rice is tender.

**FINISH THE SOUP:** While the soup is cooking, warm the olive oil in a large heavy-gauge skillet over low heat. Stir in the leek and lemon zest and cook, stirring, until the leek is soft and translucent but not browned. Increase the heat to medium, add the shrimp, season with salt and pepper, and sauté until the shrimp are cooked through.

Remove the soup from the heat and discard the bay leaves. Adjust the seasoning.

Ladle the soup into individual serving bowls. Spoon a portion of the shrimp-leek mixture over the soup and lightly drizzle with olive oil.

# Tuscan Vegetable and Rice Soup

## MINESTRONE DI RISO ALLA TOSCANA

I am a big believer in using ingredients indigenous to a region in the recipes that region is known for. If possible, purchase extra virgin olive oil produced in Tuscany for this soup. The effort will reward you with a flavor not soon forgotten. You may use canned cannellini beans rather than quick-soaked dried ones. But if you do, stir them in at the end of cooking. One more note: Although rosemary is found throughout Italy, the Tuscans seem to really gravitate to this herb, using it often and with great understanding. MAKES 8 TO 10 FIRST-COURSE SERVINGS OR 4 TO 6 MAIN-COURSE SERVINGS

**WINE PAIRING:** A simple, inexpensive Sangiovese-based red wine from Tuscany is perfect here. Chill it for 30 minutes before serving.

2 tablespoons extra virgin olive oil, preferably from Tuscany, plus more for drizzling

2 tablespoons finely chopped pancetta, both lean and fat parts

1 or 2 garlic cloves, thinly sliced on the bias to make 1 tablespoon

½ stalk celery, chopped to make ½ cup

½ small white or yellow onion, chopped to make ½ cup

½ carrot, chopped to make ½ cup

1 leek, white and light green parts only, carefully washed of any grit and chopped to make ½ cup

½ cup chopped escarole

½ zucchini (skin on), chopped to make ½ cup

1 small tomato, chopped to make ½ cup

1 bay leaf, preferably fresh

1 sprig rosemary, needles chopped to make 1 tablespoon

½ teaspoon finely ground white pepper, plus more as needed

8 cups vegetable broth (page 66)

½ cup quick-soaked and drained cannellini beans (see "Quick-Soak Method," page 83), or drained, rinsed canned beans

½ cup Arborio *superfino* rice

Finely ground sea salt

3¾ ounces Parmigiano Reggiano or Grana Padano, finely grated to make 1½ cups

Put the olive oil, pancetta, and garlic in a heavy-gauge stockpot over low heat, stirring until the pancetta and garlic are soft and translucent but not browned.

Add the celery, onion, carrot, leek, escarole, zucchini, tomato, bay leaf, rosemary, and pepper. Increase the heat to medium and cook, stirring, until the vegetables begin to soften but are not browned.

Add the vegetable broth and quick-soaked cannellini beans. (If you're using canned beans, do not add until the soup is finished.) Increase the heat and stir occasionally until the soup is boiling. Immediately lower the heat, cover the pot, and simmer until the beans are soft and tender, about 1½ hours.

Stir in the rice, cover the pot, and continue to simmer for another 25 to 30 minutes. The soup is ready when the vegetables and rice are tender.

Remove the soup from the heat and discard the bay leaf. Adjust the seasoning with salt and pepper. Ladle the soup into shallow bowls. Drizzle each serving with olive oil and serve with the grated cheese on the side.

## Quick-Soak Method for Prepping Dried Beans

IN MY EXPERIENCE, OPTIMALLY, DRIED BEANS SHOULD SOAK IN WATER IN THE REFRIGERATOR OVER-night. But if time is at a premium, use the quick-soak method. Place dried beans in a pot and cover with water to a level three inches above the beans. Heat the water to boiling over high heat. Boil for three minutes. Cover the pot and remove from the heat. Rest on a cooling rack for one hour or until cooled to room temperature. Drain. Proceed with the desired recipe to cook beans.

# Rice Soup with Soft-Poached Eggs

## MINESTRA DI RISO ALL'UOVO IN CAMICIA

The filmy appearance of egg white gently enveloping a poached egg yolk prompted someone to name this soup *in camicia*, which means "in a blouse or shirt." The flavor of pancetta combined with fresh vegetables and an elegant, soft-poached egg adds up to a harmonious soup.

**MAKES 8 TO 10 FIRST-COURSE SERVINGS OR 4 TO 6 MAIN-COURSE SERVINGS**

**WINE PAIRING:** As with the Tuscan Vegetable and Rice Soup, Tuscan Style, choose a simple, inexpensive Sangiovese-based red wine from Tuscany and chill it for 30 minutes before serving.

2 tablespoons extra virgin olive oil, plus more for drizzling

2 tablespoons finely chopped pancetta, both lean and fat parts

½ stalk celery, chopped to make ½ cup

½ carrot, chopped to make ½ cup

½ small white or yellow onion, chopped to make ½ cup

1 leek, white and light green parts only, carefully washed of any grit and chopped to make ½ cup

3 leaves Tuscan kale, center ribs removed, chopped to make ½ cup

2 bay leaves, preferably fresh

½ teaspoon finely ground sea salt, plus more as needed

1 teaspoon finely ground white pepper, plus more as needed

8 cups vegetable broth (page 66)

½ cup Arborio *superfino* rice

½ cup white wine vinegar

8 to 10 large eggs

3¾ ounces Grana Padano or Parmigiano Reggiano, finely grated to make 1½ cups

Put the olive oil and pancetta in a heavy-gauge stockpot over low heat, stirring until the pancetta becomes soft and translucent but not browned.

Add the celery, carrot, onion, leek, kale, bay leaves, salt, and pepper. Increase the heat to medium and cook, stirring occasionally, until the vegetables begin to soften but are not browned.

Add the vegetable broth and increase the heat, stirring occasionally, until the soup is boiling. Reduce the heat to maintain a low simmer and cook, covered, for 45 minutes.

Stir in the rice, cover the pot, and continue to simmer for another 25 to 30 minutes, until the rice is tender.

While the rice is cooking, poach the eggs. Fill a large pot with 4 quarts water and heat to boiling. Reduce the heat to maintain a simmer; stir in the vinegar. Crack 1 egg into a small bowl, making sure the yolk is intact. Stir the water once again to create a swirling vortex; slip the egg into the simmering vinegar-water mixture. The white will encircle the yolk. Simmer until the white is firm and the yolk is still liquid, about 3 minutes. Carefully scoop the egg out of the pot with a slotted spoon and place it in a bowl. Repeat for each egg. Set aside.

When the rice is tender, remove the soup from the heat and discard the bay leaves. Season with salt and pepper. Ladle the soup into shallow bowls. Lightly drizzle with olive oil and top each portion with a poached egg. Serve the grated cheese on the side.

# CHAPTER THREE

# RICE SALADS

INSALATE DI RISO

**Mention rice salads to someone** in the States and the image that pops to mind is an unfortunate one—something you might throw together for the Ladies' Guild potluck, probably moistened with a lot of mayonnaise. In Italy, rice salads dwell in a very different culinary universe, perhaps because rice has been held in high esteem for so long there. More akin to what Americans think of as a casserole, Italian rice salads are beloved for their gluten-free composition, and because they are an artistic expression of local *terroir*. From a warm rice and spinach salad with freshly poached chicken to my spin on the classic Risotto alla Milanese, Italian rice salads are colorful and inventive.

Initially developed and eaten only in and around the rice-growing regions of northern Italy, rice salads have spread to central and southern Italy, largely because of requests from travelers and tourists. Some of the examples I'm featuring here are based on traditional recipes; others are original, inspired by my own experiences in Italy. All are best eaten as a main plate for a casual spring, summer, or autumn lunch—perfect for *al fresco* occasions.

Italian rice salads are often pressed into tins or molds that pack the grains together into decorative shapes, which, when turned out onto serving platters, make pretty presentations. For easiest release, lightly spritz the mold with cooking spray or brush with olive oil before filling with the rice salad mixture. To serve, place a platter over the filled mold, invert, and, with a quick shake, release the salad onto the platter.

PREVIOUS SPREAD: Warm Rice Salad with Buffalo Mozzarella, Tomatoes, and Basil (see recipe, page 93).

OPPOSITE: There are two hundred rice varieties in the Italian registry of agricultural plant species; seventy are currently grown.

# Rice Salad with Seasonal Vegetables

## INSALATA DI RISO ALLA CASCINA COLOMBARA

This recipe calls for the "king of Carnaroli," Acquerello (Italian for "watercolor"), from the Colombara farm in Piedmont, where rice has been cultivated for half a millennium. The Rondolino family (owners of Colombara since 1935) developed Acquerello in the 1990s, and it is the only rice that is grown, aged, whitened, and packaged there. For that process, the unhusked, rough rice is aged for at least one year, then whitened slowly through polishing, and finally recombined with the vital germ. Aging produces rice grains that cook more evenly, reducing the chances that the grains will be cooked in the center but overcooked outside, or cooked outside but raw in the middle. I love the simplicity of this "salad," which allows each seasonal vegetable to stand out on its own: To serve, you will surround the finished bowl of Acquerello rice with individual bowls of grilled, sautéed, and blanched vegetables, plus basil pesto, a pitcher of olive oil, and fresh lemons. If dandelion greens are not available, substitute arugula. MAKES 8 TO 10 SERVINGS

**WINE PAIRING:** Pairing wine with salad—even unusual salads of the Italian-rice ilk—is quite easy, so long as you remember that the wine must be at least as acidic as the food. Luckily, Italian whites are known for their acid-forward profiles; pair this with a delicate Gavi for delicious lemon-fresh minerality.

### FOR THE RICE

1¼ cups Acquerello Carnaroli rice (see note)

4 tablespoons (½ stick) unsalted butter, cubed

1 teaspoon finely ground sea salt

### FOR THE VEGETABLES

2 red bell peppers

6 cups fresh fava bean pods, shelled, beans blanched and peeled to make 2 cups fava beans, or 2 cups fresh peeled and steamed refrigerated fava beans (see "Preparing Fresh Favas," page 72)

1 bunch asparagus spears, woody stems and papery scales (see page 95) discarded, cut into pieces to make 2 cups

2 carrots, sliced to make 2 cups

3 tablespoons extra virgin olive oil, plus more for serving

1 (7-inch) zucchini, sliced to make 2 cups

5 sage leaves, finely snipped

1 large bunch dandelion greens or arugula, leaves only, hand torn to make 2 lightly packed cups

4 lemons, sliced into quarters

Basil pesto (recipe follows), for serving

Sea salt and black pepper in grinders, for the table

**MAKE THE RICE:** In a medium heavy-gauge saucepan or pot over medium heat, combine 4¼ cups water, the rice, butter, and salt. Stir until the water comes to a boil. Reduce the heat to maintain a simmer, stirring until the rice is tender but not mushy and has absorbed almost all of the liquid. This should take 18 to 20 minutes from the simmering stage. Set aside.

*(continued)*

**MAKE THE VEGETABLES:** Meanwhile, using tongs, blister the skin of the bell peppers on all sides over a gas flame on the stovetop or under the broiler. When the roasted peppers are cool enough to handle, peel off and discard the skin. Chop the peppers and place in small serving bowl. Preheat the oven to 350°F.

In a medium heavy-gauge saucepan or pot, heat 4½ cups water to boiling over medium heat. Reduce the heat to maintain a simmer. Blanch the fava beans until al dente; scoop them out into a small serving bowl. Blanch the asparagus pieces until al dente; scoop them out into another small serving bowl. Turn off the heat and discard the cooking water.

Toss the carrots with 1 tablespoon of the olive oil; spread them out on a sheet pan. Roast in the oven until tender, about 20 minutes. Transfer to a small serving bowl.

Add 1 tablespoon of the olive oil to a medium sauté pan over medium heat. Sauté the zucchini with the sage until tender. Transfer to a small serving bowl.

Wipe out the sauté pan. Add the remaining 1 tablespoon olive oil. Sauté the dandelion greens until wilted but not soggy. Transfer to a small serving bowl.

To serve, spoon the cooked rice into a serving dish. Surround the rice with the small bowls of different vegetables. Add a small pitcher of olive oil; place the lemon wedges on a plate, and put out salt and black pepper grinders. Spoon the pesto into a small bowl. Invite guests to build their own salads.

**NOTE:** Because of the processes used to produce Acquerello, it cooks differently than other Carnaroli rice. If your local Italian specialty store doesn't have it, you can purchase online.

# Basil Pesto

MAKES 1 CUP

| | | |
|---|---|---|
| 1 large bunch basil, leaves only, to make 3 cups | 2 teaspoons sea salt | ½ cup extra virgin olive oil |
| | 1 peeled garlic clove | Finely ground sea salt and white pepper |

In a medium heavy-gauge saucepan or pot, heat 4½ cups water to boiling. Reduce the heat to maintain a simmer. Place the basil in a large-holed colander and blanch for 10 seconds. Rinse in ice-cold water.

When cool enough to handle, squeeze the water from the basil. Place the basil, salt, garlic, and olive oil into the bowl of a food processor and pulse until creamy. Season with finely ground sea salt and pepper. Transfer to a serving bowl.

# Warm Rice Salad with Buffalo Mozzarella, Tomatoes, and Basil

**INSALATA DI RISO TIEPIDA CON MOZZARELLA DI BUFALA, POMODORI E BASLICO**

Most Italian rice salads have a little additional salad, or garnish, built into the recipe. These little extras illustrate how ingredients in their prime can be used multiple ways in the same dish. Each ingredient displays different flavors and textures when raw and when cooked. Here, fresh basil, with its flavors of anise, mint, and pepper, is featured three times: once in the creamy cooked rice, again in the fresh tomato basil topping, and yet again as the crowning garnish. **MAKES 8 TO 10 SERVINGS • PHOTOGRAPH ON PAGE 86**

**WINE PAIRING:** Frascati wines are simple, light, almost "chuggable"—blissfully refreshing without distracting from your pristine tomato, basil, and mozzarella.

### FOR THE RICE

1¼ cups *superfino* rice (Arborio, Baldo, Carnaroli, or Roma)

4 tablespoons (½ stick) unsalted butter, cubed

1½ teaspoons finely ground sea salt

⅓ cup plus 1 tablespoon extra virgin olive oil

2 to 3 ripe plum or Roma tomatoes, chopped to make 1½ cups

1 bunch basil, leaves only, hand torn to make 1 lightly packed cup

½ teaspoon finely ground white pepper

### FOR THE TOPPING AND GARNISH

8 ounces fresh buffalo mozzarella in liquid (see page 20), drained and chopped

⅓ cup extra virgin olive oil

1 small bunch basil, leaves only, hand torn to make 1 lightly packed cup, plus 8 to 10 small clusters of fresh basil leaves, for garnish

Finely ground sea salt and white pepper

**MAKE THE RICE:** In a medium heavy-gauge saucepan or pot over medium heat, combine 4¼ cups water, the rice, butter, and 1 teaspoon of the salt. Stir until the water comes to a boil. Reduce the heat to maintain a simmer, stirring until the rice is tender but not mushy and has absorbed almost all of the liquid. This should take about 16 minutes from the simmering stage. Stir to cool slightly. Stir in the olive oil, tomatoes, basil, the remaining ½ teaspoon salt, and the pepper. Mound the warm rice salad onto a large platter.

**MAKE THE TOPPING:** Combine the mozzarella, olive oil, and basil leaves. Season with salt and pepper; spoon over the rice. Garnish with fresh basil clusters. Serve warm.

# Rice Salad with Fresh Brook Trout and Asparagus

## INSALATA DI RISO CON TROTA E ASPARAGI

To make this pretty creation, the rice salad mixture—a combination of the cooked *semifino* (Vialone Nano) or *superfino riso* of your choice (Carnaroli, Arborio, etc.) with lemon zest, asparagus, and olive oil—is gently pressed into a round mold, then unmolded onto a platter. You'll top it with crisply sautéed bite-size pieces of trout, blanched asparagus spears, and a fresh relish of julienned asparagus, lemon zest, and olive oil. Lake trout is native to Italy with an abundance found in the central and northern regions. As a substitute, American brook trout is best. MAKES 8 TO 10 SERVINGS

**WINE PAIRING:** Asparagus can be a challenging food for a wine pairing. Find something lean and dry, without a fruity profile. Flinty Soave would be a welcome partner to the fish and vegetable.

### FOR THE RICE

1¼ cups Vialone Nano or *superfino* rice

4 tablespoons (½ stick) unsalted butter, cubed

½ teaspoon finely ground sea salt

6 tablespoons extra virgin olive oil

Finely grated zest of 4 lemons

8 asparagus spears, woody stems and papery scales (see note) discarded, blanched and very thinly cut on the bias to make 1½ cups

½ teaspoon finely ground sea salt

½ teaspoon finely ground white pepper

### FOR THE TROUT

3½ tablespoons extra virgin olive oil

1 pound boneless, skinless trout fillets, cut into 2-inch pieces

2 ounces dry Italian white wine

Sea salt and finely ground white pepper

### FOR THE ASPARAGUS RELISH

9 asparagus spears, woody stems and papery scales (see note) discarded, blanched and cut into 1-inch pieces

3½ tablespoons extra virgin olive oil

Finely grated zest of 4 lemons

Finely ground sea salt and white pepper

Red-veined sorrel leaves for garnish (optional)

**MAKE THE RICE:** In a medium heavy-gauge saucepan or pot over medium heat, combine 4¼ cups water, the rice, butter, and salt. Stir until the water comes to a boil. Reduce the heat to maintain a simmer, stirring until the rice is tender but not mushy and has absorbed almost all of the liquid. This should take about 16 minutes from the simmering stage.

Remove the pot from the heat. Stir in the olive oil, lemon zest, and asparagus. Season with the salt and pepper. Transfer the rice salad mixture to a 2-quart round mold you have sprayed with nonstick cooking spray or brushed with olive oil. Smooth the top and press down lightly. Set aside.

**MAKE THE TROUT:** Meanwhile, in a large heavy-gauge nonstick skillet over medium heat, warm the olive oil. Being careful not to crowd the pan, add the trout pieces in batches, increase the heat to high, and sauté for 1 to 2 minutes, turning once. As each batch is fried, remove to a paper towel–lined plate and keep warm. Once all of the trout is fried, lower the heat, pour in the white wine, place all of the fish back in the pan, and cook for 1 minute more. Remove from the heat. Season with salt and pepper.

**MAKE THE ASPARAGUS RELISH:** In a small bowl, combine the asparagus, olive oil, and lemon zest and toss. Season with salt and pepper.

Unmold the rice salad mixture onto a large, round platter, Arrange the trout and the asparagus relish over the mound. Garnish with the sorrel leaves, if using.

**NOTE:** Asparagus spears have paper-like scales. For best texture, remove these with a paring knife and discard.

# Rice Salad with Bresaola and Parmigiano Reggiano

## INSALATA DI RISO CON BRESAOLA E PARMIGIANO REGGIANO

Shaved paper-thin *bresaola* is the highlight of this dish. Air-dried, top-round beef that has been defatted and cured for one to three months with a dry rub of salt and spices, *bresaola* is dark red, sweet, and tender. Although PGI (Protected Geographical Indication) *bresaola* produced from Italian beef cannot currently be imported to the States because of a USDA ban, quality *bresaola* from South America is available online. One brand to look for is Bernina, available at upscale gourmet Italian markets such as Eataly. MAKES 8 TO 10 SERVINGS

**WINE PAIRING:** The intense flavors of the bresaola and cheese need a flavorful but not too aggressive wine. Try Cerasuolo D'Abruzzo, a spicy, flavorful rosé from the central coast of Italy.

1¼ cups *superfino* rice (Arborio, Baldo, Carnaroli, or Roma)

4 tablespoons (½ stick) unsalted butter, cubed

1½ teaspoons finely ground sea salt

⅔ cup plus 1 tablespoon extra virgin olive oil

Finely grated zest of 4 lemons

1 small bunch basil, leaves only, hand torn to make ½ cup

½ teaspoon finely ground white pepper

8 ounces quality *bresaola,* sliced paper thin

2½ ounces Parmigiano Reggiano, shaved to make 1 cup

In a medium heavy-gauge saucepan or pot over medium heat, combine 4¼ cups water, the rice, butter, and 1 teaspoon of the salt. Stir until the water comes to a boil. Reduce the heat to maintain a simmer, stirring until the rice is tender but not mushy and has absorbed almost all of the liquid. This should take about 16 minutes from the simmering stage. Remove the pot from the heat; stir the rice to cool slightly.

Stir in ⅓ cup plus 1 tablespoon of the olive oil, the lemon zest, basil, the remaining ½ teaspoon salt, and the pepper. Transfer the mixture to a round 2-quart mold. Smooth the top, pressing down lightly. Set aside for 5 minutes.

Meanwhile, fold the pieces of *bresaola*, and place on a large platter. Gently brush the *bresaola* with the remaining ⅓ cup olive oil. Center and unmold the rice on top. Scatter with the cheese shavings and serve immediately.

# Warm Rice Salad with Seafood and Saffron

## INSALATA DI RISO TIEPIDO AI FRUTTI DI MARE ZAFFERANO

This is my "rice salad" version of legendary Risotto alla Milanese (see page 152 for the legend). In that dish, rich bone marrow is added. Here, however, I am choosing to keep the spotlight on seafood, which works so well with the golden threads. Saffron adds both vibrant color and subtle flavor, making this a lavish main dish. Be sure to use pre-tenderized baby octopus, available from seafood markets. If perfectly tender baby octopus is not available, substitute monkfish. MAKES 8 TO 10 SERVINGS

**WINE PAIRING:** Saffron's intense perfume benefits from wine with a bit of richness and body. Try a medium-bodied, ripe Vermentino from Tuscany—warmer and denser than Vermentinos from the northern coast or islands. Ripe pear, spice, hay, and occasionally even a touch of mild oak make for a lovely pairing to this salad.

### FOR THE SEAFOOD

¼ cup plus 1 tablespoon extra virgin olive oil

6 ounces small clams in their shells, scrubbed

6 ounces small mussels in their shells, beards removed, scrubbed

6 ounces calamari, tentacles left whole, tubes cut into ½-inch pieces

6 ounces tenderized baby octopus, tentacles only, or 6 ounces skinless monkfish, cut in 2-inch pieces

6 onces headless 21/25-count shrimp, peeled and deveined if fresh, or thawed if frozen

1 cup dry Italian white wine

1½ cups Italian tomato puree (*passata*)

1 teaspoon saffron threads (see "Worth More Than Its Weight in Gold," page 100)

6 ounces skinless, boneless trout, cut into 2-inch pieces

1 small bunch basil, leaves only, hand torn to make ½ lightly packed cup

Finely ground sea salt and white pepper

### FOR THE RICE

1¼ cups Carnaroli *superfino* or Vialone Nano *semifino* rice

1 teaspoon saffron threads

4 tablespoons (½ stick) unsalted butter, cubed

1 teaspoon finely ground sea salt

**MAKE THE SEAFOOD:** In a large heavy-gauge sauté pan or skillet, warm the olive oil over high heat. When the oil is hot but not smoking, add the clams, mussels, calamari, octopus, shrimp, wine, tomato puree, and saffron. Stir until boiling. Immediately lower the heat and simmer, stirring, until the seafood is fully cooked and the shellfish have opened, 3 to 5 minutes. Discard any unopened shellfish. In a small heavy skillet, sauté the trout, turning once until cooked. Add the trout and basil to the pan with the seafood; season with salt and pepper. Keep the pan warm while you make the rice.

**MAKE THE RICE:** In a medium heavy-gauge saucepan or pot over medium heat, combine 4¼ cups water, the rice, saffron, butter, and salt. Stir until the water comes to a boil. Reduce

the heat to maintain a simmer, stirring until the rice is tender but not mushy and has absorbed almost all of the liquid. This should take about 16 minutes from the simmering stage. Remove the pot from the heat. Stir to cool slightly.

To serve, spoon the warm saffron rice onto a large platter. Top with the warm seafood and any pan juices.

## Worth More Than Its Weight in Gold

SAFFRON, THE DRIED STIGMAS OF THE SAFFRON CROCUS (*CROCUS SATIVUS*), REMAINS THE WORLD'S costliest spice, even though it has been cultivated for seasoning, dye, fragrance, and medicine for the past 3,500 years. Its cultivation requires specific terrain and weather and, when ripe, harvesting must take place in a scant one to two weeks. Harvesting is done by hand, with 150 crocus flowers yielding only 1 gram of dry saffron threads. In cooking, saffron adds both color and flavor: slightly medicinal and metallic, with a fragrance reminiscent of the ocean and fresh hay. A little saffron goes a long way. Too much can overpower a dish. But used judiciously, saffron provides a subtle, seductive, and aromatic flavor.

# Warm Rice Salad with Chicken, Spinach, and Mushrooms

### INSALATA DI RISO TIEPIDA CON POLLO, SPINACI E FUNGHI

Because this main-course "salad" is served warm and full of savory ingredients, it more closely resembles what Stateside diners are used to enjoying in a casserole. To make it, you'll poach a whole chicken, using both the meat and the poaching liquid in the finished dish. I make the broth and the chicken the day before and cover it in the refrigerator. This speeds preparation the day I want to serve the dish. If the broth seems bland, don't worry. It will cook down as the rice simmers, intensifying flavors. You don't want to start with a salty stock, or the finished rice will be unpalatable. MAKES 8 TO 10 SERVINGS

**WINE PAIRING:** Young Barbera d'Asti provides a bright, high-acid profile and a spicy, earthy palate—a wonderful contrast to the sweet, rich casserole.

**FOR THE CHICKEN BROTH
(MAKES 6 QUARTS)**

3 tablespoons extra virgin olive oil

1 medium carrot, chopped to make at least ¾ cup

1 small white or yellow onion, chopped to make at least ¾ cup

1 small stalk celery, chopped to make at least ¾ cup

1 whole organic chicken, cleaned and giblets removed (see note)

1 sprig fresh rosemary

1 sprig thyme

1 bay leaf, preferably fresh

1 teaspoon finely ground white pepper

**FOR THE RICE**

1¼ cups *superfino* rice (Arborio, Baldo, Carnaroli, or Roma)

4 tablespoons (½ stick) unsalted butter, cubed

1½ teaspoons finely ground sea salt

¼ cup extra virgin olive oil

Finely grated zest of 2 lemons

4½ ounces white or brown button mushrooms, trimmed and very thinly sliced to make 2½ cups

½ teaspoon finely ground white pepper

**FOR THE SPINACH SALAD**

2 cups lightly packed baby spinach leaves

¼ cup extra virgin olive oil

Finely grated zest of 2 lemons

Finely ground sea salt and white pepper

**MAKE THE CHICKEN BROTH:** In a 12-quart, or larger, heavy-gauge stockpot, combine the olive oil, carrot, onion, celery, whole chicken, rosemary, thyme, bay leaf, pepper, and 2 gallons water. Bring to a boil over medium heat, ensuring that the chicken is completely immersed in water. Reduce the heat to maintain a slow simmer for 2 to 2½ hours, until the chicken is fully cooked. Transfer the chicken to a cutting board. Strain the broth through a fine-mesh sieve, reserving the broth; the vegetables can be saved for another use; set the broth aside.

*(continued)*

Remove the skin, bones, fat, and cartilage from the chicken and discard. Cut the chicken meat into 1-inch pieces. Set aside.

At this point, you may cover both the broth and the chicken meat and refrigerate them separately. When you're ready to complete the recipe, reheat the chicken gently, covered with foil, in a low oven (225°F) for just long enough to remove the chill from the meat.

**MAKE THE RICE:** In a medium heavy-gauge saucepan or pot over medium heat, combine 4½ cups of the chicken broth with the rice, butter, and 1 teaspoon of the salt. Stir until the water comes to a boil. Reduce the heat to maintain a simmer, stirring until the rice is tender but not mushy and has absorbed almost all of the liquid. This should take about 16 minutes from the simmering stage. Remove the pot from the heat and stir in the olive oil, lemon zest, and mushrooms. Season with the remaining ½ teaspoon salt and the pepper.

**MAKE THE SPINACH SALAD:** Toss the spinach, olive oil, and lemon zest together in a bowl. Season with salt and pepper.

To serve, arrange half of the chicken pieces in a ring on a large platter, leaving a few inches empty around the edge for the spinach salad. Spoon the warm rice salad mixture into the center. Arrange the spinach salad around the chicken and serve.

**NOTE:** In order for meat or poultry products to legally bear the "organic" label, they must meet USDA standards. Livestock intended to be processed and sold as organic must have been raised on certified organic land, fed certified organic feed, given no antibiotics or growth hormones, and enjoyed outdoor access. Whole organic chickens range from 3½ pounds to 4½ pounds.

# CHAPTER FOUR

# RISOTTI

**It is the perfect match: velvety** risotto—the rice dish that Italians love most—with the *japonica* rices that grow so well in Italy. While they cook, these thick, short-grained rices have the ability to soak up flavorful liquids at the same time that they release starches, an exchange that results in fully flavored dishes that are tender, toothsome, and bathed in creamy sauce.

While some chefs swear by one or another rice variety (see page 15), really, it's personal preference—and availability— that will dictate which *superfino* Italian rice you choose when making risotto. What is *not* negotiable is the origin of the rice: People ask me all the time, "Can I use . . . [insert the names of any non-Italian rices] . . . to make risotto?" The simple answer is, "No." For risotto to be risotto, you must use Italian rice.

With the exception of Vialone Nano, a *semifino* rice, I prefer using *superfino* rice for risottos. And for the sake of consistency, that is what I specify in all of these recipes. But in most cases, I leave the choice of which *superfino* up to you.

Among the varieties easily available outside of Italy, Carnaroli, "the king of rice," is perhaps more forgiving in the cooking process than Vialone Nano, but the latter cooks faster, absorbs flavor exceptionally well, and has long been the rice of choice for seafood risottos. Meanwhile, Arborio has the highest starch content,

guaranteeing a creamy texture, and is the Italian rice most easily found in the United States, making it more affordable and familiar to home cooks here. For a few recipes where I want to achieve a specific texture in the finished dish, I suggest using a specific rice, sometimes something other than Arborio.

When it comes to cooking risotto, the method I include with each recipe follows the tried-and-true traditional steps. (I've included some alternate methods for the adventuresome at the end of the chapter.) Please note that there will be some variation in how much liquid you need to make a successful risotto, depending on everything from which rice you choose to the age of the rice and the calibration of your stovetop. Factoring in a little wiggle room to allow for this, while it takes about 4½ cups simmering liquid to make a quart of risotto with 1¼ cups rice, in most recipes I specify you have 6 cups simmering liquid at the ready. Each risotto recipe begins by heating water or *brodo* (broth or stock) to a simmer in a pot, and making a *soffrito* (sautéed fat and onion) in a pan. Rice is then toasted in the *soffrito* to coat the grains, opening them up to absorb the wine and hot broth you will begin to ladle into the rice in measured doses, stirring constantly. Once the rice moves slowly across the pan *all'onda* ("with waves") as you stir it, it is ready to remove from the heat. Risottos are finished with cold butter and, sometimes, cheese. Other

*condimenti* ("ingredients") such as seafood, meats, and vegetables may be added at the beginning or at the end.

It's vital that you read each recipe all the way through before starting to cook, because once you begin, there's no stepping away. Most recipes are divided with the ingredients needed for each part, in sequence. So when you shop, you'll need to purchase ingredients listed for the stock, the *condimenti,* and the risotto. It's a good idea to prepare your stock or any roasted ingredients the day before. And when you're ready to make the risotto, set up your work surface with everything you will need already prepped, measured, and within easy reach. An easy-to-read manual timer is good to have on hand as well.

A few helpful notes: Risottos are all made with water, broth, or stock. Because the liquids reduce so much as the risotto cooks, the flavor intensifies. That's why it is so important to begin risotto with a mildly flavored, lower-sodium stock or broth. If the starting broth or stock is too intensely flavored or sodium-laden, you'll end up overpowering the flavor of the finished risotto. Also, when water is called for in a risotto recipe, I use mineral water or boiled tap water to ensure that there is no residual chlorine taste.

PREVIOUS SPREAD: Risotto with Asparagus and Taleggio (see recipe, page 110)

ABOVE: Risottos are finished with cold butter and sometimes cheese.

# Risotto with Arugula Pesto, Lemon, and Pine Nuts

**RISOTTO AL PESTO DI RUCOLA, LIMONE E PINOLI**

Outside of Italy, the best-known pesto is one made with basil and pine nuts. This one swaps out the basil for arugula. And as you will see in this chapter, pestos can be made with all manner of greens or mushrooms and a variety of seeds and nuts. This version, made with pine nuts, lemon, and peppery arugula, adds fresh flavor and verdant color to the finished risotto. Because of the easy availability of arugula, this dish can be served year-round, on its own as a light lunch, or with a *primi piatti* for a satisfying supper.  MAKES 6 SERVINGS

**WINE PAIRING:** This dish encourages some exploration *just* outside of the present-day borders of Italy: Head north to Austria. Grüner Veltliner is a great midweight white that resembles a slightly more restrained Pinot Grigio, but Grüner tends to have a delicious peppery arugula finish that will mirror the risotto's flavors marvelously.

6 cups vegetable broth (page 66)

**FOR THE ARUGULA PESTO**

⅓ cup pine nuts

3 cups lightly packed baby arugula leaves

Finely grated zest of 1 lemon

⅓ cup extra virgin olive oil

Finely ground sea salt and white pepper

**FOR THE *CONDIMENTI***

2 tablespoons extra virgin olive oil

1 slice medium white or yellow onion, finely chopped to make ¼ cup

Finely ground sea salt and white pepper

**FOR THE RISOTTO**

2 tablespoons extra virgin olive oil

1 slice medium white or yellow onion, finely chopped to make ¼ cup

Finely ground sea salt and white pepper

1¼ cups *superfino* rice (Arborio, Baldo, Carnaroli, or Roma)

⅓ cup dry Italian white wine

2 tablespoons cold unsalted butter

2½ ounces Parmigiano Reggiano or Grana Padano, finely grated to make 1 cup

Extra virgin olive oil

⅓ cup lightly packed arugula leaves

Shaved curls of Parmigiano Reggiano or Grana Padano, for garnish

In a medium heavy-gauge saucepan or pot over medium heat, bring the broth to a boil; reduce the heat to maintain a slow simmer.

**MAKE THE PESTO:** In the work bowl of a food processor, combine the pine nuts, arugula, lemon zest, and olive oil. Pulse until creamy and smooth. Season with salt and pepper. Refrigerate until needed.

**MAKE THE *CONDIMENTI*:** In a medium heavy-gauge sauté pan or skillet at least 3 inches deep (with lid handy), combine the olive oil and onion over low heat. Cook, stirring frequently, until the onion is soft and translucent but not browned. It's okay to add 2 tablespoons water to help the onion soften without browning, just be sure the water has all evaporated before moving to the next step. Season with salt and pepper. Stir in ½ cup of the arugula pesto. Transfer to a bowl and cover to keep warm while you prepare the rice.

**MAKE THE RISOTTO:** Wipe out the pan and place it over low heat. Add the olive oil and onion and cook, stirring frequently, until the onion is soft and translucent but not browned. It's okay to add 2 tablespoons water to help the onion soften without browning, just be sure the water has evaporated before moving to the next step. Season with salt and pepper. Add the rice and stir for 2 minutes, until the kernels are well coated. Pour in the white wine and stir until the wine has completely evaporated. Ladle ½ cup of the broth into the rice and stir until the broth has reduced by two thirds. Add another ladleful of broth, again stirring until reduced by two thirds. Repeat this process until most of the broth has been absorbed by the rice and the rice is tender, but not mushy, with a creamy consistency. (You may have as much as a cup of broth left unused.) When stirred, the rice should move across the pan in slow waves (*all'onda*). This should take about 14 minutes from the time you begin ladling the broth into the rice.

Remove the risotto from the heat. Stir in the *condimenti* and cover the pot for 2 minutes. Add the butter and grated cheese and stir until creamy. Adjust the seasoning with salt and pepper.

Spoon the risotto onto a serving platter, drizzle with olive oil, and top with the arugula leaves and shaved cheese curls. Serve immediately.

# Risotto with Asparagus and Taleggio

### RISOTTO AGLI ASPARAGI E TALEGGIO

Asparagus stars in this dish in two ways: The stalk trim is used to make the broth. And paper-thin slices of the tender parts of the stalks go into the risotto itself. Nothing goes to waste. While you may substitute vegetable broth for homemade asparagus broth, making it from scratch adds an extra flavor dimension to this risotto. Taleggio is a semisoft, washed-rind ripened cheese with a strong aroma but mild, almost fruity, flavor. To cook with Taleggio, remove the rind, or wash it very well with clean cotton cloths. **MAKES 6 SERVINGS • PHOTOGRAPH ON PAGE 104**

**WINE PAIRING:** To successfully match a wine with the funky, savory cheese and notoriously difficult-to-pair asparagus in this risotto, I'd recommend something demure and restrained. Look for a high-quality Pinot Grigio from Alto Adige or the Dolomiti—something young, mineral-driven, and highly acidic to keep your mouth watering, but with simple, linear flavors that will happily play "chorus line" to the starring role of the risotto.

### FOR THE ASPARAGUS BROTH

1 tablespoon unsalted butter

1 tablespoon extra virgin olive oil

1 medium white or yellow onion, chopped

5 sprigs Italian flat-leaf parsley

1 stalk celery, chopped

1 pound chopped asparagus spear bottoms (trimmed from 2 pounds asparagus; save asparagus tops from 1 pound of the asparagus for the *condimenti*; save the rest for another use)

12 whole white peppercorns

1 teaspoon sea salt

2 lemon slices

### FOR THE ASPARAGUS CONDIMENTI

4-inch tops from 1 pound trimmed asparagus, sliced paper-thin on a bias

### FOR THE RISOTTO

2 tablespoons extra virgin olive oil, plus more for drizzling

1 slice medium white or yellow onion, finely chopped to make ¼ cup

1 teaspoon finely ground sea salt, plus more as needed

½ teaspoon finely ground white pepper, plus more as needed

1¼ cups Carnaroli *superfino* rice

⅓ cup dry Italian white wine

2 tablespoons cold unsalted butter

4 ounces Taleggio cheese, at room temperature, rind removed, cut into small cubes to make 1 cup

**MAKE THE ASPARAGUS BROTH:** In a large heavy-gauge saucepan or pot, warm the butter and olive oil over medium heat. Add the onion, parsley, celery, and asparagus spear bottoms and cook, stirring frequently, until the vegetables are tender and translucent but not browned. Add 8½ cups water, the peppercorns, salt, and lemon slices; heat to boiling. Reduce the heat to maintain a simmer and cook, partially covered, until the broth is flavorful and somewhat reduced, 1 to 1½ hours.

*(continued)*

**MAKE THE ASPARAGUS *CONDIMENTI*:** Place the 1 pound of thinly sliced asparagus in a strainer or colander and immerse it in the hot broth pot for 3 minutes. Rinse the tenderized asparagus in cold water. Set aside.

Pour the broth through a fine-mesh sieve into a medium saucepan, reserving the broth and discarding the solids. You should have 6½ to 7 cups broth. At this point, you can cool the broth to room temperature, cover it, and refrigerate for later use, if you like.

**MAKE THE RISOTTO:** Bring 6 cups of the asparagus broth to a boil over medium heat. Reduce the heat to maintain a very low simmer.

In a medium heavy-gauge sauté pan or skillet at least 3 inches deep (with lid handy), warm the olive oil over low heat. Add the onion and cook, stirring frequently, until soft and translucent but not browned. It's okay to add 2 tablespoons water to help the onion soften without browning, just be sure the water has evaporated before moving to the next step. Season with the salt and pepper. Add the rice and stir for 2 minutes, until the kernels are well coated. Pour in the white wine and stir until the wine has completely evaporated. Ladle ½ cup of the simmering asparagus broth into the rice and stir until the broth has reduced by two thirds. Add another ladleful of broth, again stirring until reduced by two thirds. Repeat this process until most of the broth has been absorbed by the rice and the rice is tender but not mushy, with a creamy consistency. (You may have as much as a cup of broth left unused.) When stirred, the rice should move across the pan in slow waves (*all'onda*). This should take about 14 minutes from the time you begin ladling the broth into the rice.

Remove the risotto from the heat. Stir in the sliced asparagus *condimenti*; cover the pot for 2 minutes. Stir in the butter and Taleggio until the cheese has melted and the risotto is creamy. Season with salt and pepper. Spoon the risotto into a serving bowl or individual dishes. Drizzle with olive oil and serve immediately.

# Risotto Amatrice Style with Aged Pecorino

### RISOTTO ALL'AMATRICIANA MANTECATO CON PECORINO STAGIONATO

Pasta Amatriciana is a well-known Italian specialty that takes its name from the town of Amatrice near Rome. I fashioned this risotto to feature the primary ingredients typically used in that pasta sauce: guanciale (cured pork jowl or cheeks), tomatoes, red chili pepper, and black pepper. While Stagionata (an aged sheep's milk cheese) is traditionally used, I specify Pecorino Romano here, since it's easier to find. Guanciale is a central Italian specialty of Lazio and Umbria. It has a more delicate texture than pancetta, but a more assertive flavor. During cooking, guanciale fat melts, adding its flavor to the finished dish. If you can't find guanciale, substitute pancetta. If you find that making the Pecorino Romano cheese curls is too difficult, simply shave the cheese into shards. MAKES 6 SERVINGS

WINE PAIRING: Assertive dishes like this one do well with a good Italian rosato. Look to southern Italy for a rosato made from Aglianico. Rosé wines made from Aglianico are bright and floral with sweet raspberry notes and a compelling herbal finish; they are able to stand up to the flavors in this risotto, while still proving light and refreshing.

### FOR THE GUANCIALE TOMATO SAUCE

2 tablespoons extra virgin olive oil

3½ ounces guanciale, finely chopped to make ⅔ cup

2 slices medium white or yellow onion, finely chopped to make ⅓ cup

2 cups canned, chopped San Marzano tomatoes, juice included

¼ to ½ teaspoon minced, seeded red chili pepper

1 teaspoon finely ground black pepper

### FOR THE RISOTTO

1¼ cups *superfino* rice, preferably Carnaroli

⅓ cup dry Italian white wine

2 tablespoons cold unsalted butter

2½ ounces Pecorino Romano, finely grated to make 1 cup, plus Pecorino Romano curls or shaved shards, for garnish

Finely ground sea salt and black pepper

Extra virgin olive oil for drizzling

Fresh-cracked black pepper

**MAKE THE GUANCIALE TOMATO SAUCE:** In a large heavy-gauge sauté pan or skillet over low heat, combine the olive oil, guanciale, onion, tomatoes, red chili pepper, and black pepper. Cook, stirring frequently, until the onion is soft and the sauce coats the back of a spoon, 20 to 25 minutes. Sert aside.

**MAKE THE RISOTTO:** In a medium heavy-gauge saucepan or pot, bring 6 cups water to a boil over medium heat. Reduce the heat to maintain a very low simmer.

*(continued)*

When the guanciale tomato sauce is done, add the rice to the sauce and stir for 2 minutes, until the kernels are well coated. Pour in the white wine and stir until the wine has completely evaporated. Ladle ½ cup of the water into the rice and stir until the water has reduced by two thirds. Add another ladleful of water, again stirring until reduced by two thirds. Repeat this process until most of the water has been absorbed by the rice and the rice is tender but not mushy, with a creamy consistency. (You may have as much as a cup of water left unused.) When stirred, the rice should move across the pan in slow waves (*all'onda*). This should take about 14 minutes from the time you begin ladling the water into the rice.

Remove the risotto from the heat and cover for 2 minutes. Add the butter and grated cheese and stir until the risotto is creamy. Season with salt and ground pepper. Spoon the risotto into a serving bowl; drizzle with olive oil and top with a few grinds of pepper. Garnish with cheese curls and serve immediately.

# Venetian Seafood Risotto

## RISOTTO AI FRUTTI DI MARE ALLA VENEZIANA

At the mention of Venice, lapped by the waves of the Adriatic Sea, I immediately imagine canals, gondoliers, St. Mark's Square, and pigeons. All that, and the beautiful seafood that is so much a part of Venetian cuisine. This Venetian-style risotto, flavored by shrimp stock and tomato, includes five kinds of seafood. To make it most authentically Italian, use *semi-fino* Vialone Nano rice. And, if possible, make the shrimp stock from scratch. If too pressed for time, substitute high-quality purchased seafood stock. It takes three pounds of shrimp to make the pound of heads, tails, and shells needed for the stock. You'll use a pound of the bodies for the risotto and can save the rest for another use. MAKES 6 SERVINGS

**WINE PAIRING:** Pair this classic seafood risotto with Soave, a classic wine from the same region. Soave whites made from the Garganega grape are citrusy, mineral-driven, and clean.

### FOR THE SHRIMP STOCK

¼ cup extra virgin olive oil

1 small white or yellow onion, finely chopped to make 1 cup

4 garlic cloves

1 pound shells, heads, and tails from 3 pounds 21/25-count shrimp (reserve 1 pound of the shrimp bodies for the risotto; refrigerate the rest for another use)

½ cup dry Italian white wine

### FOR THE SEAFOOD
### CONDIMENTI

⅓ cup extra virgin olive oil

6 ounces small clams in shells, scrubbed

6 ounces small mussels in shells, beards removed, scrubbed

6 ounces calamari, tubes cut into ½-inch pieces, tentacles left whole

1 pound 21/25-count headless shrimp, peeled and deveined (reserved from making the shrimp stock)

6 ounces tenderized baby octopus tentacles (optional)

⅓ cup dry Italian white wine

½ cup canned, chopped, drained San Marzano tomatoes

1 very small bunch basil, leaves only, roughly chopped to make 2 tablespoons

1 large sprig Italian flat-leaf parsley, leaves only, roughly chopped to make 1 tablespoon

### FOR THE RISOTTO

2 tablespoons extra virgin olive oil, plus more for drizzling

1 slice medium white or yellow onion, finely chopped to make ¼ cup

Finely ground sea salt and white pepper

1¼ cups Vialone Nano *semifino* rice

⅓ cup dry Italian white wine

2 tablespoons cold unsalted butter

**MAKE THE SHRIMP STOCK:** In a heavy-gauge stockpot, combine the olive oil, onion, and garlic; shrimp shells, heads, and tails; wine; and 8 cups water. Heat to a simmer over medium heat, stirring. (Do not boil.) Lower the heat to maintain a very low simmer and cook for 45 minutes. Strain the stock through a fine-mesh sieve into a saucepan, reserving the stock and discarding the solids. Rinse the pot and refill with the stock. You should have 6½ to 7 cups. Keep at a gentle simmer over very low heat.

*(continued)*

**MAKE THE SEAFOOD *CONDIMENTI*:** In a 12-inch heavy-gauge sauté pan over medium heat, warm the olive oil. Add the clams, mussels, calamari, shrimp, tenderized octopus, wine, tomatoes, basil, and parsley. Sauté, stirring, until the shellfish have opened and the seafood is cooked through but not rubbery. Discard any unopened shellfish. Remove from the heat and cover to keep the seafood warm while the rice is cooking.

**MAKE THE RISOTTO:** In a medium heavy-gauge sauté pan or skillet at least 3 inches deep (with lid handy), warm the olive oil over low heat. Add the onion. Stir until the onion is tender and translucent but not browned. It's okay to add 2 tablespoons water to help the onion soften without browning, just be sure the water has evaporated before moving to the next step. Season with salt and pepper. Add the rice and stir for 2 minutes, until the kernels are well coated. Pour in the wine and stir until the wine has completely evaporated. Ladle ½ cup of the simmering shrimp stock into the rice and stir until the stock has reduced by two thirds. Add another ladleful of stock, again stirring until reduced by two thirds. Repeat this process until most of the stock has been absorbed by the rice and the rice is tender but not mushy, with a creamy consistency. (You may have as much as a cup of stock left unused.) When stirred, the rice should move across the pan in slow waves (*all'onda*). This should take about 14 minutes from the time you begin ladling the stock into the rice.

Remove the risotto from the heat. Gently fold in the seafood and cover for 2 minutes. Add the butter and stir until creamy. Season with salt and pepper. Spoon the risotto into a serving bowl or individual dishes and drizzle with olive oil. Serve immediately.

# Risotto with Gorgonzola, Apples, and Walnuts

### RISOTTO AL GORGONZOLA, MELE E NOCI

Apples, blue cheese, and walnuts are a popular combination in many culinary traditions. This Italian risotto combines Granny Smith apples, toasted walnuts, and Gorgonzola, the famous blue-veined cow's milk cheese from northern Italy. Aged Gorgonzola piccante has a sharper, more intense flavor than dolce, which is sweeter. Either will work well in this dish.

MAKES 6 SERVINGS

**WINE PAIRING:** Mimic the apple and walnut flavors in this risotto dish with a rich chardonnay that has some oak to it.

2 tablespoons extra virgin olive oil, plus more for drizzling

1 slice medium white or yellow onion, finely chopped to make ¼ cup

½ teaspoon finely ground sea salt, plus more as needed

½ teaspoon finely ground white pepper, plus more as needed

1¼ cups *superfino* rice, preferably Carnaroli

⅓ cup dry Italian white wine

1 Granny Smith apple, peeled, cored, and finely chopped to make 1¼ cups

1 cup raw walnuts, toasted (see recipe introduction page 49) and coarsely chopped

2 tablespoons cold unsalted butter

4 ounces Gorgonzola dolce or piccante, at room temperature, crumbled to make 1 cup

In a medium heavy-gauge saucepan or pot, bring 6 cups water to a boil over medium heat. Reduce the heat to maintain a low simmer.

In a medium heavy-gauge sauté pan or skillet at least 3 inches deep (with lid handy), warm the olive oil over low heat. Add the onion and cook, stirring frequently, until the onion is translucent and tender but not browned. Season with the salt and pepper. Add the rice and stir for 2 minutes, until the kernels are well coated. Pour in the white wine and stir until the wine is completely evaporated. Ladle ½ cup of the simmering water into the rice. Stir until the liquid has reduced by two thirds. Repeat until most of the water has been absorbed by the rice and the rice is tender but not mushy, with a creamy consistency. (You may have as much as a cup of water left unused.) This should take about 14 minutes from the time you begin ladling the simmering water into the rice.

Remove the risotto from the heat; add ¾ cup of the apple and all but ½ cup of the walnuts, and cover the pot for 2 minutes. Stir in the butter and cheese until the risotto is creamy. Season with salt and pepper. Spoon the risotto into a serving bowl or individual dishes, drizzle with olive oil, and top with the remaining apples and nuts. Serve immediately.

# Risotto with Leeks and Grana Padano

## RISOTTO CON PORRI E GRANA PADANO

The French sometimes call leeks "poor man's asparagus," but in my opinion, there is nothing "poor" about these mild, long-shanked onions. Their mild flavor, brightened with spring onion and emboldened by Grana Padano, makes this a sprightly, nuanced risotto that's very approachable. I like to make it in the spring when both onions and leeks first appear. You'll garnish the dish with curls of Grana Padano. If you find these are too difficult to make, shards of the cheese will work. **MAKES 6 SERVINGS**

**WINE PAIRING:** A savory white with a bit of body pairs nicely with the sweet leeks and cheese in this risotto. For that? Head to Tuscany for a Vermentino di Toscana with a honeyed, apple pie depth.

### FOR THE SPRING ONION–LEEK *CONDIMENTI*

2 tablespoons extra virgin olive oil

3 spring onions or scallions, cut in half lengthwise, and finely chopped

4 slices leek, white and light green parts only, carefully washed of any grit or dirt, finely chopped to make ¼ cup

½ teaspoon finely ground sea salt

½ teaspoon finely ground white pepper

### FOR THE RISOTTO

6 cups vegetable broth (page 66)

2 tablespoons extra virgin olive oil, plus more for drizzling

1 slice medium white or yellow onion, finely chopped to make ¼ cup

Finely ground sea salt and white pepper

1¼ cups *superfino* rice (Arborio, Baldo, Carnaroli, or Roma)

⅓ cup dry Italian white wine

2 tablespoons cold unsalted butter

2½ ounces Grana Padano, finely grated to make 1 cup, plus Grana Padano shaved curls or shards, for garnish

**MAKE THE SPRING ONION–LEEK *CONDIMENTI*:** In a medium heavy-gauge sauté pan or skillet at least 3 inches deep (with lid handy), combine the olive oil, spring onions, and leek. Cook slowly over low heat until the onions and leek are soft but not browned. It's okay to add 2 tablespoons water to help the onion and leek soften without browning, just be sure the water has evaporated before moving to the next step. Season with the salt and pepper. Transfer the *condimenti* to a bowl. Wipe out the pan; set aside.

**MAKE THE RISOTTO:** In a medium heavy-gauge saucepan or pot over medium heat, bring the vegetable broth to a boil over medium heat. Reduce the heat to maintain a gentle simmer.

In the pan used to make the *condimenti*, combine the olive oil and onion over low heat. Cook, stirring frequently, until the onion is soft and translucent but not browned. It's okay to add 2 tablespoons water to help the onion soften without browning, just be sure the water has evaporated before moving to the next step. Season with salt and pepper. Add the rice and stir for 2 minutes, until the kernels are well coated. Pour in the white wine and stir continuously until the wine has completely evaporated. Ladle ½ cup of the hot vegetable broth into the rice and stir until reduced by two thirds. Add another ladleful of hot broth, again stirring until reduced by two thirds. Repeat this process until most of the vegetable broth has been absorbed and the rice is tender but not mushy, with a creamy consistency. (You may have as much as a cup of broth left unused.) When stirred, the rice should move across the pan in a slow wave (*all'onda*). This should take about 14 minutes from the time you begin to ladle the simmering broth into the rice.

Remove the risotto from the stovetop, stir in the spring onion–leek *condimenti*, and cover for 1 minute. Add the butter and grated cheese and stir until creamy. Season with salt and pepper.

Spoon the risotto into a serving bowl or individual dishes. Drizzle with olive oil and garnish with the cheese curls. Serve immediately.

# Risotto with Lemony Spinach Pesto and Parmigiano Reggiano

### RISOTTO AL PESTO DI SPINACI E PARMIGIANO REGGIANO

A lemon-zesty spinach pesto gives this risotto vibrant flavor and color, and snipped fresh spinach leaves, extra texture. Baby spinach leaves are tender and don't need to have their stems removed. More mature leaves will work, too, although it's important to remove and discard their stems. I suggest stirring in just ¼ cup of the pesto, but you can add more if you like. Any left over works well with pasta or bruschetta.  MAKES 6 SERVINGS

**WINE PAIRING:** Lemon and spinach call for Verdicchio and its fresh green notes. Find a young, lightweight option from Le Marche, like Fulvia Tombolini, for a simple, successful pairing.

### FOR THE SPINACH PESTO

3 cups baby spinach leaves or mature spinach leaves with stems removed

Finely grated zest of 1 lemon

⅓ cup extra virgin olive oil

Finely ground sea salt and white pepper

### FOR THE RISOTTO

2 tablespoons extra virgin olive oil, plus more for drizzling

1 slice medium white or yellow onion, finely chopped to make ¼ cup

1¼ cups *superfino* rice (Arborio, Baldo, Carnaroli, or Roma)

⅓ cup dry Italian white wine

¼ cup loosely packed fresh-snipped baby spinach leaves

2 tablespoons cold unsalted butter

2½ ounces Parmigiano Reggiano, finely grated to make 1 cup, plus shaved curls of Parmigiano Reggiano, for garnish

Finely ground sea salt and white pepper

In a medium heavy-gauge saucepan or pot over medium heat, bring 6 cups water to a boil; reduce the heat to maintain a slow simmer.

**MAKE THE PESTO:** In the work bowl of a food processor, combine the spinach, lemon zest, and olive oil. Pulse until creamy and smooth. Season with salt and pepper. Refrigerate until needed.

**MAKE THE RISOTTO:** In a medium heavy-gauge sauté pan or skillet at least 3 inches deep (with lid handy), combine the olive oil and onion over low heat. Cook, stirring frequently, until the onion is soft and translucent but not browned. It's okay to add 2 tablespoons water to help the onion soften without browning, just be sure the water has evaporated before moving to the next step. Season with the salt and pepper. Add the rice and stir for 2 minutes, until the kernels are well coated. Pour in the white wine and stir continuously until the wine has completely evaporated. Ladle ½ cup of the simmering water into the rice and stir until the water has reduced by two thirds. Add another ladleful of water, again stirring until reduced by two thirds. Repeat this process until most of the water has been absorbed and the rice is tender but not mushy, with a creamy consistency. (You may have as much as a cup of water left unused.) When stirred, the rice should move across the pan in slow waves (*all'onda*). This should take about 14 minutes from the time you begin ladling the simmering water into the rice.

Remove the risotto from the heat. Stir in ¼ cup of the spinach pesto and cover for 2 minutes (save any remaining pesto for another use). Add the snipped spinach, butter, and grated cheese; stir until creamy. Season with salt and pepper. Spoon the risotto onto a serving dish or into individual bowls, drizzle with olive oil, and top with the cheese curls. Serve immediately.

# Risotto with Beets and Castelmagno

**RISOTTO ALLA BARBABIETOLE E CASTELMAGNO**

The earthy sweetness of beets and the rich, deep flavors of this very special blue-veined cheese come together in this brightly hued risotto. Castelmagno cheese DOP has been produced in the Piedmont region of Italy since 1277 or earlier. The cheese, which has a semihard texture, is made from the milk of a Piedmontese breed of cattle, pastured in meadows or grasslands. It has a pronounced flavor—not as strong as Gorgonzola, but one that stands up to the earthy sweetness of beets.  MAKES 6 SERVINGS

**WINE PAIRING:** Beets are notoriously tricky to pair with wine; their earthy sweetness often makes wine seem bitter or strangely metallic. A good way around this is to go with a slightly chilled red wine from Schiava. Bright and simple, these have the perfumed flavors of roses, strawberry, and lemon drops.

### FOR THE BEET BROTH

8 cups vegetable broth (page 66)

3 large beets, scrubbed, stemmed, and roots trimmed

### FOR THE RISOTTO

2 tablespoons extra virgin olive oil, plus more for drizzling

1 slice medium white or yellow onion, finely chopped to make ¼ cup

½ teaspoon finely ground sea salt, plus more as needed

½ teaspoon finely ground white pepper, plus more as needed

1¼ cups *superfino* rice, preferably Carnaroli

⅓ cup dry Italian white wine

2 tablespoons cold unsalted butter

3½ ounces Castelmagno cheese, at room temperature, cubed to make ¾ cup

**MAKE THE BEET BROTH:** In a medium heavy-gauge saucepan or pot, combine the vegetable broth and beets. Heat to simmering over medium heat. Lower the heat to maintain a low simmer and cook until the beets are tender when pierced with a fork, about 45 minutes. Using a slotted spoon, remove the beets from the broth and set aside. Keep the beet broth at a slow simmer. Peel one of the reserved beets and finely chop it to make 1 cup; set aside. (Refrigerate the remaining 2 beets for another use.)

**MAKE THE RISOTTO:** In a medium heavy-gauge sauté pan or skillet at least 3 inches deep (with lid handy), warm the olive oil over low heat. Add the onion and cook, stirring frequently, until the onion is translucent and tender but not browned. It's okay to add 2 tablespoons water to help the onion soften without browning, just be sure the water has evaporated before moving to the next step. Season with the salt and pepper. Add the rice and stir for 2 minutes, until the kernels are well coated. Pour in the wine, stirring until completely evaporated. Ladle ½ cup of the beet broth into the rice and stir continuously until the broth has reduced by two thirds. Repeat with another ladleful, again stirring until the broth has reduced by two thirds. Repeat until most of the beet broth has been incorporated and the rice is tender but not mushy, with a creamy consistency. (You may have as much as a cup of beet broth left unused.) When stirred, the rice should move across the pan in slow waves (*all'onda*). This should take about 14 minutes from the time you begin ladling the broth into the rice.

Remove the risotto from the heat. Add ½ cup of the finely chopped beets; cover the pot for 2 minutes. Stir in the butter and cheese until the risotto is creamy. Season with salt and pepper. Spoon the risotto into a serving bowl or individual dishes, garnish with the remaining ½ cup chopped beets, and drizzle with olive oil. Serve immediately.

# Risotto with Butternut Squash

## RISOTTO ALLA ZUCCA

Golden and richly flavorful, this is one of my favorite risottos, made with a lemony squash pesto that you'll stir in just before serving. I recommend microwave-roasting the squash for the pesto the day before you plan to make the risotto. MAKES 6 SERVINGS

**WINE PAIRING:** A Tuscan Sangiovese from Montalcino brings a nice, bright sour cherry bite, a bit of tannic grip, and a lovely clove-thyme-tobacco finish that will keep a sweet-flavored dish from becoming cloying.

### FOR THE SQUASH PESTO

1 small butternut squash

Finely grated zest of 1 lemon

3 tablespoons extra virgin olive oil

½ teaspoon finely ground sea salt

½ teaspoon finely ground white pepper

### FOR THE RISOTTO

6 cups vegetable broth (page 66) or water

2 tablespoons extra virgin olive oil, plus more for drizzling

1 slice medium white or yellow onion, finely chopped to make ¼ cup

¼ teaspoon finely ground sea salt, plus more as needed

½ teaspoon finely ground white pepper, plus more as needed

1¼ cups *superfino* rice, preferably Baldo, Carnaroli, or Roma, not Arborio

⅓ cup dry Italian white wine

2 tablespoons cold unsalted butter

2 ounces Parmigiano Reggiano or Grana Padano, finely grated to make ¾ cup

**MAKE THE SQUASH PESTO:** Pierce the squash all over with a paring knife. Place in a large microwave-safe dish with 2 tablespoons water and cover with plastic wrap. Microwave until cooked through, 20 to 25 minutes. Discard the wrap. When cool enough to handle, cut the squash in half; discard the seeds and membranes. Scoop the flesh into a small saucepan; discard the skin. Mash the squash until smooth. Place the saucepan over low heat and stir the mashed squash until some of the moisture has evaporated, 2 to 3 minutes. Remove from the heat; let cool slightly. Measure 1 cup of the squash into a food processor along with the lemon zest, olive oil, salt, and pepper. (Refrigerate any remaining squash for another use.) Pulse the pesto until smooth. Set aside in the refrigerator.

**MAKE THE RISOTTO:** In a medium heavy-gauge saucepan or pot, bring the vegetable broth to a boil over medium heat. Reduce the heat to maintain a slow simmer.

In a medium heavy-gauge sauté pan or skillet at least 3 inches deep (with lid handy), warm the olive oil over low heat. Stir in the onion and cook, stirring frequently, until the onion is tender and translucent but not browned. It's okay to add 2 tablespoons water to help

the onion soften without browning, just be sure the water has evaporated before moving to the next step. Season with the salt and pepper. Add the rice and stir for 2 minutes, until the kernels are well coated. Pour in the wine, stirring until completely evaporated. Ladle ½ cup of the hot vegetable broth into the rice and stir until reduced by two thirds. Add another ladleful and again stir until reduced by two thirds. Repeat this process until most of the vegetable broth has been incorporated and the rice is tender but not mushy, with a creamy consistency. (You may have as much as a cup of broth left unused.) When stirred, the rice should move across the pan in a slow wave (*all'onda*). This should take about 14 minutes from the time you begin ladling the broth into the rice.

Remove the risotto from the heat and stir in the ½ cup of squash pesto (save the remainder for another use). Cover for 2 minutes. Add the butter and cheese and stir until the risotto is creamy. Season with salt and pepper. Spoon the risotto into a serving bowl or individual dishes. Drizzle with olive oil and serve immediately.

# Risotto with Fresh Ricotta

## RISOTTO ALLA RICOTTA FRESCA

I like to make this simple and light risotto in the summer, serving it on its own or with a salad. This is a good recipe for trying your hand at adding your own *condimenti*, such as fresh peas with a little mint, or tiny fresh tomatoes with basil. MAKES 6 SERVINGS

**WINE PAIRING:** A dish as soft and creamy as this one gives you the opportunity to show off a wine of real panache: Spend a few extra dollars and try a Franciacorta—Italy's answer to Champagne. Franciacorta is made with almost the exact same restrictions and specifications as top-level Champagne (and, in some cases, requires even more aging). These wines are beautifully structured, rich, ripe, and complex.

6 cups vegetable broth (page 66)

2 tablespoons extra virgin olive oil, plus more for drizzling

1 slice medium white or yellow onion, finely chopped to make ¼ cup

½ teaspoon finely ground sea salt, plus more as needed

½ teaspoon finely ground white pepper, plus more as needed

1¼ cups *superfino* rice (Arborio, Baldo, Carnaroli, or Roma)

⅓ cup dry Italian white wine

2 tablespoons cold unsalted butter

½ cup plus ⅓ cup ricotta

In a medium heavy-gauge saucepan or pot, bring the vegetable broth to a boil over medium heat. Reduce the heat to maintain a simmer.

In a medium heavy-gauge sauté pan or skillet at least 3 inches deep (with lid handy) warm the olive oil over low heat and add the onions. Cook, stirring frequently, until the onions are soft and translucent but not browned. It's okay to add 2 tablespoons of water to help the onion soften without browning, just be sure the water has evaporated before moving to the next step. Season with the salt and pepper. Add the rice and stir for 2 minutes, until the kernels are well coated. Pour in the wine and stir until completely evaporated. Ladle ½ cup of the hot vegetable broth into the rice, stirring until reduced by two thirds. Add another ladleful of broth into the pot, again stirring until reduced by two thirds. Repeat this process until most of the vegetable broth has been absorbed into the rice and it is tender, but not mushy, with a creamy consistency. (You may have as much as a cup of broth left unused.) When stirred, the rice should move across the pan in a slow wave (*all'onda*). This should take about 14 minutes from the time you begin ladling the broth into the rice.

Remove the risotto from the heat. Cover for 1 minute. Add the butter and ½ cup ricotta and stir until creamy. Season with salt and pepper. Spoon the risotto into a serving bowl or individual dishes. Drizzle with olive oil and dot with the remaining ⅓ cup of fresh ricotta. Serve immediately.

# Risotto with Black-Eyed Peas

## RISOTTO CON I FAGIOLI DELL'OCCHIO

Inexpensive, nourishing, and filling, this flavorful Italian rendition of beans-and-rice is enriched with the melting texture and assertive flavor of guanciale (cured pork jowl and cheeks), tomato, and Pecorino Romano. Make sure to soak the black-eyed peas the night before you plan to make the risotto and simmer them in the morning. If time-pressed, you may substitute canned black-eyed peas. MAKES 6 SERVINGS

**WINE PAIRING:** Higher in alcohol, earthy, and loaded with dried herb and citrus peel flavors, a Gaglioppo rosé from Calabria would be a fabulously fascinating pairing here.

2 tablespoons extra virgin olive oil, plus more for drizzling

3½ ounces guanciale, finely chopped to make ⅔ cup

1 thick slice medium white or yellow onion, finely chopped to make ⅓ cup

1 cup canned diced Italian tomatoes

½ teaspoon finely ground sea salt, plus more as needed

½ teaspoon finely ground black pepper, plus more as needed

1¼ cups *superfino* rice (Arborio, Baldo, Carnaroli, or Roma)

⅓ cup dry Italian white wine

1½ cups cooked black-eyed peas (made from ½ cup dried), or substitute drained and rinsed canned

2 tablespoons cold unsalted butter

2 ounces Pecorino Romano, finely grated to make ¾ cup, plus Pecorino Romano curls or shavings, for garnish

In a medium heavy-gauge saucepan or pot bring 6 cups water to a boil over medium heat. Reduce the heat to maintain a simmer.

In a medium heavy-gauge sauté pan or skillet at least 3 inches deep (with lid handy) combine the olive oil, guanciale, onion, and tomatoes over low heat. Cook, stirring frequently, until the onion is soft and translucent and the mixture heavily coats the back of a spoon. Season with the salt and pepper. Add the rice and stir for 2 minutes, until the kernels are well coated. Pour in the white wine and stir continuously until the wine is completely evaporated. Ladle ½ cup of the simmering water into the rice and stir until the water is reduced by two thirds. Add another ladleful of water, again stirring until reduced by two thirds. Repeat this process until most of the water has been absorbed by the rice and the rice is tender, but not mushy, with a creamy consistency. (You may have as much as a cup of water left unused.) When stirred, the rice should move across the pan in slow waves (*all'onda*). This should take about 14 minutes from the time you begin ladling the broth into the rice.

Remove the risotto from the heat. Cover for 1 minute. Add 1 cup of the black-eyed peas, the butter, and the grated cheese. Stir until creamy. Season with salt and pepper.

Spoon the risotto into a serving bowl or individual dishes. Sprinkle with the remaining ½ cup black-eyed peas. Drizzle with olive oil, sprinkle with a few grinds of black pepper, and arrange the pecorino curls on top. Serve immediately.

# Risotto with Tomato Pesto and Fresh Mozzarella

## RISOTTO AL PESTO DI POMODORI E FIOR DI LATTE

Soft and mild, fresh mozzarella is made on such a large scale in Italy, people purchase it at their local dairies daily. In the States, "fresh-made daily" mozzarella is not as easy to find, but specialty stores such as Eataly and other Italian groceries do have it. Be sure to keep the cheese well chilled until you are ready to use it, and drain and discard the liquid it comes in. This recipe contrasts the mildness of the cheese with the lemony brightness of a tomato pesto. Add tiny basil leaves as a garnish, if you like. **MAKES 6 SERVINGS**

**WINE PAIRING:** Fresh, southern Italian flavors sing when paired with a Campagnese white. Try a Falanghina from just over the mountains of Naples, delicate and perfumed, with bright acidity and a fresh peach-melon flavor that shows off fresh cuisine with aplomb.

### FOR THE TOMATO PESTO

4 plum or Roma tomatoes, cored, blanched, seeded, and chopped to make 2 cups (or 2 cups diced canned and drained Italian tomatoes)

Finely grated zest of 1 lemon

3 tablespoons extra virgin olive oil

Finely ground sea salt and white pepper

### FOR THE TOMATO *CONDIMENTI*

2 tablespoons extra virgin olive oil

1 slice medium white or yellow onion, finely chopped to make ¼ cup

Finely ground sea salt and white pepper

1 small plum or Roma tomato, cored, seeded, blanched, skinned, and chopped to make ¼ cup (or ¼ cup diced canned and drained Italian tomatoes)

### FOR THE RISOTTO

2 tablespoons extra virgin olive oil, plus more for drizzling

1 slice medium white or yellow onion, finely chopped to make ¼ cup

1¼ cups *superfino* rice (Arborio, Baldo, Carnaroli, or Roma)

⅓ cup dry Italian white wine

2 tablespoons cold unsalted butter

6 ounces *fior di latte* (fresh cow's milk mozzarella in liquid; see page 20) drained and chopped to make 1 cup

Finely ground sea salt and white pepper

Basil leaves, for garnish (optional)

In a medium heavy-gauge saucepan or pot over medium heat, bring 6 cups water to a boil; reduce the heat to maintain a slow simmer.

**MAKE THE TOMATO PESTO:** In the work bowl of a food processor, combine the tomatoes, lemon zest, and olive oil. Pulse until creamy and smooth. Season with salt and pepper. Refrigerate until needed.

**MAKE THE TOMATO *CONDIMENTI*:** In a medium heavy-gauge sauté pan or skillet at least 3 inches deep (with lid handy), combine the olive oil, onion, ⅓ cup of the tomato pesto, and the chopped tomato over low heat. Cook, stirring continuously, until the vegetables are soft. Transfer to a bowl and cover to keep warm while you make the rice.

**MAKE THE RISOTTO:** Wipe out the sauté pan and return it to the stove over low heat. Combine the olive oil and onion and cook, stirring frequently, over low heat until the onion is soft and translucent but not browned. It's okay to add 2 tablespoons water to help the onion soften without browning, just be sure the water has all evaporated before moving to the next step. Season with the salt and pepper. Add the rice and stir for 2 minutes, until the kernels are well coated. Pour in the white wine and stir until the wine has completely evaporated. Ladle ½ cup of the simmering water into the rice and stir until the water has reduced by two thirds. Add another ladleful of water, again stirring until reduced by two thirds. Repeat this process until most of the simmering water has been absorbed by the rice and the rice is tender but not mushy, with a creamy consistency. (You may have as much as a cup of water left unused.) When stirred, the rice should move across the pan in slow waves (*all'onda*). This should take about 14 minutes from the time you begin ladling the broth into the rice.

Remove the risotto from the heat. Stir in the tomato *condimenti* and cover the pot for 2 minutes. Add the butter and mozzarella and stir until creamy. Season with salt and pepper. Spoon the risotto into a serving bowl or individual dishes, drizzle with olive oil, and—if you like—garnish with basil leaves. Serve immediately.

# Risotto with Fresh Black Truffles

## RISOTTO AL TARTUFI NERI

Beautiful to behold, celestial to eat, this risotto is actually among the easiest risottos in the chapter to prepare. It's easy because the risotto is a basic preparation, but extravagant because fresh black truffles, which are harvested in Italy from fall through early winter, can be exorbitant in price. **MAKES 6 SERVINGS**

**WINE PAIRING:** To show off a bounty of black truffles, we need a wine that can work in tandem with, but not overshadow, our star ingredient. Choose a Reserve Franciacorta, with all of its foamy richness and intensity. Who doesn't like Champagne with their truffles?

6 cups vegetable broth
(page 66)

2 tablespoons extra virgin
olive oil, plus more for drizzling

1 slice medium white or yellow
onion, finely chopped to make
¼ cup

½ teaspoon finely ground
sea salt, plus more as needed

½ teaspoon finely ground
white pepper, plus more as
needed

1¼ cups Carnaroli *superfino*
rice, preferably Acquerello

⅓ cup dry Italian white wine

2 tablespoons cold unsalted
butter

2 ounces Parmigiano Reggiano
or Grana Padano, finely grated
to make ¾ cup

1 ounce black truffle

In a medium heavy-gauge saucepan or pot over medium heat, bring the broth to a boil. Reduce the heat to maintain a slow simmer.

In a medium heavy-gauge sauté pan or skillet at least 3 inches deep (with lid handy), warm the olive oil over low heat. Add the onion and cook, stirring frequently, until the onion is soft and translucent but not browned. It's okay to add 2 tablespoons water to help the onion soften without browning, just be sure the water has evaporated before moving to the next step. Season with the salt and pepper. Add the rice and stir for 2 minutes, until the kernels are well coated. Add the wine, stirring until it has completely evaporated. Ladle ½ cup of the hot vegetable broth into the pan and stir continuously until reduced by two thirds. Add another ladleful, again stirring until reduced by two thirds. Repeat the process until most of the broth has been used and the rice is tender but not mushy, with a creamy consistency. (You may have as much as a cup of broth left unused.) When stirred, the rice should move across the pan in slow waves (*all'onda*). This should take about 14 minutes from the time you begin ladling the broth into the rice.

Remove the risotto from the heat; cover for 2 minutes. Stir in the butter and cheese until the risotto is creamy. Season with salt and pepper. Spoon the risotto into a serving bowl or individual dishes, drizzle with olive oil, and shave the entire truffle, paper thin, over the risotto. Serve immediately.

# Risotto with Butter and Sage

## RISOTTO AL BURRO E SALVIA

This risotto, fragrant with herbs and citrus, makes a tasty light lunch or a nice prelude to a *secondi* of roast turkey or chicken. You'll use fresh sage in the pesto and pretty little fried sage leaves as the garnish. MAKES 6 SERVINGS

**WINE PAIRING:** Italian Pinot Nero is a strange creature: earthy and savory like a French pinot, but with a much brighter and fruitier profile. Exploring the far northern areas of Italy, such as Friuli and Trentino, you find some elegant Pinot Nero–based wines that are perfect for this dish.

**FOR THE SAGE PESTO**

⅓ cup pine nuts

4 bunches sage, leaves only, very roughly chopped to make 2 cups

Finely grated zest of 1 lemon

⅓ cup extra virgin olive oil

½ teaspoon finely ground sea salt

½ teaspoon finely ground white pepper

**FOR THE FRIED SAGE LEAF GARNISH**

12 small sage leaves

½ cup extra virgin olive oil

**FOR THE RISOTTO**

6 cups vegetable broth (page 66)

2 tablespoons extra virgin olive oil, plus more for drizzling

1 slice medium white or yellow onion, finely chopped to make ¼ cup

Finely ground sea salt and white pepper

1¼ cups *superfino* rice (Arborio, Baldo, Carnaroli, or Roma)

⅓ cup dry Italian white wine

2 tablespoons cold unsalted butter

2½ ounces Parmigiano Reggiano or Grana Padano, finely grated to make 1 cup, plus shavings for garnish

**MAKE THE SAGE PESTO:** In the work bowl of a food processor, combine the pine nuts, sage, lemon zest, olive oil, salt, and pepper. Pulse into a creamy paste. Refrigerate until needed.

**MAKE THE FRIED SAGE LEAVES:** In a small heavy skillet over medium-high heat, warm the oil. Add the sage leaves and fry until crispy. Transfer to paper towels to drain.

**MAKE THE RISOTTO:** In a medium heavy-gauge saucepan or pot over medium heat, bring the vegetable broth to a boil over medium heat. Reduce the heat to maintain a gentle simmer.

In a medium heavy-gauge sauté pan or skillet at least 3 inches deep (with lid handy), warm the olive oil over low heat. Add the onion and cook, stirring frequently, until soft and translucent but not browned. It's okay to add 2 tablespoons water to help the onion soften without browning, just be sure the water has evaporated before moving to the next step. Season with salt and pepper. Add the rice and stir for 2 minutes, until the kernels are well coated. Pour in the white wine and stir continuously until the wine has completely evaporated. Ladle ½ cup of the hot vegetable broth into the rice and stir until the broth has reduced by two thirds. Add another ladleful of broth, again stirring until reduced by two thirds. Repeat this process until most of the broth has been absorbed by the rice and the rice is tender but not mushy, with a creamy consistency. (You may have as much as a cup of broth left unused.) When stirred, the rice should move across the pan in slow waves (*all'onda*). This should take about 14 minutes from the time you begin ladling the broth into the rice.

Remove the risotto from the heat. Stir in ⅓ cup of the sage pesto (save any remaining pesto for another use). Cover for 2 minutes. Add the butter and grated cheese and stir until creamy. Season with salt and pepper. Spoon the risotto into a serving bowl or individual dishes. Drizzle with olive oil and top with the fried sage leaves and cheese shavings. Serve immediately.

# Risotto with Dried Mushrooms and Mascarpone

## RISOTTO AI FUNGHI SECCHI E MASCARPONE

A specialty of Lombardy that originated near Milan in the late sixteenth century, soft, sweet mascarpone cheese was once made with fresh cream and acid from the bottom of wine barrels. Perhaps best known outside of Italy for its starring appearance in desserts such as *tiramisù*, satiny-white mascarpone has also long been used instead of butter and Parmigiano Reggiano in Lombardy risottos like this one. I love how this recipe balances mascarpone's sweetness with the zing of lemon and depth of dried mushrooms. Be sure to soak the dried mushrooms ahead of time to reconstitute; a few hours will do the job but overnight is ideal. MAKES 6 SERVINGS

**WINE PAIRING:** Lambrusco Grasparossa di Castelvetro, a fizzy red with a fresh blackberry and mushroom profile, goes well here. Make sure to choose a "secco" version, indicating a dry wine, and avoid anything labeled "amabile," which indicates a significant amount of sweetness.

1½ ounces (44 grams) dried porcini or chanterelle mushrooms, brushed free of any dust or sand to make 1 loosely packed, mounded cup; once soaked and chopped, mushrooms will measure 1½ cups

### FOR THE MUSHROOM PESTO

Finely grated zest of 1 lemon

⅓ cup extra virgin olive oil

Finely ground sea salt and white pepper

### FOR THE RISOTTO

2 tablespoons extra virgin olive oil, plus more for drizzling

1 slice medium white or yellow onion, finely chopped to make ¼ cup

½ teaspoon finely ground sea salt, plus more as needed

½ teaspoon finely ground white pepper, plus more as needed

1¼ cups *superfino* rice (Arborio, Baldo, Carnaroli, or Roma)

⅓ cup dry Italian white wine

¾ cup mascarpone, at room temperature

**RECONSTITUTE THE MUSHROOMS:** To soak the dried mushrooms, place them in a medium bowl and cover with fresh water. Top with a small plate that fits within the bowl to keep the mushrooms submerged. Soak until soft, for several hours if possible; overnight is optimal. When the mushrooms are soft and pliant, strain through a coffee filter into a measuring cup. You can use the filtered soaking water as part of the water for the risotto, for a richer flavor. Rinse the mushrooms once more to ensure you've removed any residual sand or grit, pat dry, and mince. Divide into two equal portions. Set aside.

**MAKE THE MUSHROOM PESTO:** In the work bowl of a food processor, combine ¾ cup of the reconstituted chopped mushrooms with the lemon zest and olive oil. Puise until a creamy paste forms. Season with salt and pepper. Refrigerate until needed.

**MAKE THE RISOTTO:** In a medium heavy-gauge saucepan or pot, bring 6 cups water to a boil over medium heat. Reduce the heat to maintain a simmer.

In a medium heavy-gauge sauté pan or skillet, warm the olive oil over medium heat. Add the onion and the remaining reconstituted chopped mushrooms and cook, stirring frequently, until the onion is soft and translucent and the mushrooms are lightly browned. Season with the salt and pepper. Add the rice and stir for 2 minutes, until the kernels are well coated. Pour in the white wine and stir continuously until the wine has completely evaporated. Ladle ½ cup of the simmering water into the rice and stir until the water has reduced by two thirds. Add another ladleful of water, again stirring until reduced by two thirds. Repeat this process until most of the simmering water has been absorbed and the rice is tender but not mushy, with a creamy consistency. (You may have as much as a cup of water left unused.) When stirred, the rice should move across the pan in slow waves (*all'onda*). This should take about 14 minutes from the time you begin ladling the water into the rice.

Remove the risotto from the heat. Stir in ½ cup of the mushroom pesto and cover the pot for 1 minute. Add ½ cup of the mascarpone and stir until creamy. Season with salt and pepper. Spoon the risotto into a serving bowl or individual dishes. Drizzle with olive oil and dollop with the remaining ¼ cup mascarpone. Serve immediately.

Variation: Here's another delicious version of this classic mushroom risotto, with butter and cheese replacing the mascarpone: After you remove the risotto from the heat, stir in ½ cup plus 2 tablespoons mushroom pesto, along with 2 tablespoons room-temperature unsalted butter and 2½ ounces finely grated Parmigiano Reggiano or Grana Padano. Stir until creamy, season with salt and pepper, drizzle with olive oil, and serve immediately.

# Risotto with Radicchio

## RISOTTO AL RADICCHIO ROSSO

The peppery flavor of radicchio is very popular in Italy. Cooking it slightly mellows the taste of the vegetable. While there are many varieties grown in Italy, the variety most prevalent elsewhere is *radicchio di chioggia*, a small round head with white and maroon leaves—a fine choice for this dish. Another variety, *radicchio di Treviso*, which resembles a large, red Belgian endive, is nice here, too. Be sure to core the heads and remove the stems—you'll only be using the leaves in the recipe. MAKES 6 SERVINGS

WINE PAIRING: Any fruity, earthy, medium-weight red would be delicious here, but if you'd like to get nerdy, this is a perfect opportunity to hunt down a Teroldego. From the same corner of northern Italy that made radicchio popular, Teroldego wines are a straightforward, uncomplicated balance of acid driven fruit and smoky minerality, with clear flavors of pomegranate, blackberry, and licorice, and a nicely bittersweet tannic finish.

### FOR THE RADICCHIO PESTO

½ cup coarsely chopped almonds, skin on or off

1 large or 2 small heads radicchio, cored and stemmed, leaves roughly chopped to make 3 cups

⅓ cup extra virgin olive oil

Finely grated zest of 1 lemon

½ teaspoon finely ground sea salt

½ teaspoon finely ground white pepper

### FOR THE RISOTTO

6 cups vegetable broth (page 66) or water

2 tablespoons extra virgin olive oil, plus more for drizzling

1 slice medium white or yellow onion, finely chopped to make ¼ cup

½ teaspoon finely ground sea salt, plus more as needed

½ teaspoon finely ground white pepper, plus more as needed

1¼ cups *superfino* rice, preferably Baldo, Carnaroli, or Roma, not Arborio

⅓ cup dry Italian red wine

½ large head radicchio, cored and stemmed, leaves thinly sliced to make 1⅓ cups, plus extra for garnish

2 tablespoons cold unsalted butter

2 ounces Parmigiano Reggiano or Grana Padano, finely grated to make ¾ cup, plus curls or shavings for garnish

**MAKE THE PESTO:** In the work bowl of a food processor, combine the almonds, radicchio, olive oil, lemon zest, salt, and pepper. Pulse to process into a smooth puree. Set aside.

**MAKE THE RISOTTO:** In a medium heavy-gauge saucepan or pot, heat the vegetable broth to boiling over medium heat. Reduce the heat to maintain a slow simmer.

    In a medium heavy-gauge sauté pan or skillet at least 3 inches deep (with lid handy), warm the olive oil over low heat. Add the onion and sauté, stirring frequently, until the onion is tender and translucent but not browned. It's okay to add 2 tablespoons water to help the onion soften without browning, just be sure the water has evaporated before moving to the next step. Season with the salt and pepper. Add the rice and stir for 2 minutes, until the kernels are well coated. Pour in the red wine, stirring until the wine has completely evaporated.

*(continued)*

Ladle ½ cup of the hot vegetable broth into the rice and stir until reduced by two thirds. Add another ladleful and again stir until reduced by two thirds. Repeat this process until most of the vegetable broth has been incorporated and the rice is tender but not mushy, with a creamy consistency. (You may have as much as a cup of broth left unused.) When stirred, the rice should move across the pan in a slow wave (*all'onda*). This should take about 14 minutes from the time you begin ladling the broth into the rice.

Remove the risotto from the heat. Stir in ½ cup of the radicchio pesto; reserve the remaining pesto for another use. Cover the pot for 2 minutes. Add the thinly sliced radicchio leaves, butter, and cheese and stir until creamy. Season with salt and pepper. Spoon the risotto into a serving bowl or individual dishes. Drizzle with olive oil. Sprinkle with additional sliced radicchio, if desired, and cheese curls or shavings. Serve immediately.

# Risotto with
# Sea Scallops and Peas

**RISOTTO ALLE CAPESANTE E PISELLI**

The sweetly elegant combination of fresh green peas and soft white sea scallops makes this a celebratory Venetian risotto. In the best Italian seafood risotto tradition, use Vialone Nano, a *semifino* rice that I like for its ability to absorb liquid so well, making for a very creamy risotto. If fresh English peas (sometimes called "sweet peas") are unavailable, substitute very-best-quality frozen green peas, thawed and unblanched. Ensure the sea scallops you purchase are scrupulously fresh: They will be sliced very thin, and served raw over the cooked risotto.

MAKES 6 SERVINGS

**WINE PAIRING:** Sicilian Carricante—the "dry Riesling of Sicily"—is mineral-driven, high-acid, and relatively light-weight with delicious green pear and chamomile flavors; perfect for the sweet scallops and fresh peas. Make sure you find a young, unoaked example.

2½ cups fresh shelled garden peas (English) or frozen, thawed green peas

**FOR THE PEA PESTO**

Finely grated zest of 2 lemons

⅓ cup extra virgin olive oil

½ teaspoon finely ground sea salt

½ teaspoon finely ground white pepper

**FOR THE RISOTTO**

2 tablespoons extra virgin olive oil, plus more for drizzling

1 slice medium white or yellow onion, finely chopped to make ¼ cup

½ teaspoon finely ground sea salt, plus more as needed

½ teaspoon finely ground white pepper, plus more as needed

1¼ cups Vialone Nano *semifino* rice

⅓ cup dry Italian white wine

4 tablespoons (½ cup) cold unsalted butter

6 large sea scallops, sliced into paper-thin rounds

**BLANCH THE PEAS:** In a medium heavy-gauge saucepan or pot, bring 6 cups water to a boil over medium heat. Reduce the heat to maintain a slow simmer. Place the peas in a mesh strainer; immerse in the simmering water to blanch for 1 minute; transfer to a bowl. Leave the water at a very slow simmer.

**MAKE THE PEA PESTO:** Place 2 cups of the blanched peas in the work bowl of a food processor with the lemon zest, olive oil, salt, and pepper. Pulse until pureed into a creamy paste. Transfer to a bowl and refrigerate until ready to use.

**MAKE THE RISOTTO:** In a medium heavy-gauge sauté pan or skillet at least 3 inches deep (with lid handy) warm the olive oil over low heat. Add the onion and cook, stirring frequently, until the onion is translucent but not browned. It's okay to add 2 tablespoons water to help the onion soften without browning, just be sure the water has evaporated before moving to the next step. Season with the salt and pepper. Add the rice and stir for 2 minutes, until the kernels are well coated. Pour in the wine, stirring until completely evaporated. Ladle ½ cup of the simmering water from blanching the peas into the rice and cook, stirring continuously, until reduced by two thirds. Add another ladleful, again stirring until the cooking water has reduced by two thirds. Repeat the process until most of the water has been incorporated and the rice kernels are tender, but not mushy, with a creamy consistency. (You may have as much as a cup of water left unused.) When stirred, the rice should move across the pan in a slow wave (*all'onda*). This should take about 14 minutes from the time you begin ladling the water into the rice.

Remove the risotto from the heat. Stir in ½ to ⅓ cup pea pesto and the remaining blanched peas; reserve any remaining pesto for another use. Cover for 2 minutes. Stir in the butter until creamy. Season with salt and pepper. Spoon the risotto into a serving bowl or individual dishes. Top with the sliced sea scallops. Drizzle with olive oil. Sprinkle with a bit of finely ground white pepper. Serve immediately.

# Risotto with Cuttlefish Ink, Squid, and Tomatoes

## RISOTTO AL NERO DI SEPIA, CALAMARI IN UMIDO

Calamari, tomato, and wine in risotto is a classic southern Italian combination. The addition of cuttlefish ink adds a dramatic, dark hue to the finished dish. You can purchase cuttlefish ink at specialty markets and online. As with the other seafood risottos in this chapter, do try to make the fish stock from scratch, unless you are time-pressed and must use store-bought. Use Vialone Nano rice. MAKES 6 SERVINGS

**WINE PAIRING:** Choose a high-quality Greco di Tufo, with both freshness and intensity, plus a bit of savory bitterness. The Greco grape creates wines of lush citrus fruit, bright acidity, and savory herbs.

### FOR THE CALAMARI CONDIMENTI

½ cup extra virgin olive oil

11 ounces calamari (tubes and tentacles), cleaned, tubes chopped, tentacles left whole

⅓ cup dry Italian white wine

½ cup canned, chopped Italian tomatoes, drained

### FOR THE RISOTTO

6 cups fish stock (page 158 or substitute best-quality store-bought)

2 tablespoons extra virgin olive oil, plus more for drizzling

1 slice medium white or yellow onion, finely chopped to make ¼ cup

½ teaspoon finely ground sea salt, plus more as needed

½ teaspoon finely ground white pepper, plus more as needed

1¼ cups Vialone Nano *semifino* rice

⅓ cup dry Italian white wine

1 teaspoon cuttlefish ink

2 tablespoons cold unsalted butter

**MAKE THE CALAMARI *CONDIMENTI*:** In a medium heavy-gauge sauté pan or skillet at least 3 inches deep (with lid handy), combine the olive oil, calamari, white wine, and tomatoes. Gently warm over low heat until the calamari is cooked but tender. Transfer to a bowl and cover to keep warm. Wipe out the pan.

**MAKE THE RISOTTO:** In a medium heavy-gauge saucepan or pot, bring the fish stock to a boil over medium heat. Reduce the heat to maintain a gentle simmer.

Return the pan you used for the *condimenti* to the stovetop over low heat. Add the olive oil and onion and cook, stirring frequently, until the onion is soft and translucent but not browned. It's okay to add 2 tablespoons water to help the onion soften without browning, just be sure the water has evaporated before moving to the next step. Season with the salt and pepper. Add the rice and stir for 2 minutes, until the kernels are well coated. Pour in the white wine and stir continuously until the wine has completely evaporated. Ladle ½ cup of the hot fish stock and the cuttlefish ink into the rice and stir until the stock has reduced by two thirds. Add another ladleful of stock, again stirring until reduced by two thirds. Repeat this process until most of the stock has been absorbed by the rice and the rice is tender but not mushy, with a creamy consistency. (You may have as much as a cup of stock left unused.) When stirred, the rice should move across the pan in slow waves (*all'onda*). This should take about 14 minutes from the time you begin ladling the stock into the rice.

Remove the risotto from the heat. Cover for 1 minute. Stir in the butter until creamy. Season with salt and pepper. Spoon the risotto into a serving bowl or individual dishes. Top with the calamari *condimenti*. Drizzle with olive oil and serve immediately.

# Vicenza Salted Cod Risotto

## RISOTTO CON IL BACCALÀ ALLA VINCENTINA

This is one of my favorite rice dishes to make with salted cod. While you have to soak the cod a few days before you are ready to make the risotto, it is worth it: The texture and flavor salted cod adds to rice is uniquely satisfying. Once you've tried this dish, you'll want to make the Rice Tart with Salted Cod (page 61) from the appetizer chapter as well. You will soak the salted cod whole, in milk, until soft before dicing it for the recipe. MAKES 6 SERVINGS

**WINE PAIRING:** *Baccalà* has a delicious intensity to it and requires a stand-up wine: Try a Pinot Bianco–based wine. These embrace a savory, hazelnut-scented elegance with bright orchard fruit and keening acidity. They're also very affordable.

### FOR THE SALTED COD

1 (6-inch) piece boneless, skinless salted cod (*baccalà*)

2½ cups plus 2 tablespoons whole milk

⅔ cup all-purpose flour

¼ cup extra virgin olive oil

2 slices medium white or yellow onion, finely chopped to make ⅓ cup

½ teaspoon finely ground sea salt

½ teaspoon finely ground white pepper

### FOR THE RISOTTO

2 tablespoons extra virgin olive oil, plus more for drizzling

2 slices medium white or yellow onion, finely chopped to make ⅓ cup

2 salted anchovies, finely chopped to make 2 tablespoons

Finely ground sea salt and white pepper

1¼ cups Vialone Nano *semifino* rice

⅓ cup dry Italian white wine

2 tablespoons cold unsalted butter

**MAKE THE COD:** Place the salted cod and 1¼ cups milk in a nonreactive bowl, cover, and refrigerate for 18 hours. Drain the salted cod; discard the milk. Cover with an additional 1¼ cups milk. Refrigerate for another 18 hours. Drain. Using paper towels, dry the fish well. Chop the cod and measure it to ensure you have 1¼ cups fish. Put the flour in a shallow bowl and dredge the fish pieces in the flour; dust off any excess. Heat the olive oil in a heavy-gauge sauté pan over medium heat. Add the onion and sauté until tender. Add the floured cod pieces to the pan. Lightly brown the fish. Season with the salt and pepper. Remove the onion and cod from the pan and set aside; cover to keep warm.

**MAKE THE RISOTTO:** In a medium heavy-gauge saucepan or pot, bring 6 cups of water to a boil over medium heat. Reduce the heat to maintain a slow simmer.

In a medium heavy-gauge sauté pan or skillet at least 3 inches deep (with lid handy), warm the olive oil over low heat. Add the onion and anchovies and cook, stirring, until the onion is soft and translucent but not browned. It's okay to add 2 tablespoons water to help the onion soften without browning, just be sure the water has evaporated before moving to the next step. Season with salt and pepper. Add the rice and stir for 2 minutes, until the kernels are well coated. Pour in the white wine and stir until the wine has completely evaporated. Ladle ½ cup of the simmering water into the rice and stir until the water has reduced by two thirds. Add another ladleful of water into the rice, again stirring until reduced by two thirds. Repeat this process until most of the water has been incorporated and the rice is tender but not mushy, with a creamy consistency. (You may have as much as a cup of water left unused.) When stirred, the rice should move across the pan in slow waves (*all'onda*). This should take about 14 minutes from the time you begin ladling the simmering water into the rice.

Remove the risotto from the heat, add the fried cod and onion, and cover for 1 minute. Stir in the butter. Season with salt and pepper. Arrange the risotto on a platter and drizzle with olive oil. Serve immediately.

# The Legend of Risotto alla Milanese

**THE LEGEND OF THE FIRST AND MOST FAMOUS RISOTTO IS CHARMINGLY ONCE-UPON-A-TIME.**
It goes like this:

There was once a Belgian artist named Valerius of Flanders, master of the magical stained-glass windows being made for the many-splendored Cathedral Duomo in Milan. So magnificent was this cathedral that artisans and craftsmen from throughout the realm, and all of Europe, came to be part of the work. Among them, one young apprentice was known above all for his uncanny ability to mix vibrant colors—the richest scarlets, deepest blues, and beryl-bright yellows, sparkling citrine in the sun. Although the young chromatic genius kept his methods to himself, the whispered rumors were that he achieved the brilliance of the yellows with saffron. A pinch here, a pinch there, so many pinches in so many panes, all glittering magnificently in the sun. Valerius knew the boy's secret, and took to teasing him, finally saying, "Stay your hand, or you will be sprinkling saffron in your soup!" Irked by the taunts, the color-clever lad planned a prank. That very week, during the wedding feast of Valerius's daughter, the young man colluded with the cook, who marched to the table with a steaming platter of saffron-hued rice. Marveling, the guests drew in their collective breath, and with that, the beguiling scent of saffron. They *had* to taste the beautiful food and declared it most excellent. And so it became known as *risotto alla Milanese*, still made today with a plentiful pinch of saffron.

# Risotto with Saffron and Beef Bone Marrow

## RISOTTO ALLA MILANESE

Milan's signature recipe, this golden-hued dish, traditionally enriched with bone marrow and served alongside osso buco (braised veal shanks), has a long and storied history (see opposite page). Saffron, the precious spice worth more than its weight in gold, is central here. Made from the hand-harvested dried stigmas of the *Crocus sativus* flower, saffron has an intensely yellow hue and earthy, pleasant aroma and flavor. It's best to purchase saffron threads and then carefully pulverize these into a fine powder using a mortar and pestle, so as to get the best color saturation throughout the dish. For richest flavor, I make the beef and veal stocks in this recipe from scratch, including some leg soup bones in the stock ingredients. To make the process manageable, you can split up the tasks: Make the stocks a few days before you want to serve the risotto; the gremolata and osso buco can be prepared the day before.  MAKES 6 TO 8 SERVINGS

**WINE PAIRING:** Ripasso-style winemaking indicates a wine that is made over the must of a previous pressing (i.e., the skins and seeds of the first batch are *ripasso*, or "revisited," with a new batch of grapes). A wine made ripasso thus has more tannic intensity and a bit more "chew" to its fruit character. One of the best-known ripasso-style wines is Valpolicella Ripasso from the Veneto. The spiced-plum richness and tannin-acid balance of a nice Valpolicella Ripasso makes a lovely pairing for the beefy richness of the bone marrow.

### FOR THE WHITE (VEAL) STOCK (4 QUARTS)

6 pounds veal knucklebones, split and washed under cold water

1 pound yellow onions, finely chopped

1 pound leeks, carefully washed of any grit or dirt, trimmed and finely chopped

1 pound celery, trimmed and finely chopped

2 bay leaves, preferably fresh

3 whole garlic cloves, peeled

1 small bunch Italian flat-leaf parsley, stems only, finely chopped to make 2 tablespoons (reserve leaves for the gremolata sauce)

1 teaspoon fresh thyme

1 teaspoon whole black peppercorns

### FOR THE BROWN (BEEF) STOCK (4 QUARTS)

2 tablespoons extra virgin olive oil

6 pounds veal knucklebones, split and washed under cold water

1 pound yellow onions, finely chopped

1 pound leeks, carefully washed of any grit or dirt, trimmed, finely chopped

1 pound celery, finely chopped

1 cup dry red Italian wine

¼ cup tomato paste, preferably Carmelina brand

2 bay leaves, preferably fresh

3 whole garlic cloves, peeled

1 small bunch Italian flat-leaf parsley, stems only, finely chopped to make 2 tablespoons (reserve leaves for the gremolata sauce)

Leaves from 1 sprig fresh thyme (1 teaspoon)

6 to 8 whole black peppercorns ( 1 teaspoon)

### FOR THE GREMOLATA SAUCE

¼ cup minced Italian flat-leaf parsley leaves, reserved from making stock

1 large garlic clove, minced to make 1 tablespoon

1 teaspoon finely grated lemon zest

1 teaspoon finely grated orange zest

2 tablespoons extra virgin olive oil

### FOR THE OSSO BUCO

4 pounds veal hind-shank (osso buco), cut into 8 portions

2 tablespoons finely ground sea salt

1 tablespoon finely ground white pepper

1 cup (2 sticks) unsalted butter

1 cup dry Italian white wine

1 stalk celery, finely chopped to make ¾ cup

1 small white or yellow onion, finely chopped to make ¾ cup

1 small carrot, finely chopped to make ¾ cup

1 bouquet garni, made with 2-inch piece of lemon peel, 1 sprig fresh rosemary, and 1 peeled garlic clove

### FOR THE RISOTTO

.4 grams saffron threads, carefully crushed into a powder to make 1 teaspoon

2 tablespoons extra virgin olive oil, plus more for drizzling

1 slice medium white or yellow onion, finely chopped to make ¼ cup

½ teaspoon finely ground sea salt, plus more as needed

½ teaspoon finely ground white pepper, plus more as needed

1¼ cups *superfino* rice (Arborio, Baldo, Carnaroli, or Roma)

⅓ cup dry Italian white wine

2 tablespoons cold unsalted butter

2½ ounces Parmigiano Reggiano or Grana Padano, finely grated to make 1 cup

**MAKE THE WHITE STOCK:** In a heavy-gauge stockpot over medium heat, combine the white stock ingredients. Add water to cover, ensuring that the water comes at least an inch above the contents of the pot. Bring to a boil over medium heat. Lower the heat to maintain a slow simmer and cook for 8 to 10 hours. (Longer cook times result in a more-reduced, richer stock.) Skim off any fat or foam. Replenish the water if the level dips below the tops of the bones during simmering. Remove the bones and discard. Strain the stock into a bowl through a fine-mesh sieve or a colander lined with cheesecloth. Discard the solids.

**MAKE THE BROWN STOCK:** Preheat the oven to 375°F. Place the oil in a large roasting pan and toss the bones in the oil. Scatter the onions, leeks, and celery over the bones; toss. Roast the bones and the vegetables in the oven for 1 hour 15 minutes to 1 hour 30 minutes until everything is well browned and deeply caramelized. Transfer the roasted ingredients to a large stockpot; set aside.

Pour the red wine into the roasting pan and deglaze over medium heat, scraping up any browned bits from the bottom of the pan. Stir in the tomato paste and 3 tablespoons water, whisking to dissolve the paste. Pour the tomato liquid over the bones in the stockpot. Add the bay leaves, garlic, parsley stems, thyme, and peppercorns to the stockpot. Cover with water, ensuring that the water comes at least 1 inch above the contents of the pot. Bring to a boil over medium heat; reduce the heat to maintain a slow simmer. Simmer for 8 to 10 hours. (Longer cook times result in a more-reduced, richer stock.) Skim off any foam or fat as needed. Replenish the water if the level dips below the tops of the bones during simmering. Remove the bones and discard. Strain the stock into a bowl through a fine-mesh sieve or a colander lined with cheesecloth. Discard the solids.

**MAKE THE GREMOLATA:** In a small marble or stone mortar, combine the parsley, garlic, lemon and orange zests, and olive oil. Use the pestle to crush the mixture into a paste. If you do not have a mortar and pestle, use a food processor and pulse in short bursts until a paste forms. Allow the completed gremolata to rest overnight in the refrigerator.

**MAKE THE OSSO BUCO:** Season the veal with the salt and pepper. Melt the butter in a large, heavy, oven-safe skillet (with lid) over medium heat. Brown the veal in the butter until caramelized on all sides. Transfer the meat from the pan to a platter and set aside. Pour off and discard the fat from the skillet.

Preheat the oven to 325°F. Return the skillet to the stovetop over medium heat, pour in the white wine, and whisk, scraping up any browned bits from the bottom of the pan. Once most of the wine has evaporated, return the meat to the pan. Add the celery, onion, and carrot, 2 cups of the brown (beef) stock, and the bouquet garni. Simmer for 5 minutes. Remove the skillet from the heat; cover. Roast for 6 hours, or until the osso buco is fork-tender. Remove from the oven.

Once the bones are cool enough to handle, scoop the marrow from the cooked osso buco bones and finely chop. Set ¼ cup of the marrow aside for the risotto. Reserve the rest for another use. Place the meat and vegetables on a platter; keep warm. Strain the cooking liquids into a skillet on the stovetop. Over medium heat, reduce the liquid to a sauce consistency. Stir in the gremolata, cover, and keep warm.

**MAKE THE RISOTTO:** In a medium heavy-gauge saucepan or pot over medium heat, combine 2 cups of the white stock, 4 cups of the brown stock, and the saffron. Bring to a boil over medium heat. Reduce the heat to maintain a gentle simmer.

In a medium heavy-gauge sauté pan or skillet at least 3 inches deep (with lid handy) warm the olive oil and onion over low heat. Cook, stirring frequently, until the onion is soft and translucent but not browned. It's okay to add 2 tablespoons water to help the onion soften without browning, just be sure the water has evaporated before moving to the next step. Season with the salt and white pepper. Add the rice and stir for 2 minutes, until the kernels are well coated. Pour in the white wine and stir continuously until the wine has completely evaporated. Ladle ½ cup of the hot stock into the rice and stir continuously until reduced by two thirds. Add another ladleful of stock, again stirring continuously until reduced by two thirds. Repeat this process until most of the stock has been absorbed and the rice is tender but not mushy, with a creamy consistency. (You may have as much as a cup of stock left unused.) When stirred, the rice should move in a slow wave across the bottom of the pot (*all'onda*). This should take about 14 minutes from the time you begin ladling the stock into the rice.

Remove the risotto from the heat and cover for 1 minute. Stir in the butter, cheese, and ¼ cup of the veal marrow until creamy. Season with salt and white pepper.

To serve, spoon the sauce over portions of osso buco and serve with the risotto Milanese. Serve immediately.

# Risotto with Shrimp, Zucchini, and Sun-Dried Tomatoes

## RISOTTO CON GAMBERI, ZUCCHINE E POMODORI SECCHI

This unusual risotto blends the riches of earth and sea—shrimp, garden-fresh zucchini, and sun-dried tomatoes—building layers of sweetness, salt, and vegetal mellowness. I usually make the shrimp stock a day or more ahead of time, refrigerating it until I'm ready to make the risotto. It takes three pounds of shrimp to make the one pound of tails, heads, and shells you need for the stock. You'll use a pound of the shelled bodies for the risotto. Save the other two pounds for another use—or grill them to eat alongside the risotto. Don't peel the zucchini— the color and texture of the peel adds to the dish. And when selecting sun-dried tomatoes, look for a brightly colored, semisoft product, avoiding any that are overly dark or dry. MAKES 6 SERVINGS

**WINE PAIRING:** Show off the island cuisine with an island wine like Vermentino from Sardinia, which brings a lovely green-melon freshness and simplicity that allow the flavors of the risotto to stand tall.

6 cups shrimp stock (see recipe, page 117)

**FOR THE SHRIMP AND ZUCCHINI *CONDIMENTI***

⅓ cup extra virgin olive oil

1 small skin-on zucchini, finely chopped to make 1 cup

1 pound medium-sized shrimp, heads and tails removed, peeled and deveined (reserved from making the shrimp stock)

½ cup sun-dried tomatoes, finely chopped

⅓ cup dry Italian white wine

1 small bunch basil, leaves only, roughly chopped to make 2 tablespoons

2 sprigs Italian flat-leaf parsley, leaves only, roughly chopped to make 1 tablespoon

**FOR THE RISOTTO**

2 tablespoons extra virgin olive oil, plus more for drizzling

1 slice medium white or yellow onion, finely chopped to make ¼ cup

½ teaspoon finely ground sea salt, plus more as needed

½ teaspoon finely ground white pepper, plus more as needed

1¼ cups Vialone Nano *semifino* rice

⅓ cup dry Italian white wine

2 tablespoons cold unsalted butter

In a medium heavy-gauge saucepan or pot, bring the shrimp stock to a boil over medium heat. Reduce the heat to maintain a gentle simmer.

**MAKE THE *CONDIMENTI*:** In a medium heavy-gauge sauté pan or skillet at least 3 inches deep (with lid handy), combine the olive oil, zucchini, shrimp, sun-dried tomatoes, white wine, basil, and parsley. Cook over very low heat, stirring frequently, until the vegetables are tender but not mushy and the shrimp is cooked through. Transfer the *condimenti* to a bowl and wipe out the pan. Keep the *condimenti* warm while you make the rice.

**MAKE THE RISOTTO:** Return the pan to the stovetop over low heat. Add the olive oil and onion. Cook, stirring frequently, until the onion is soft and translucent but not browned. It's okay to add 2 tablespoons water to help the onion soften without browning, just be sure the water has evaporated before moving to the next step. Season with the salt and pepper. Add the rice and stir for 2 minutes, until the kernels are well coated. Pour in the white wine and stir continuously until the wine has completely evaporated. Ladle ½ cup of the hot shrimp stock into the rice and stir until the stock has reduced by two thirds. Add another ladleful of stock, again stirring until reduced by two thirds. Repeat this process until most of the stock has been absorbed by the rice and the rice is tender but not mushy, with a creamy consistency. (You may have as much as a cup of stock left unused.) When stirred, the rice should move across the pan in slow waves (*all'onda*). This should take about 14 minutes from the time you begin ladling the stock into the rice.

Remove the risotto from the heat. Add the shrimp and zucchini *condimenti* and cover for 2 minutes. Stir in the butter until creamy. Season with salt and pepper. Spoon the risotto into a serving bowl or individual dishes. Drizzle with olive oil and serve immediately.

# Risotto with Oysters and Prosecco

## RISOTTO ALLE OSTRICHE E PROSECCO

While all the risottos in this book follow the classic tradition of simmering toasted rice in just a small amount of dry white wine before adding broth, there is a legacy of *risotti* made with generous cupfuls of other prized Italian wines, from Amarone and Chianti to Marsala and Barolo. This is one of them, and it stars Prosecco, Italy's beloved bubbly, which, for the first time, in 2013, surpassed Champagne in worldwide sales. Light-bodied with a bit of acidity and effervescence, Prosecco goes very well with the brininess of oysters, such as the Belon variety I've specified. Do try to find Prosecco from the Conegliano-Valdobbiadene area—it's the best. This recipe begins with a flavor-enhancing fish stock—I recommend making it a day ahead of time. If you are time-pressed, substitute store-bought fish stock. And, as with any Italian seafood risotto, the rice to use is Vialone Nano. MAKES 6 SERVINGS

**WINE PAIRING:** The wine pairing is quite obvious here: more Prosecco! Preferably, find a *superiore* version, which will have extra flavor and ripeness to stand up to the meal.

### FOR THE FISH STOCK

2 tablespoons extra virgin olive oil

1 small white or yellow onion, chopped to make 1 cup

4 whole garlic cloves, peeled

1 pound fish bones, preferably from red snapper or white fish, rinsed well

½ cup dry Italian white wine

### FOR THE RISOTTO

¼ cup extra virgin olive oil, plus more for drizzling

1 slice white or yellow onion, finely chopped to make ¼ cup

½ teaspoon finely ground sea salt, plus more as needed

½ teaspoon finely ground white pepper, plus more as needed

1¼ cups Vialone Nano *semifino* rice

1 cup Italian Prosecco, such as Conegliano-Valdobbiadene

4 tablespoons (½ stick) cold unsalted butter

36 Belon oysters, shucked and shelled

**MAKE THE FISH STOCK:** In a heavy-gauge stockpot over medium heat, combine the olive oil, onion, garlic, fish bones, and wine. Pour in 9 cups water to cover and bring to a very slow simmer. (Do not boil.) Lower the heat to maintain a gentle simmer and cook for 45 minutes. Strain through a fine-mesh strainer, discarding the solids. You should have 6½ to 7 cups stock. If you plan to finish the risotto at a later time, cool the stock and store it in a covered container in the refrigerator until ready to use.

**MAKE THE RISOTTO:** In a medium heavy-gauge saucepan or pot, bring 6 cups of the fish stock (homemade or store-bought) to a simmer over medium-low heat. (Do not boil.) Adjust heat to maintain a gentle simmer.

In a medium heavy-gauge sauté pan or skillet at least 3 inches deep (with lid handy) combine 2 tablespoons of the olive oil and the onion over low heat. Cook, stirring frequently, until the onion is soft and translucent but not browned. It's okay to add 2 tablespoons water to help the onion soften without browning, just be sure the water has evaporated before moving to the next step. Season with the salt and pepper. Add the rice and stir for 2 minutes, until the kernels are well coated. Pour in ½ cup of the Prosecco and stir continuously until the wine has completely evaporated. Ladle ½ cup of the hot fish stock into the rice and stir until the stock has reduced by two thirds. Add another ladleful of stock, again stirring until reduced by two thirds. Repeat this process until most of the broth has been incorporated and the rice is tender but not mushy, with a creamy consistency. (You may have as much as a cup of stock left unused.) When stirred, the rice should move across the pan in slow waves (*all'onda*). This should take about 14 minutes from the time you begin ladling the stock into the rice.

Remove the risotto from the heat. Cover for 1 minute. Stir in the butter until creamy. Season with salt and pepper.

In a heavy-gauge skillet over low heat, warm the remaining 2 tablespoons olive oil. Add the oysters and remaining ½ cup Prosecco, season with salt and pepper, and cook for 1 to 2 minutes, until the oysters are semifirm. Remove the oysters from the pan to a holding platter. Spoon the risotto into a serving bowl or individual dishes. Using a slotted spoon, arrange the oysters over all. Drizzle with olive oil and serve immediately.

# Risotto with Spring Vegetables

## RISOTTO ALLA PRIMAVERA

If, like me, you are a farmers market fan, or buy shares in a local farm's CSA, this is the perfect way to highlight the sweet fresh vegetables you bring home in season. The vegetable mix includes fava beans, synonymous with spring in Italy. Favas can get really big—save the huge ones for another recipe. For this one, try to find smaller pods enclosing beans each no more than an inch long. MAKES 6 SERVINGS

**WINE PAIRING:** Rich risotto with fresh vegetables needs a contradiction-filled wine that has both richness and freshness: The answer? A chilled rosé from Sangiovese with cherry-raspberry richness and an herbal freshness.

### FOR THE SPRING VEGETABLE *CONDIMENTI*

¼ cup extra virgin olive oil

1 spring onion or scallion, sliced

3 or 4 fresh fava bean pods, shelled, blanched, and peeled to make ¼ cup beans, or ¼ cup peeled refrigerated fava beans (see "Preparing Fresh Favas," page 72)

¼ cup shelled and blanched fresh garden peas (English) or frozen, thawed green peas

2 asparagus spears, woody stems discarded, remainder thinly sliced on a bias

4 baby carrots, thinly cut on a bias

4 canned baby artichokes, drained, cut into pieces

Finely ground sea salt and white pepper

### FOR THE RISOTTO

6 cups vegetable broth (page 66)

2 tablespoons extra virgin olive oil, plus more for drizzling

1 slice medium white or yellow onion, finely chopped to make ¼ cup

Finely ground sea salt and white pepper

1¼ cups *superfino* rice (Arborio, Baldo, Carnaroli, or Roma)

⅓ cup dry Italian white wine

2 tablespoons cold unsalted butter

4 ounces Parmigiano Reggiano or Grana Padano, finely grated to make 1 cup

**MAKE THE SPRING VEGETABLE *CONDIMENTI*:** In a medium heavy-gauge sauté pan or skillet at least 3 inches deep (with lid handy), warm the olive oil over low heat. Add the spring onion, fava beans, peas, asparagus, baby carrots, and baby artichokes; cook slowly, stirring continuously, until the vegetables are tender but not browned. Season with salt and pepper. Remove from the heat; transfer to a bowl. Wipe out the pan.

**MAKE THE RISOTTO:** In a medium heavy-gauge saucepan or pot, bring the vegetable broth to a boil over medium heat. Lower the heat to maintain a gentle simmer.

In the pan used to make the *condimenti*, combine the olive oil and onion over low heat. Cook, stirring frequently, until the onion is soft and translucent but not browned. It's okay to add 2 tablespoons water to help the onion soften without browning, just be sure the water has evaporated before moving to the next step. Season with salt and pepper. Add the rice and stir for 2 minutes, until the kernels are well coated. Pour in the wine and stir continuously until the wine has completely evaporated. Ladle ½ cup of the broth into the rice and stir continuously until the broth has reduced by two thirds. Add another ladleful of broth and again stir until reduced by two thirds. Repeat this process until most of the broth has been absorbed by the rice and the rice is tender but not mushy, with a creamy consistency. (You may have as much as a cup of broth left unused.) When stirred, the rice should move across the pan in slow waves (*all'onda*). This should take about 14 minutes from the time you begin ladling the broth into the rice.

Remove the risotto from the heat. Stir in the spring vegetable *condimenti*. Cover for 2 minutes. Add the butter and cheese and stir until creamy. Season with salt and pepper. Spoon the risotto into a serving bowl or individual dishes. Drizzle with olive oil and serve immediately.

# Risotto with Guanciale, Egg Yolk, and Pecorino Romano

## RISOTTO ALLA CARBONARA

The word *carbonara* means "charcoal burner" in Italian, which has some food historians theorizing that the dish was named for coal miners. Use pancetta if you have any trouble sourcing guanciale. MAKES 6 SERVINGS

**WINE PAIRING:** Morellino di Scansano, a ripe red from southern Tuscany made with a local variant of Sangiovese is the best wine here. Ripe black cherries, dusty herbs, and bright acids will pair well with this flavorful risotto.

**FOR THE GUANCIALE CONDIMENTI**

2 tablespoons extra virgin olive oil

2 slices medium white or yellow onion, finely chopped to make ⅓ cup

3½ ounces guanciale, chopped to make ⅔ cup

Finely ground sea salt and black pepper

**FOR THE RISOTTO**

1¼ cups *superfino* rice (Arborio, Baldo, Carnaroli, or Roma)

⅓ cup dry Italian white wine

2 tablespoons cold unsalted butter

2½ ounces Pecorino Romano, finely grated to make 1 cup, plus Pecorino Romano shavings for garnish

6 large egg yolks, beaten (refrigerate whites for another use)

Finely ground sea salt and black pepper

Extra virgin olive oil

½ teaspoon freshly cracked black pepper

In a medium heavy-gauge saucepan or pot over medium heat, bring 6 cups water to a boil; reduce the heat to maintain a slow simmer.

**MAKE THE *CONDIMENTI*:** In a medium heavy-gauge sauté pan or skillet at least 3 inches deep (with lid handy), combine the olive oil, onion, and guanciale over very low heat. Cook until the onion is soft and translucent and the guanciale is lightly browned. Season with salt and pepper.

**MAKE THE RISOTTO:** Add the rice to the guanciale *condimenti* and stir for 2 minutes, until the kernels are well coated. Pour in the white wine and stir until the wine has completely evaporated. Ladle ½ cup of the simmering water into the rice and stir until the water has reduced by two thirds. Repeat this process until most of the simmering water has been absorbed and the rice is tender but not mushy, with a creamy consistency. This should take about 14 minutes from the time you begin ladling the water into the rice.

Remove the risotto from the heat. Cover for 2 minutes. Add the butter, grated cheese, and egg yolks and stir until creamy. Season with salt and pepper. Spoon the risotto into a serving bowl or individual dishes. Drizzle with olive oil, sprinkle with cracked black pepper, and top with cheese shavings. Serve immediately.

# Risotto with Pancetta and Savoy Cabbage

## RISOTTO CON PANCETTA E VERZA

Savoy cabbage has a more delicate leaf, elevating this cabbage-and-rice dish. Spring onions and vegetable broth enhance the lighter balance in the dish. MAKES 6 SERVINGS

**WINE PAIRING:** Join the cabbage and pancetta together in unity and hunt down a Merlot from Friuli. Italian wine-makers do wonders with this international grape, creating bright, silky, smoky reds with a fresh-plum juiciness.

6 cups vegetable broth (page 66)

**FOR THE PANCETTA-CABBAGE *CONDIMENTI* STIR-IN**

¼ cup extra virgin olive oil

3½ ounces pancetta, finely chopped to make ⅔ cup

2 spring onions or scallions, peeled, blanched, and cut in half lengthwise

½ small head savoy cabbage, core removed, chopped to make 2 cups

Finely ground sea salt and black pepper

**FOR THE RISOTTO**

2 tablespoons extra virgin olive oil, plus more for drizzling

1 slice medium white or yellow onion, finely chopped to make ¼ cup

Finely ground sea salt and white pepper

1¼ cups *superfino* rice (Arborio, Baldo, Carnaroli, or Roma)

⅓ cup dry Italian white wine

2 tablespoons cold unsalted butter

4 ounces Parmigiano Reggiano, finely grated to make 1 cup

In a medium heavy-gauge saucepan or pot over medium heat, bring the vegetable broth to a boil; reduce the heat to maintain a simmer.

**MAKE THE PANCETTA-CABBAGE *CONDIMENTI*:** In a medium heavy-gauge sauté pan or skillet at least 3 inches deep (with lid handy), combine the olive oil, pancetta, spring onions, and cabbage over low heat. Season with salt and pepper. Cook slowly, stirring frequently, until soft. Transfer to a bowl and keep warm. Wipe out the pan.

**MAKE THE RISOTTO:** Return the pan to the stovetop over low heat. Add the olive oil and onion and cook, stirring frequently, until the onion is soft and translucent but not browned. It's okay to add 2 tablespoons water to help the onion soften without browning, just be sure the water has evaporated before moving to the next step. Season with salt and pepper. Add the rice and stir for 2 minutes, until the kernels are well coated. Pour in the white wine and stir until the wine has completely evaporated. Ladle ½ cup of the hot vegetable broth into the rice and stir until the broth has reduced by two thirds. Repeat this process until most of the broth has been absorbed and the rice is tender but not mushy, with a creamy consistency. This should take about 14 minutes from the time you begin ladling the broth into the rice.

Remove the risotto from the stovetop. Stir in the pancetta-cabbage *condimenti*. Cover for 1 minute. Add the butter and cheese and stir until creamy. Season with salt and pepper. Spoon the risotto into a serving bowl or individual dishes, drizzle with olive oil, and serve.

# Risotto with Guanciale and Tuscan Kale

## RISOTTO CON GUANCIALE E CAVOLO NERO

Pairing guanciale, Italy's famed cured pork jowl and cheek, with the deep, dark flavor of Tuscan kale gives this risotto bold taste. I make it with spring onions and vegetable broth, but you can substitute scallions and chicken broth (page 101) or brown stock (page 153) for an even heartier fall or winter preparation. MAKES 6 SERVINGS

**WINE PAIRING:** Show off this Tuscan dish with a Tuscan wine—a Chianti Classico Riserva would be a delicious spicy pairing for the hearty flavors of this recipe.

6 cups vegetable broth (page 66)

**FOR THE GUANCIALE-KALE** *CONDIMENTI*

¼ cup extra virgin olive oil

3½ ounces guanciale, finely chopped to make ⅔ cup

2 spring onions or scallions, blanched and cut in half lengthwise

4 leaves Tuscan kale, stems removed, chopped to make 2 cups

Finely ground sea salt and black pepper

**FOR THE RISOTTO**

2 tablespoons extra virgin olive oil, plus more for drizzling

1 slice medium white or yellow onion, finely chopped to make ¼ cup

Finely ground sea salt and white pepper

1¼ cups *superfino* rice (Arborio, Baldo, Carnaroli, or Roma)

⅓ cup dry Italian white wine

2 tablespoons cold unsalted butter

2½ ounces Parmigiano Reggiano or Grana Padano, finely grated to make 1 cup

In a medium heavy-gauge saucepan or pot over medium heat, bring the vegetable broth to a boil; reduce the heat to maintain a simmer.

**MAKE THE GUANCIALE-KALE** *CONDIMENTI:* In a medium heavy-gauge sauté pan or skillet at least 3 inches deep (with lid handy), combine the olive oil, guanciale, onion, and kale over low heat. Cook slowly, stirring frequently, until the mixture is tender but not browned. Season with salt and pepper. Transfer to a bowl, cover, and keep warm.

**MAKE THE RISOTTO:** Wipe out the pan. Return the pan to the stovetop over low heat, add the olive oil and onion, and cook, stirring, until the onion is soft and translucent. It's okay to add 2 tablespoons water to help the onion soften without browning, just be sure the water has evaporated before moving to the next step. Season with salt and pepper. Add the rice and stir for 2 minutes, until the kernels are well coated. Pour in the white wine and stir continuously until the wine has completely evaporated. Ladle ½ cup of the hot vegetable broth into the rice and stir until the broth has reduced by two thirds. Add another ladleful of broth, again stirring until reduced by two thirds. Repeat this process until most of the broth has been absorbed by the rice and the rice is tender but not mushy, with a creamy consistency. (You may have as much as a cup of broth left unused.) When stirred, the rice should move across the pan in slow waves (*all'onda*). This should take about 14 minutes from the time you begin ladling the broth into the rice.

Remove the risotto from the heat. Stir in the guanciale-kale *condimenti*. Cover the pot for 1 minute. Add the butter and cheese and stir until creamy. Season with salt and pepper. Spoon the risotto into a serving bowl or individual dishes, drizzle with olive oil, and serve immediately.

# Risotto with Shaved Bottarga

## RISOTTO ALLA RASATO DI BOTTARGA

Bottarga, salted, cured fish roe from mullet or tuna, is an Italian delicacy most often associated with Sicily and Sardinia. There, you'll often see it served with lemon and olive oil as a topping for crostini. But it's delicious finely grated or shaved as an accent over pasta or vegetable dishes, or added to risotto as we've done here. For best flavor, do make the fish stock from scratch if you can. If time-pressed, use store-bought. The rice of choice should be Vialone Nano. MAKES 6 SERVINGS

**WINE PAIRING:** Follow the old adage "if it grows together, it goes together" by serving a simple Sardininan Vermentino. The apple/pear fruit, and tart, herbal body, complement the bottarga well.

6 cups fish stock (page 158, or substitute best-quality store-bought)

2 tablespoons extra virgin olive oil, plus more for drizzling

1 slice medium white or yellow onion, finely chopped to make ¼ cup

½ teaspoon finely ground sea salt, plus more as needed

½ teaspoon finely ground white pepper, plus more as needed

1¼ cups Vialone Nano *semifino* rice

⅓ cup dry Italian white wine

2 tablespoons cold unsalted butter

1 ounce bottarga

In a medium heavy-gauge saucepan or pot, bring the fish stock to a boil over medium heat. Reduce the heat to maintain a gentle simmer.

In a medium heavy-gauge sauté pan or skillet at least 3 inches deep (with lid handy), combine the olive oil and onion over low heat. Cook, stirring frequently, until the onion is soft and translucent but not browned. It's okay to add 2 tablespoons water to help the onion soften without browning, just be sure the water has evaporated before moving to the next step. Season with the salt and pepper. Add the rice and stir for 2 minutes, until the kernels are well coated. Pour in the white wine and stir continuously until the wine has completely evaporated. Ladle ½ cup of the hot fish stock into the rice and stir until the stock has reduced by two thirds. Add another ladleful of stock, again stirring until reduced by two thirds. Repeat this process until most of the stock has been absorbed by the rice and the rice is tender, but not mushy, with a creamy consistency. (You may have as much as a cup of stock left unused.) When stirred, the rice should move across the pan in slow waves (*all'onda*). This should take about 14 minutes from the time you begin ladling the stock into the rice.

Remove the risotto from the heat. Cover for 1 minute. Stir in the butter until creamy. Season with salt and pepper. Spoon the risotto into a serving bowl or individual serving dishes. Grate or shave the bottarga over the risotto, drizzle with olive oil, and serve immediately.

# Oven-Parcooked Risotto

While the traditional method of preparing risotto is my favorite, parcooking rice ahead of time cuts down on cleanup and prep time the day you want to make risotto. Try it!

**MAKES 6 SERVINGS**

1 tablespoon extra virgin olive oil

1¼ cups *superfino* rice (Arborio, Baldo, Carnaroli, or Roma)

½ cup dry Italian white wine

2¼ cups plus ⅔ cup vegetable or chicken broth, or shrimp or brown (beef) stock (see pages 66, 101, 117, or 153), or water

1 small onion, studded with 9 cloves

Cooked *condimenti* of choice

5⅓ tablespoons (⅓ cup) cold unsalted butter, cubed

2½ ounces Parmigiano Reggiano or Grana Padano, finely grated to make 1 cup

Finely ground sea salt and white pepper

Preheat the oven to 350°F.

In a heavy-gauge, enamel-coated Dutch oven over low heat, combine the olive oil and rice and stir, toasting the rice for 2 minutes, until the kernels are well coated.

Pour in the white wine; it will bubble up and simmer. Continue to simmer until the wine has been absorbed by the rice, about 2 minutes. Add 2¼ cups of your broth of choice and the clove-studded onion. Cover the pot and parcook the rice in the oven for 12 minutes, until about two thirds of the broth has been absorbed and the rice is still quite firm but beginning to tenderize. Let cool, uncovered, at room temperature for 30 minutes. Discard the onion. As the rice cools it will absorb most, if not all, of the liquid, and will remain slightly under-cooked. Transfer the parcooked rice to an airtight container and refrigerate for up to 4 days.

When you're ready to prepare risotto, place the parcooked rice in a heavy-gauge pot and add the remaining ⅔ cup broth; cook over medium heat until the broth begins to simmer. Reduce the heat to low. Add your cooked *condimenti* of choice, such as vegetables, pesto, sea-food, or meat. Continue cooking the rice for a scant 3 minutes, until tender but not mushy. Stir in the butter and cheese until creamy. Cover the pot for 2 minutes. Season with salt and pepper. Spoon into a serving bowl or individual serving dishes and serve immediately.

# No-Stir Stovetop Risotto

Purists may raise eyebrows, but in my opinion, it is possible to make a good risotto without all of the traditional stirring. Be sure to use an enameled Dutch oven and best-quality ingredients. **MAKES 6 SERVINGS**

½ cup dry Italian white wine

2¼ cups vegetable or chicken broth, or shrimp or brown (beef) stock (see pages 66, 101, 117, or 153), or water

1 small onion, studded with 9 cloves

1 cup *superfino* rice (Arborio, Baldo, Carnaroli, or Roma)

Cooked *condimenti* of choice

5⅓ tablespoons (⅓ cup) cold unsalted butter, cubed

2½ ounces Parmigiano Reggiano or Grana Padano, finely grated to make 1 cup

Finely ground sea salt and white pepper

In a heavy-gauge, enamel-coated Dutch oven, combine the wine, broth, and clove-studded onion and heat to boiling over medium heat. Add the rice in a mound in the center of the pot. Reduce the heat to maintain a simmer. Cover and simmer for 1 minute. Stir. Flatten the rice in an even layer across the bottom of the pan. Cover the pot, reduce the heat to the lowest setting, and cook for 40 minutes.

Stir in your cooked *condimenti* of choice, such as vegetables, pesto, seafood, or meat. Once the stir-ins are heated through and the rice is tender but not mushy, with a creamy texture, remove the pot from the heat. Stir in the butter and cheese. Cover for 2 minutes. Season with salt and pepper. Spoon into a serving dish or individual bowls and serve immediately.

# No-Stir Oven-Cooked Risotto

In this risotto cooking method, you'll toast the rice in oil as you do in traditional risotto preparation, opening up the rice so that it will better absorb the liquid, but the recipe merges the wine and broth stir-ins into one step. A time-saver. MAKES 6 SERVINGS

1 tablespoon extra virgin olive oil

1 cup *superfino* rice (Arborio, Baldo, Carnaroli, or Roma)

½ cup dry Italian white wine

2¼ cups vegetable or chicken broth, or shrimp or brown (beef) stock (see pages 66, 101, 117, or 153), or water

1 small onion, studded with 9 cloves

Cooked *condimenti* of choice

5⅓ tablespoons (⅓ cup) cold unsalted butter, cubed

2½ ounces Parmigiano Reggiano or Grana Padano, finely grated to make 1 cup

Finely ground sea salt and white pepper

In a heavy-gauge, enamel-coated Dutch oven over low heat, combine the olive oil and rice and stir, toasting the rice for 2 minutes, until the kernels are evenly coated. Remove from the heat and set aside.

In another heavy-gauge pot over high heat, combine the wine, broth, and clove-studded onion. Bring to a rapid boil over high heat. Carefully pour the boiling broth mixture into the Dutch oven containing the toasted rice. Stir. Put the rice mixture back on the heat on low, cover the pot, and cook for 15 minutes.

Stir in your cooked *condimenti* stir-in of choice, such as vegetables, pesto, seafood, or meat. Once the stir-ins are heated through and the rice is tender but not mushy, with a creamy texture, remove the pot from heat. Stir in the butter and cheese. Cover the pot for 2 minutes. Season with salt and pepper. Spoon into a serving dish or individual bowls and serve immediately.

# CHAPTER FIVE

# ONE-DISH MEALS

PIATTI UNICI

When I was growing up in Queens, Mom's family dinners were a well-orchestrated daily event. As the morning bloomed, the large, Formica-topped table in our kitchen would be covered with just-shaped gnocchi, or some other kind of handmade pasta. On the counter, you'd see jars full of preserved tomatoes, vegetables, and olives. And bubbling on the stovetop? The beginning of a tomato ragu in the front, chicken stock slowly simmering at the back, and vegetables being blanched on another burner.

Today, all-day meal prep in the United States is a thing of the past, and even in Italy, the long progression of dishes has been abbreviated by utilizing the time-saving Italian piatti *unici* or "single dish," which combines the *primo* and *secondo* courses in one dish. I think even my mom would have appreciated the *piatti unici* I'm featuring here.

All fall into three rice-dish categories:

- Rice dishes cooked in parchment paper (*al cartoccio*)

- Rustic or saucy/hearty rice stews

- Rice-filled or stuffed meat, vegetable, and poultry dishes

Of these, the *bracioli* (filled meat rolls) and stuffed poultry dishes are the heartiest offerings, while the *al cartoccio* dishes are lighter.

When you see *al cartoccio* on a menu at an Italian restaurant, it refers to a dish cooked in pretty parchment paper packets, or sometimes in heat-resistant film bundles. *Al cartoccio* cooking may feature anything from whole fish to fish fillets, shellfish, meats, game, vegetables, pasta, and rice.

**PREVIOUS SPREAD:** Artichokes with Lemon and Thyme Risotto (see recipe, pages 201–202)

# Rice from Vercelli with Lardo, Red Wine, Borlotti Beans, and Dried Salami

## LA PANISSA DEL VERCELLESE

In 1949, Dino De Laurentiis's Academy Award–nominated film *Riso Amaro* ("Bitter Rice") immortalized the life of *le mondine*, the female rice workers who painstakingly planted, weeded, and hand-harvested northern Italy's rice fields. The film stars Silvana Mangano as *la mondina*, who befriends two petty thieves and plans to help one of them carry out a rice heist. Love, lust, murder, and suicide ensue before the credits roll. Although Silvana's portrayal was criticized by some for being oversexualized, her role did bring to light the difficult working conditions *le mondine* endured. From May through July, these women stood daily in cold water and under hot sun, prey to leeches and mosquitos. They lived during the summer in dormitorics on the rice plantations and their main sustenance was this dish—a bean, rice, and sausage medley known as *panissa*—cooked in the open courtyard. In Vercelli (the rice capital of Italy) at La Tenuta Colombara, a historic farm and modern rice-producing facility, this dish is still prepared to honor the memory of *le mondine*. Originally, the dish was prepared with saluggia beans and a soft, confit-cured *salam d'la Duja*, but neither of these ingredients are readily available outside of Italy. In their place, flavorful borlotti beans and crumbled salami (such as an aged Ciauscolo or young Strolghino di Culatello) make tasty substitutions.

MAKES 6 TO 8 SERVINGS

**WINE PAIRING:** With the rich, savory profile of this rice dish, an intense Nebbiolo-based wine would be perfect. A spicy Barbaresco from the Piedmont, loaded with mouth-watering sour cherry flavors, would keep the palate excited for each next bite. Try Produttori del Barbaresco for a great everyday option.

1 cup dried borlotti beans, soaked in 4 cups water overnight in the refrigerator

4 cups vegetable broth (page 66)

½ pound young salami (see suggestions above), casing removed (if possible), crumbled or chopped to make about 2 lightly packed cups

⅓ cup lightly packed, finely chopped lardo (see page 20)

1 medium white or yellow onion, finely chopped to make 1 cup

1¼ cups Carnaroli *superfino* rice, preferably Acquerello

1 cup dry Italian red wine

Transfer the soaked beans and their soaking liquid to a large heavy-gauge saucepan or pot (with lid handy). Add the vegetable broth and salami. Heat to boiling over medium heat. Lower the heat to maintain a gentle simmer. Simmer, stirring occasionally, until the beans are tender and cooked through, about 1 hour. You will have 6 cups liquid remaining with the beans when you are done with this step. Remove from the heat and keep warm while you prepare the rice.

In a medium heavy-gauge sauté pan or skillet over low heat, melt the lardo. When the lardo begins to sizzle and release its fat, add the onion and cook, stirring, until the onion is tender and translucent but not browned. It's okay to add 2 tablespoons water to help the onion soften without browning, just be sure the water has all evaporated before moving to the next step. Add the rice and stir for 2 minutes, until the kernels are well coated. Pour in the red wine and simmer, stirring, for another 2 minutes. Scoop all of this into the bean pot. Simmer, uncovered, for about 1 hour, until the rice is tender, but not mushy. The mixture will be porridge-like, but still a bit loose. Remove the pot from the heat; cover with a lid. Let rest for 10 minutes. Place a wooden spoon upright in the center of the pan. If the spoon begins to lean over just a bit, the dish is perfectly cooked and ready to be served. (If still too loose, cover and let set up a bit more.) Traditionally, if there are any little crispy bits of rice and sausage at the bottom of the pot they are served last, by special request.

# Avocado Cups with
# Black Venus Rice and Seafood

**TAZZE DI AVOCADO RIPIENO DI RISO VENERE ALLA PESCATORE**

Black Venus rice, a whole-grain, minimally milled Italian rice, is a fairly recent variety. Developed in the 1990s in Vercelli, a cross of Italian varietals and the Chinese black "Forbidden Rice," Black Venus is mineral rich, nutty, and sweet. Purple when cooked, the rice provides a dramatic contrast to most foods. Tastewise and texturally, I like it very much with seafood. Here, I've featured this rice paired with seafood in avocado cups, a pleasant recipe for a light lunch. MAKES 8 SERVINGS

**WINE PAIRING:** Seafood and white wine naturally go together, and with this delicious seafood panoply, something loaded with fruity, citrusy, saline flavors is the best choice. Try a Gavi from the Piedmont for a stunning pairing that balances bright acidity with bold lemon-candy aromas.

### FOR THE RICE

⅔ cup Black Venus rice

2 tablespoons unsalted butter

1 teaspoon finely ground sea salt

### FOR THE SEAFOOD

2 tablespoons extra virgin olive oil, plus more for drizzling

6 ounces smallest-available Manila, pastaneck, or littleneck clams, scrubbed until free of all visible dirt (see notes)

6 ounces mussels, beards removed, scrubbed free of all visible dirt

4 ounces calamari, tentacles left whole, tubes cut into ½-inch-thick rings

6 ounces 26/30-count fresh peeled and deveined, or frozen/thawed uncooked shrimp

4 ounces pre-tenderized baby octopus, tentacles only (optional; see notes)

¼ cup dry Italian white wine

⅓ cup bottled Italian tomato puree (*passata*)

Leaves from 3 sprigs basil, hand-torn to make ¼ cup loosely packed

Finely ground sea salt and white pepper

### FOR THE AVOCADO CUPS

4 cups very cold water

Juice of 1 lemon

4 large ripe avocados

Extra virgin olive oil, for drizzling

**MAKE THE RICE:** In a medium heavy-gauge saucepan or pot over medium heat, combine 4 cups water, the rice, butter, and salt. Heat to simmering, stirring continuously. Reduce the heat to maintain a slow simmer and stir again. Cover and simmer until the rice has absorbed almost all the water, about 45 minutes. Remove the lid and check the rice for doneness. If it hasn't absorbed most of the water, allow it to simmer a bit longer. When the rice is done, remove the pot from the heat and uncover it. Set aside.

**MAKE THE SEAFOOD:** In a medium heavy-gauge nonstick skillet over medium heat, warm the olive oil and add the clams, mussels, calamari, shrimp, and octopus (if using). Pour in the wine and tomato puree and increase the heat to high; cover the pan. Simmer briskly, until all of the shellfish have opened, 5 to 10 minutes. Remove and discard any unopened shells. Reduce the heat. Using tongs or a slotted spoon, move the opened shellfish to a large platter. Remove the clams and mussels from their shells, returning the meat to the sauce and discarding the shells. Simmer until all the seafood is fully cooked. Add the basil; season with salt and pepper. Gently mix the seafood and sauce into the reserved rice and set aside.

**PREPARE AND STUFF THE AVOCADO CUPS:** Cut the avocados in half lengthwise, and remove and discard the pits. At this point you can fill the avocados and serve, or, if desired, carefully peel the avocado halves to create cups. Combine the cold water and lemon juice in a large, nonreactive bowl. Slip the avocado halves into the lemon water and let marinate for 1 minute. Remove the avocado halves from the lemon water one at a time and pat them dry with paper toweling. Trim the bottoms level so the cups are stable and transfer them to a large serving platter. Using a tablespoon, fill the avocado cavities with the seafood-rice mixture, mounding the filling as high as possible. Drizzle with olive oil and serve immediately.

**NOTES:**

• Manila clams from Japan accidentally reached U.S. waters in the 1920s but have acclimated well. They are now widely available and are very easy to order on the Internet. Although they can grow large, Manila clams are usually harvested early and sold at a smaller size than littleneck clams. Pastaneck and littleneck clams are the smallest native American clams.

• Some fish markets sell baby octopus already tenderized, which I highly recommend; otherwise, it can be exceptionally chewy.

# Baked Gratin of Rice with Four Cheeses

## GRATINATO DI RISO AI QUATTRO FORMAGGI

This comforting, custardy preparation of rice with cheeses is rich—serve it alongside a nice salad or with some vegetables as a light meal. You can also mix in sliced and sautéed fresh mushrooms or blanched fresh peas or asparagus tips to vary the preparation a bit. Each of the four cheeses brings something a bit different to the dish—creamy texture from the ricotta, mild mellowness from the fresh mozzarella, and depth of flavor from the pecorino and Parmigiano. While I have specified making this in individual 4-ounce cups, you might also bake it in a single gratin dish to serve family style. For extra indulgence, dot the *gratinato* with a little extra ricotta and fresh mozzarella before garnishing with the grated hard cheeses. You will need eight 4-ounce oven-safe ramekins or one 1½-quart casserole dish to bake the gratins. MAKES 8 SERVINGS

**WINE PAIRING:** All that creamy cheese needs some serious acid as a counterpoint. Explore Sicilian whites that show a bit of body, like a Cataratto or Carricante from a great producer. For example? Planeta's Carricante is a fabulous wine with the character of an elegant, bright chardonnay.

2 tablespoons extra virgin olive oil

½ small white or yellow onion, finely chopped to make ½ cup

Finely ground sea salt and black pepper

1¼ cups Arborio or Carnaroli *superfino* rice

⅓ cup dry Italian white wine

2 tablespoons cold unsalted butter, plus more for greasing the ramekins

1½ ounces Pecorino Romano, finely grated to make ¾ cup

1½ ounces Parmigiano Reggiano, finely grated to make ¾ cup

3½ ounces *fior di latte* (fresh cow's milk mozzarella in liquid; see page 20) drained and chopped to make ½ cup

¼ cup ricotta cheese

6 egg yolks (refrigerate whites for another use), beaten

In a medium heavy-gauge saucepan or pot, bring 4½ cups water to a simmer over medium heat. Keep the water at a very low simmer.

Meanwhile, in a medium heavy-gauge sauté pan or skillet at least 3 inches deep (with lid handy), combine the olive oil and onion. Cook over low heat, stirring frequently, until the onion is soft and translucent but not browned. It's okay to add 2 tablespoons water to help the onion soften without browning, just be sure the water has evaporated before moving to the next step. Season with salt and pepper. Add the rice and stir for 2 minutes, until the kernels are well coated. Pour in the white wine; simmer until the wine has evaporated. Ladle ½ cup of the simmering water into the rice and stir until the water has reduced by two thirds. Add another ladleful and stir again until the water has reduced by two thirds. Repeat until most of the water has been absorbed into the rice, which should take about 14 minutes from the time you begin adding the water to the rice. At this point, the rice should be tender, but not mushy, with a creamy consistency. (You may have as much as a cup of water left unused.)

Remove the risotto from the stovetop; cover the pot with a lid for 2 minutes. Remove the lid from the risotto and stir in the butter, ½ cup each of the pecorino and Parmigiano cheeses, the mozzarella, ricotta, and egg yolks. Season with salt and pepper.

Preheat the oven to 400°F. You will have 4 cups of risotto. Lightly butter eight 4-ounce ramekins, or one casserole dish, and set the prepared dishes on a large rimmed sheet pan. Spoon the risotto into the ramekins, distributing it evenly. Top each dish with the remaining ¼ cup each pecorino and Parmigiano. Bake for 25 minutes. Serve hot or at room temperature.

# Porcini Pesto Risotto in Parchment Paper Packets

## RISO CON PESTO DI FUNGHI PORCINI AL CARTOCCIO

I am a big fan of *al cartoccio* (parchment paper packet) cooking, especially when the recipe includes creamy risotto. Filling parchment paper bundles with a blend of rice, cheeses, and, in this case, sautéed fresh porcini (which means "piglets" in Italian), plus a lemony porcini pesto allows the food to steam in its own microenvironment. The rice sets up well, and presented on the plate for the guest to cut open, the packets retain heat until opened, releasing a showy cloud of fragrant steam. Use fresh porcini mushrooms if you can—they are exceptionally aromatic. Get them in season from the mushroom forager at your farmers market. If they are not available, cremini mushrooms can be substituted. To make the packets, eight 9-inch paper cake-pan liners are easiest, but you can also cut eight 10-inch parchment paper squares into circles, too. MAKES 8 SERVINGS

**WINE PAIRING:** Choose a youthful, delicate Arneis from the Piedmont. This wine beautifully balances graceful minerality with peachy acidity.

### FOR THE PESTO

3 ounces fresh porcini mushrooms, stems and caps brushed free of all visible dirt and lightly rinsed in cool water, chopped to make 1 cup

Finely grated zest from 1 lemon

½ cup extra virgin olive oil

1 teaspoon finely ground sea salt

½ teaspoon finely ground white pepper

### FOR THE RISOTTO

2 tablespoons extra virgin olive oil, plus more for the packets

½ small white or yellow onion, finely chopped to make ½ cup

6 ounces fresh porcini mushrooms, brushed free of any visible dirt, rinsed in cool water, and cut into ¼-inch-thick slices (about 2 cups)

Finely ground sea salt and white pepper

1¼ cups Arborio or Carnaroli *superfino* rice

⅓ cup dry Italian white wine

2 tablespoons cold unsalted butter

1½ ounces Parmigiano Reggiano or Grana Padano, finely grated to make ¾ cup

**MAKE THE PESTO:** In the work bowl of a food processor, pulse the porcini mushrooms with the lemon zest, olive oil, salt, and pepper until a creamy paste forms. Refrigerate until needed.

**MAKE THE RISOTTO:** In a medium heavy-gauge saucepan or pot, bring 4½ cups water to a simmer over medium heat. Reduce the heat to maintain a very low simmer.

In a medium heavy-gauge sauté pan or skillet at least 3 inches deep (with lid handy), combine the olive oil, onion, and porcini mushrooms. Stir over low heat until the onion is soft and translucent and the mushrooms are lightly browned. Season with salt and pepper. Add the rice and stir for 2 minutes, until the kernels are well coated. Pour in the white wine and simmer until the wine has evaporated. Ladle ½ cup of the simmering water into the rice, stirring until the water has reduced by two thirds. Add another ladleful and stir again until the water has reduced by two thirds. Repeat until most of the water has been absorbed into the rice, which should take about 14 minutes from the time you begin adding the water. At this point, the rice should be tender, but not mushy, with a creamy consistency. (You may have as much as a cup of water left unused.)

Remove the risotto from the stovetop. Stir in all the porcini pesto and cover with the lid for 1 minute. Remove the lid and stir in the butter and cheese until creamy. Season with salt and pepper. Cover and let rest for 2 minutes.

**ASSEMBLE AND BAKE THE PACKETS:** Preheat the oven to 350°F. Place the stack of parchment paper sheets or cake-pan liners (see recipe introduction) on your work surface. If using square sheets: Trace the bottom of a 9-inch cake pan onto each sheet, cut out each circle; fold each in half. If using cake-pan liners: Fold each in half.

Open one of the parchment paper circles. Sprinkle with olive oil and close the paper to spread the oil. Spoon ¼ cup of risotto into the center of one half. Place flat on your work surface, as if the circle were a taco lying on its side. Working from one end to the other, fold and roll the open edge of the parchment paper in little consecutive pleats until the packet is completely closed, tucking the last flap under. Finished, the packet will look like a Spanish empanada pastry. Repeat with the remaining risotto and parchment paper.

Place the filled packets on a large, rimmed sheet pan and bake for 5 minutes. Immediately serve the packets on individual serving plates, cutting them open at the table.

*Al cartoccio* refers to a dish cooked in parchment paper packets. Packets retain heat until opened, releasing a showy cloud of fragrant steam.

**1.** To make the packets, I either cut squares of parchment into rounds, or use pre-rounded parchment cake-pan liners.

**2.** Fold each sheet (or round) in half and then open and sprinkle with olive oil.

**3.** Briefly close (to spread the oil).

**4.** Re-open the oiled parchment and fill it with the ingredients to be steamed.

**5, 6, 7.** Working from one end to the other, I fold and roll the open edge of the parchment paper packet in little consecutive pleats until the packet is completely closed, tucking the last flap under. Finished, the packet will look like a Spanish empanada pastry.

# Sea Bream and Vegetable Risotto in Parchment Paper Packets

### ORATA CON RISO DI VERDURE AL CARTOCCIO

The tradition of baking in parchment paper has a long history. Many are familiar with the French version, *en papillote*. In Italy the equivalent is *al cartoccio*. *Al cartoccio* cooking is infinitely varied, ranging from simple rice and cheese preparations to one-dish meals like this beautiful dish. Bursting with spring flavors, this recipe is light—with no cheese in the risotto—and bright from the colors of fresh fava beans, peas, and asparagus. Sea bream is prized in Italy for its depth of flavor and is readily available elsewhere, which is why I feature it here. But you can substitute red snapper or sea bass, if necessary. If you can't find fresh favas, substitute Melissa's brand peeled and steamed favas. And if fresh peas aren't in season, use high-quality frozen green peas. To make the packets, eight 9-inch paper cake-pan liners are easiest, but you can also cut eight 10-inch parchment paper squares into circles, too. Note: You will have several extra servings of the risotto filling. Save for later, or serve in a bowl on the table as extra helpings. MAKES 8 SERVINGS

**WINE PAIRING:** Wines with fresh, green flavors are foolproof pairings for vegetable dishes. Here, a grassy, high-acid Vermentino will act like a spritz of lemon on this beautiful fish dish. Look to Sardinia for this wonderful summery white that pairs with vegetables and seafood flawlessly.

### FOR THE VEGETABLES

¼ cup extra virgin olive oil

2 spring onions or scallions, finely chopped to make ½ cup

½ cup fresh shelled green peas (English, sometimes called sweet peas) or frozen thawed green peas

2 asparagus spears, woody stems and papery scales (see page 95) discarded, cut on the bias into 1-inch pieces to make ½ cup

½ whole carrot or equivalent of baby carrots, cut on the bias into ¼-inch-thick slices to make ½ cup

½ teaspoon finely ground sea salt

½ teaspoon finely ground white pepper

### FOR THE RISOTTO

4½ cups vegetable broth (page 66)

2 tablespoons extra virgin olive oil, plus more for the packets

1 slice medium white or yellow onion, finely chopped to make ¼ cup

½ teaspoon finely ground sea salt, plus more as needed

½ teaspoon finely ground white pepper, plus more as needed

1¼ cups Arborio or Carnaroli *superfino* rice

⅓ cup dry Italian white wine

2 tablespoons cold unsalted butter

### FOR THE FISH

8 boneless, skinless sea bream fillets

Finely ground sea salt and white pepper

3 tablespoons extra virgin olive oil

**MAKE THE VEGETABLES:** Heat the olive oil in a medium heavy-gauge sauté pan or skillet over medium-low heat. Add the spring onions, peas, asparagus, carrot, salt, and pepper. Cook, stirring continuously, until the vegetables are tender but not browned. Remove from the heat; place the vegetables in a bowl. Wipe out the pan.

**MAKE THE RISOTTO:** In a medium heavy-gauge saucepan or pot over medium heat, bring the vegetable broth to a simmer over medium heat. Reduce the heat to maintain a very low simmer.

Place the pan you cooked the vegetables in on the stovetop. Add the olive oil and onion and stir until the onion is soft and translucent but not browned. It's okay to add 2 tablespoons water to help the onion soften without browning, just be sure the water has evaporated before moving to the next step. Season with the salt and pepper. Add the rice and stir for 2 minutes, until the kernels are well coated. Pour in the white wine and simmer until the wine has evaporated. Ladle ½ cup of the simmering broth into the rice; stir until reduced by two thirds. Repeat with another ladleful and continue until most of the broth has been incorporated into the risotto. This should take about 14 minutes from the time you begin adding the broth to the rice. At this point, the rice should be tender, but not mushy, with a creamy consistency. (You may have as much as a cup of broth left unused.)

Remove the risotto from the heat. Stir in ½ cup of the vegetables. Cover the pot for 2 minutes. Remove the lid and stir in the butter until the risotto is creamy. Season with salt and pepper. Set aside.

**ASSEMBLE AND BAKE THE PACKETS:** Preheat the oven to 400°F. Place the stack of parchment paper sheets or cake-pan liners (see recipe introduction) on your work surface. If using square sheets: Use a 9-inch cake pan to trace a circle on each sheet. Cut out each circle and fold it in half. If using cake-pan liners: Fold each in half.

Open one of the parchment paper circles and place it flat on your work surface. Sprinkle with the olive oil and close the paper to spread the oil. Spoon 1 heaping tablespoon of the vegetables into the center, just to the right of the fold. Place a fish fillet on top and sprinkle with salt and pepper. Spoon an even layer of risotto (about 2 tablespoons) on top of the fillet. Top with another tablespoon of vegetables and drizzle lightly with olive oil. Fold the left side of the parchment paper circle over the fillet. Working from one end of the half-moon to the other, fold and roll the open edge in little consecutive pleats until the packet is completely closed, tucking the last flap under. Finished, the packet will look like a Spanish empanada pastry. Repeat the process with all the parchment paper packets.

Using a spatula, carefully transfer the filled packets onto a large rimmed sheet pan (you may need two); bake for 15 minutes. Immediately serve the packets on individual plates, cutting them open at the table.

# Onion Cups Filled with Garden Vegetable Risotto

**TAZZE DI CIPOLLE RIPIENE CON RISO DI VERDURE**

I've always thought onions looked a bit like the globes teachers used in elementary school to teach us geography. Longitudinal lines neatly demarcate slices of countries, top to bottom, pole to pole, with the equator encircling the middle latitudinally. That visual comes in handy when halving onions to stuff for this recipe. Rather than cutting them horizontally (through the imaginary equator), cut them longitudinally, from pole to pole. This puts the stem and root ends sideways, rather than at the top and bottom of the cups, making the filled onion cups easier to balance on the tray while they're cooking. It's also easier to separate and remove the inner layers using this cut. Try both ways, you'll see. For this recipe, the filling is best made with fresh spring onions, favas, and peas, but if you can't locate these, scallions, high-quality frozen green peas, and Melissa's brand of peeled, steamed fava beans can be substituted. Fava beans can get really big—for this recipe, avoid those big boys and choose small fava pods (3 or 4 inches long) with the beans inside them no longer than 1 inch.

**MAKES 8 SERVINGS (2 ONION CUPS EACH)**

**WINE PAIRING:** Lambrusco di Sorbara is a deep pink sparkling wine from Emilia-Romagna with good acidity, a clean, flinty finish, and herbal strawberry flavors. Simple and refreshing, it provides a nice counterpoint to the savory vegetables in this dish.

**FOR THE ONION CUPS**

2 large white onions, unpeeled

**FOR THE VEGETABLE CONDIMENTI**

¼ cup extra virgin olive oil

1 spring onion or scallion, trimmed and sliced to make ¼ cup

¼ cup fresh shelled, blanched and peeled fava beans, or peeled and steamed refrigerated favas (see "Preparing Fresh Favas," page 72)

¼ cup shelled fresh green peas (English) or frozen thawed peas

2 asparagus spears, woody stems and papery scales (see page 95) discarded, cut on the bias into 1-inch pieces

3 baby carrots, thinly cut on the bias to make ½ cup

½ teaspoon finely ground sea salt

½ teaspoon finely ground white pepper

**FOR THE RISOTTO**

4½ cups vegetable broth (page 66) or water

2 tablespoons extra virgin olive oil, plus more for oiling the dish and drizzling

½ teaspoon finely ground kosher or sea salt, plus more as needed

½ teaspoon finely ground white pepper, plus more as needed

1¼ cups Arborio or Carnaroli *superfino* rice

⅓ cup dry Italian white wine

2 tablespoons cold unsalted butter

1½ ounces Grana Padano, finely grated to make ¾ cup

Thyme sprigs for garnish

**MAKE THE ONION CUPS:** Preheat the oven to 375°F. Using a paring knife, carefully trim away the root and stem ends of each onion and discard with the peel, leaving as much of the onion intact as possible. Slice the onions in half, from root to stem end (pole to pole). Separate and pull out all but the last four layers of onion from the inside of each onion half. Carefully separate the last four layers of onion to make "cups." You will have 4 "cups" from each onion half for a total of 16 "cups." Finely chop the onion centers to make ½ cup and set aside for the risotto. Place the onion cups in a 9 x 13-inch casserole with 1 cup water at the bottom. Cover with foil. Roast for 15 minutes, until the cups are hot and just beginning to tenderize. Remove from the oven and discard the water. Keep the oven on. Place the onion cups in a bowl and oil the same casserole dish. Put the onion cups back in the casserole. Set aside.

**MAKE THE VEGETABLE *CONDIMENTI*:** In a medium heavy-gauge sauté pan or skillet at least 3 inches deep (with lid handy), heat the olive oil over low heat. Stir in the spring onion, fava beans, peas, asparagus, carrots, salt, and pepper. Cook, stirring frequently, until the vegetables are tender but not browned. Remove from the heat; place the vegetables in a bowl. Wipe out the pan and set aside.

**MAKE THE RISOTTO:** In a medium heavy-gauge saucepan or pot, bring the vegetable broth to a simmer over medium heat. Reduce the heat to low to maintain a slow simmer.

Place the pan you used to cook the *condimenti* over low heat. Warm the olive oil and add the reserved ½ cup chopped onion. Cook, stirring frequently, until the onion is translucent but not browned. It's okay to add 2 tablespoons water to help the onion soften without browning, just be sure the water has all evaporated before moving to the next step. Season with the salt and pepper. Add the rice and stir for 2 minutes, until the kernels are well coated. Pour in the white wine, stirring until the wine has evaporated. Ladle ½ cup of the hot broth into the rice and stir until the broth has reduced by two thirds. Add another ladleful and stir again until the broth has reduced by two thirds. Repeat the procedure until most of the broth has been incorporated, about 14 minutes from the time you begin adding the broth to the rice. At this point, the rice should be tender, but not mushy, with a creamy consistency. (You may have as much as a cup of broth left unused.) Remove the risotto from the heat and stir in the *condimenti*. Cover the pot for 2 minutes. Remove the lid and add the butter and cheese, stirring until creamy. Season with salt and pepper.

Spoon the risotto into the onion cups, mounding it slightly in the middle of each cup. Lightly drizzle with olive oil. Bake until the onions are just heated through, about 5 minutes. Garnish with thyme leaves. Serve hot.

# Sweet Red Bell Peppers Filled with Pancetta, Tomato, and Lentil Risotto

**PEPERONE RIPIENE AL RISO DI PANCETTA, POMODORI E LENTICCHIE**

In the same way that black-eyed peas are eaten on New Year's Day as a good-luck dish in the southern region of the United States, lentils are thought to usher in prosperity and good fortune in Italy. When I was a kid, during the first weeks of January my mom made so many lentils, I'd say, "Mom, how much good luck do we need?" But that aside, I still love lentils. The most famous lentils in Italy are from the valley of Castelluccio in Umbria, where they have been organically grown for hundreds of years. Small, texturally perfect, and full of flavor, they are frequently prepared with onion and tomato, as I have done in this tasty dish. Do use Umbrian lentils, available online or from purveyors of specialty Italian food products, if possible. If not, buy organic French or European lentils. **MAKES 8 SERVINGS**

**WINE PAIRING:** Spicy, smoky, and full of bitter herbs and chewy tannins, a young Aglianico-based wine would show quite nicely here. Or go with a medium-bodied Lacryma Christi to play a little exciting counterpoint with the peppers and zingy tomato.

**FOR THE RED PEPPERS**

8 medium-sized red bell peppers, 1 inch of tops sliced off and saved as lids, cored and seeded

Extra virgin olive oil, for greasing and drizzling

Finely ground black pepper

**FOR THE RISOTTO**

2 tablespoons extra virgin olive oil

1 slice medium white or yellow onion, finely chopped to make ¼ cup

3½ ounces pancetta, chopped to make ⅔ cup

1 cup canned, drained, chopped Italian tomatoes

½ teaspoon finely ground sea salt, plus more as needed

½ teaspoon finely ground black pepper, plus more as needed

1¼ cups Carnaroli *superfino* rice

⅓ cup dry Italian white wine

2 tablespoons cold unsalted butter

3 ounces finely grated Pecorino Romano, finely grated to make ¾ cup

⅔ cup Umbrian lentils, cooked according to package directions

**MAKE THE RED PEPPERS:** Preheat the oven to 375°F. Very thinly slice off the base of each pepper to create a level surface for standing. Place the peppers in a 9 x 13-inch casserole; stand the pepper "lids" sideways along the inside edges of the casserole. Pour 1 cup water into the casserole, cover with foil and roast for 20 minutes. Remove from the oven, but keep the oven on; discard the water. Transfer the peppers to a bowl; dry and grease the casserole. Return the peppers to the casserole.

*(continued)*

**MAKE THE RISOTTO:** In a medium heavy-gauge saucepan or pot, bring 4½ cups water to a simmer over medium heat. Reduce the heat to maintain a slow simmer.

In a medium heavy-gauge sauté pan or skillet at least 3 inches deep (with lid handy), warm the olive oil over low heat. Stir in the onion and pancetta and cook, stirring frequently, until the onion is translucent but not browned and the pancetta has released some of its fat. Stir in the tomatoes, salt, and black pepper. Cook, stirring occasionally, until the mixture is thick enough to coat the back of a spoon. Add the rice and stir for 2 minutes, until the kernels are well coated. Pour in the white wine and stir until the wine has completely evaporated. Ladle ½ cup of the simmering water into the rice and stir until reduced by two thirds. Add another ladleful and stir again until the water has reduced by two thirds. Repeat until most of the water has been absorbed into the rice, which should take about 14 minutes from the time you began adding the water to the rice. At this point, the rice should be tender, but not mushy, with a creamy consistency. (You may have as much as a cup of water left unused.)

Remove the risotto from the heat and cover the pot for 2 minutes. Remove the lid and add the butter, cheese, and cooked lentils, stirring until creamy. Season with salt and black pepper.

Spoon ¾ cup of the risotto into each of the pepper cups. Top each pepper with its lid. Bake just until the peppers are heated through and tender but not limp, about 5 minutes. Lightly drizzle with olive oil, sprinkle with black pepper, and serve.

# Rice Timbale with Neapolitan Sauce and Poached Egg

### TIMBALLO DI RISO CON UOVA IN CAMICIA E SALSA NAPOLETANA

Outside Italy, few cooks, even foodies, had heard of timballo before the 1996 movie *The Big Night* came out. In the film, the *timballo* is called *timpani* and provides a pivotal dramatic moment. Since then, *timballos* have made more frequent appearances on menus, catching up just the slightest bit with their equivalents in Italy, where regional variations have existed since the seventeenth century. Baked in a dome or springform pan, these elegant, layered constructions are built with pasta, rice, or potatoes and bound with eggs and cheese. When done properly, a perfectly shaped, unmolded *timballo* is a source of pride and well worth the effort. You will need 8 individual timbale forms or ⅔ cup ramekins. One note: I recommend making the *Salsa Napoletana* a day before you plan to serve the dish to allow the flavors to develop.

**MAKES 8 TIMBALES**

**WINE PAIRING:** Bring out the big guns: A meaty, smoky Aglianico from Taurasi (or a more economical Aglianico del Vulture) will parry the heat of the chile, wrestle the fatty meats into submission, and show off the savory flavors of the cheeses.

### FOR THE *SALSA NAPOLETANA*

1 tablespoon extra virgin olive oil

1 slice medium white or yellow onion, finely chopped to make ¼ cup

3½ ounces pork belly, chopped to make ½ cup

Just under 1 ounce pancetta, chopped to make 2 tablespoons

4 ounces beef shoulder meat, chopped to make about ⅔ cup

¾ teaspoon crushed red pepper flakes

⅓ cup dry Italian red wine

2 cups canned crushed Italian tomatoes in puree

Leaves from 3 sprigs basil, hand-torn to make ¼ cup loosely packed

½ teaspoon finely ground sea salt

½ teaspoon finely ground black pepper

### FOR THE RICE TIMBALES

2 tablespoons extra virgin olive oil, plus more for oiling the molds

2 slices white or yellow onion, finely chopped to make ⅓ cup

½ teaspoon finely ground sea salt, plus more as needed

½ teaspoon finely ground black pepper, plus more as needed

1¼ cups Arborio or Carnaroli *superfino* rice

⅓ cup dry Italian white wine

1 ounce Pecorino Romano, finely grated to make ½ cup

1 ounce Parmigiano Reggiano, finely grated to make ½ cup

8 egg yolks (reserve whites for another use), beaten

Boiling water for hot-water bath

8 poached eggs, edges trimmed (see Rice Soup with Soft-Poached Eggs, page 85)

**MAKE THE *SALSA NAPOLETANA*:** In a medium heavy-gauge saucepan or pot, combine the olive oil and onion. Cook over low heat, stirring frequently, until the onion is tender and translucent but not browned.  It's okay to add 2 tablespoons water to help the onion soften without browning, just be sure the water has evaporated before moving to the next step. Add the pork belly, pancetta, and beef; increase the heat to high. Stir in the red pepper flakes and cook, stirring frequently, until the meats are browned and caramelized. Stir in the red wine, tomatoes, and basil and reduce the heat to low. Cover and simmer the sauce very slowly, stirring occasionally, for 30 minutes. Taste and adjust the seasoning with salt and pepper. Add ½ cup water. Simmer for an additional 30 minutes. Remove from the heat and keep warm or, if making the sauce in advance, cool and refrigerate until ready to use. Rewarm when ready to use.

**MAKE THE RICE TIMBALES:** In a medium heavy-gauge saucepan or pot over medium heat, bring 4½ cups water to a boil. Reduce the heat to maintain a slow simmer.

In a medium heavy gauge sauté pan or skillet, combine the olive oil and onion. Cook over low heat, stirring frequently, until the onion is tender and translucent but not browned. It's okay to add 2 tablespoons water to help the onion soften without browning, just be sure the water has evaporated before moving to the next step. Season with the salt and pepper. Add the rice and stir for 2 minutes, until the kernels are well coated. Pour in the white wine and stir until the wine has evaporated. Ladle ½ cup of the simmering water into the rice, stirring continuously until the water has reduced by two thirds. Add another ladleful and stir again until the water has reduced by two thirds. Repeat the process until most of the water has been incorporated into the rice, which should take about 14 minutes from the time you begin adding the water to the rice. At this point, the rice should be tender, but not mushy, with a creamy consistency. (You may have as much as a cup of water left unused.)

Remove the risotto from the heat; cover the pot for 2 minutes. Remove the lid and add the cheeses and the egg yolks, stirring until creamy. Season with salt and pepper.

Preheat the oven to 325°F. Brush the timbale forms or ramekins with olive oil. Evenly distribute the risotto among the forms, pressing lightly to ensure there are no empty spaces or air pockets. Spray two large sheets of aluminum foil with nonstick cooking spray. Cut these into 8 squares. Cover each ramekin with a square of foil, cooking spray side down.

Put the filled timbales in a roasting pan and place the roasting pan on the center oven rack. Before closing the oven door, carefully pour the boiling water into the roasting pan until the water comes halfway up the sides of the timbale forms. Bake for 45 minutes, until the timbales are firm but creamy.

Remove the timbales from the hot water bath; let rest on a work surface for 10 minutes. Run a thin spatula around the inside edges of the molds. Invert to unmold each timbale onto a serving plate. Top each with a poached egg. Spoon warmed *Salsa Napoletana* over all and serve.

# Zucchini Boats Filled with Risotto, Pancetta, Salami, and Borlotti Beans

**BARCHETTA DI ZUCCHINE RIPIENE DI RISO, PANCETTA, SALAME E FAGIOLI BORLOTTI**

When I was growing up, my mom used to cut zucchini into long strips, dip them in egg batter, and deep-fry them by the platterful. Simply salted and peppered, these were our "French fries" and we loved them. But in Italy and elsewhere, when home gardens swell with dozens of these firm, green squash, everyone is continually in search of new ways to prepare them. When creating this recipe, my thought was to make a zucchini dish with earthy, rich flavors that was comforting, not intimidating. Carved into little boats, fresh zucchini are clever edible vessels for this Italian potage of Carnaroli rice, sausage, and flavorful borlotti beans, which I've also featured in a main-course version in this book (see page 175). You'll need to start the beans soaking the night before you want to make this dish. MAKES 8 SERVINGS

**WINE PAIRING:** Cerasuolo di Vittoria, a blend of Sicilian indigenous varietals, has an exciting, racy profile of fresh berries, dried herbs, aromatic spices, and volcanic ash. Find a bottling with some muscle, such as the offering from Planeta, and you'll have a perfect pairing for this dish.

### FOR THE BEANS

½ cup dried borlotti (cranberry) beans (see "Quick-Soak Method," page 83)

2 cups vegetable broth (page 66)

4½ ounces young salami, such as an aged Ciauscolo or young Strolghino di Culatello, casing removed, crumbled or chopped to make 1 cup

### FOR THE ZUCCHINI BOATS

8 small or 4 large zucchini

Extra virgin olive oil, for oiling and drizzling

### FOR THE RISOTTO

1¼ ounces pancetta, finely chopped to make ¼ cup

2 slices medium white or yellow onion, finely chopped to make ⅓ cup

1 cup Carnaroli *superfino* rice

½ cup dry Italian red wine

2 tablespoons cold unsalted butter

1 ounce Parmigiano Reggiano or Grana Padano, finely grated to make ½ cup

Finely ground sea salt and white pepper

**MAKE THE BEANS:** The night before you want to serve this dish, place the beans and 3 cups water in a nonreactive bowl, cover the bowl, and refrigerate. The following day, transfer the beans and their soaking liquid to a heavy-gauge pot over low heat. Add the vegetable broth and crumbled salami and simmer until the beans are tender and cooked through, about 1 hour. Remove from the heat and set aside.

**MAKE THE ZUCCHINI BOATS:** Preheat the oven to 350°F. Slice each zucchini in half lengthwise. Using an apple or tomato corer, carefully scoop the flesh out of the zucchini, making hollowed-out canoes. Chop 1 cup of the zucchini flesh and reserve it for use in the risotto.

Save the rest for another use. Place the zucchini boats in a 9 x 13-inch casserole dish. Pour 1 cup water into the dish. Cover with foil. Roast for 20 minutes, until the zucchini are hot and beginning to tenderize but not cooked through. Pour off the water; transfer the zucchini to a bowl. Dry and oil the casserole dish. Return the boats to the casserole. Set aside.

**MAKE THE RISOTTO:** In a medium heavy-gauge saucepan or pot over low heat, add the pancetta, and stir until the pancetta begins to sizzle. Add the onion and reserved 1 cup chopped zucchini. Cook, stirring, until the onion is soft and translucent but not browned. Add the rice and stir for 2 minutes, until well coated. Pour in the red wine and simmer for 2 minutes. Scoop all of this into the bean pot, stir once, and set the pot over the lowest heat. Simmer very slowly for about 1 hour, until the rice is tender, but not mushy, and most of the liquid has been absorbed. Remove the pot from the heat, cover, and let rest for 5 minutes. Stir in the butter and cheese. Season with salt and pepper. Cover and let rest for another 3 minutes.

**ASSEMBLE AND BAKE THE BOATS:** Preheat the oven to 350°F. Fill the zucchini boats with the rice and bean mixture. Bake for 7 to 10 minutes, until the zucchini are cooked through but not mushy. Remove from the oven and transfer to a serving platter. Drizzle with olive oil and serve.

# Artichokes with Lemon and Thyme Risotto

## CARCIOFI RIPIENE DI RISO AL LIMONE E TIMO

Grassy, nutty, asparagus-like but earthier, with a refreshingly tangy finish on the palate, the flavor of fresh artichokes is sublime and Italian preparations are myriad: Artichokes may be preserved in oil, shaved on salads, puréed and spread on bruschetta, or, as in this recipe, filled or stuffed with creamy risotto. Despite their elaborate appearance, filled artichokes are actually easy to prepare. Just be sure to use a sharp knife and kitchen shears. Also, take care when you remove the hairy choke before stuffing the artichokes: The tender inner bottom of the vegetable right underneath the hairy choke is the best part, so you want to leave that intact. Please note: The risotto portion of this recipe makes 4 cups of filling, enough to use 1 cup for each of 4 large globe artichokes—½ cup in the center and ½ cup stuffed between the leaves. Double the recipe for a larger crowd. MAKES 4 SERVINGS • PHOTOGRAPH ON PAGE 170

**WINE PAIRING:** Artichokes contain an enzyme that can spoil fruity flavors in wine. Avoid this pitfall by choosing a wine that's famously non-fruity: Verdicchio. With its lean, mineral-driven palate of green herbs and tart citrus, a young Verdicchio pairs perfectly with this dish and won't be altered by the artichokes' notorious alchemy.

### FOR THE ARTICHOKES

¼ teaspoon kosher or sea salt

1 lemon, thinly sliced

4 large globe artichokes

### FOR THE VEGETABLE CONDIMENTI

2 tablespoons extra virgin olive oil

1 spring onion or scallion, coarsely chopped to make ¼ cup

Leaves from 1 small bunch thyme (1 tablespoon)

Finely grated zest of 2 lemons

½ teaspoon finely ground sea salt

½ teaspoon finely ground white pepper

### FOR THE RISOTTO

4½ cups vegetable broth (page 66) or water

2 tablespoons extra virgin olive oil, plus more for greasing and drizzling

2 slices white or yellow onion, finely chopped to make ⅓ cup

½ teaspoon finely ground sea salt, plus more as needed

½ teaspoon finely ground white pepper, plus more as needed

1¼ cups Arborio or Carnaroli *superfino* rice

⅓ cup dry Italian white wine

2 tablespoons cold unsalted butter

1½ ounces Grana Padano, finely grated to make ¾ cup

**MAKE THE ARTICHOKES:** In a very large pot over high heat, bring 5 quarts water to boiling. Reduce the heat to low to maintain a slow simmer. Add the salt and lemon slices.

Using a very sharp knife, cut off and discard all but 1 inch of the artichoke stems. Discard the bottom layer of leaves. Using sharp kitchen shears, cut off the tip of each remaining leaf. Place the artichokes in the simmering water, ensuring that they are completely covered. If they float, you can weight them with a heavy lid that's just a bit smaller than the circumference of the pot. Simmer for 1 hour or until you can insert a knife tip easily into the bottom of an artichoke. Remove the artichokes from the water and drain in colander; let cool. When cool enough to handle, pull out and discard the central inner leaves. Using a spoon, carefully remove and discard the hairy choke underneath. Transfer the finished artichokes to a large rimmed sheet pan; set aside.

**MAKE THE VEGETABLE *CONDIMENTI*:** In a medium heavy-gauge sauté pan or skillet at least 3 inches deep (with lid handy), warm the olive oil over low heat. Stir in the spring onion, thyme, lemon zest, salt, and pepper. Cook, stirring frequently, until the onion is soft but not browned. Transfer the mixture to a bowl and keep warm. Wipe out the pan.

**MAKE THE RISOTTO:** In a medium heavy-gauge saucepan or pot, bring the vegetable broth to a simmer over medium heat. Reduce the heat to maintain a low simmer.

Place the pan you used to cook the *condimenti* over low heat and warm the olive oil. Stir in the onion. Cook, stirring frequently, until the onion is translucent but not browned. It's okay to add 2 tablespoons water to help the onion soften without browning, just be sure the water has evaporated before moving to the next step. Season with the salt and pepper. Add the rice and stir for 2 minutes, until the kernels are well coated. Pour in the white wine and stir until the wine has evaporated. Ladle ½ cup of the simmering broth into the rice and stir until the broth has reduced by two thirds. Add another ladleful and stir again until reduced by two thirds. Repeat the procedure until most of the broth has been incorporated, which should take about 14 minutes from the time you begin adding the broth to the rice. At this point, the rice should be tender, but not mushy, with a creamy consistency. (You may have as much as a cup of broth left unused.)

Remove the risotto from the heat and stir in the vegetable *condimenti*. Cover the pot for 2 minutes. Remove the lid and add the butter and cheese, stirring until creamy. Season with salt and pepper.

Preheat the oven to 375°F. Using a teaspoon, fill each artichoke with ½ cup of risotto in the center and another ½ cup tucked between the leaves. Place each filled artichoke in a lightly oiled, shallow casserole dish. Lightly drizzle the artichokes with olive oil. Bake just until the artichokes are heated through, about 5 minutes.

# Braised Pork Rolls with Pine Nut–Raisin Risotto

## BRACIOLE DI MAIALE RIPIENE CON RISO DI PINOLI E ALL'UVETTE PASSITA

*Braciole*, little bundles of poultry, beef, or pork stuffed with fillings, are a specialty in southern Italy. There, for centuries, inexpensive cuts of meat from the shoulder and leg have been pounded flat, salted and peppered, filled, and braised in tomato sauce. Stuffing slices of pork shoulder with the special risotto filling detailed here elevates these rolls to main-course status. This recipe, with raisins and pine nuts in a rich tomato sauce, is one of my favorites: a new take on an old classic. MAKES 6 TO 8 SERVINGS

**WINE PAIRING:** When raisins are used in a savory dish, Ripasso Valpolicella from the Veneto makes a delicious wine pairing. And in this case, Ripasso—a bright, extracted wine akin to a baby Amarone—echoes the sweetness of the raisins and savory flavors of the cheese and onions while supporting the weight of the braised pork.

### FOR THE RISOTTO

4½ cups vegetable broth (page 66)

2 tablespoons extra virgin olive oil

2 slices medium white or yellow onion, finely chopped to make ⅓ cup

Finely ground sea salt and white pepper

1¼ cups Arborio or Carnaroli *superfino* rice

⅓ cup dry Italian white wine

1½ ounces Pecorino Romano, finely grated to make ¾ cup

⅔ cup dark raisins

⅔ cup golden raisins

⅓ cup pine nuts

### FOR THE *BRACIOLE*

12 to 16 slices of pork shoulder (2 to 3 ounces each), pounded to ¼-inch thickness

12 to 16 pieces of thin butcher's or baker's twine (2 to 3 feet each; see note)

3 tablespoons extra virgin olive oil

⅓ cup dry Italian white wine

1 (24-ounce) bottle Italian tomato puree (*passata*)

**MAKE THE RISOTTO:** In a medium heavy-gauge saucepan or pot over medium heat, bring the vegetable broth to a boil. Reduce the heat to maintain a slow simmer.

In a medium heavy-gauge sauté pan or skillet at least 3 inches deep (with lid handy), combine the olive oil and onion over low heat. Cook, stirring frequently, until the onion is soft and translucent but not browned. It's okay to add 2 tablespoons water to help the onion soften without browning, just be sure the water has evaporated before moving to the next step. Season with salt and pepper. Add the rice and stir for 2 minutes, until the kernels are well coated. Pour in the white wine and stir until the wine has evaporated. Ladle ½ cup of the simmering broth into the rice and stir until reduced by two thirds. Add another ladleful and stir again until the broth has reduced by two thirds. Repeat until most of the broth has been absorbed into the rice, which should take about 14 minutes from the time you begin adding the broth to the rice. At this point, the rice should be tender, but not mushy, with a creamy consistency. (You may have as much as a cup of broth left unused.)

Remove the risotto from the heat and cover the pot for 2 minutes. Remove the lid and add the cheese, dark and golden raisins, and the pine nuts, stirring until creamy. Season with salt and pepper.

**MAKE THE *BRACIOLE*:** Spread out a sheet of parchment paper on a clean work surface. Arrange the pork slices, widest ends facing you, on top of the parchment paper. Scoop a rounded tablespoonful of the risotto onto the wide end of each slice. Carefully tucking and folding, roll toward the narrow end of the slice until you finish with a little bundle. Grab a length of twine in one hand and wrap and spiral the twine around the bundle, holding the bundle with your other hand to ensure the filling is enclosed as much as possible and tying the loose ends of the twine when finished. Repeat with the remaining pork slices and filling.

Preheat the oven to 350°F. On the stovetop, heat the olive oil in a heavy-gauge ovensafe skillet with lid or large Dutch oven over medium heat. Place the *braciole* in the pan and sear on all sides. Reduce the heat to low, pour in the white wine, and simmer until the wine has reduced by half. Add the tomato puree. Remove for the heat. Cover the skillet or Dutch oven and roast for 45 minutes. Let cool slightly. Remove the twine from the *braciole*. Serve each bundle whole, or slice into several circular pieces and fan out on serving plates. Top each serving with some of the tomato sauce.

NOTE: Be sure to precut your lengths of twine and make them plenty long—2 to 3 feet of twine per bundle is not too much. Using some extra twine makes shaping the bundles a little easier, and you'll be removing the twine before you serve the *braciole* anyway.

# Chicken Breasts Stuffed with Prosciutto and Spinach Pesto Risotto

## PETTO DI POLLO RIPIENE CON PROSCIUTTO CRUDO E RISO AL PESTO DI SPINACI

Layered with prosciutto and filled with spinach pesto risotto, these tender stuffed breasts are oven-roasted until juicy inside with crispy skin outside. Pretty to look at and satisfyingly filling, they are truly a one-dish meal. MAKES 8 SERVINGS

**WINE PAIRING:** With its richness, bright acidity, and round apricot-almond flavors, Friulano is a famous pairing for prosciutto and is a perfect wine to enjoy alongside this dish. If you prefer red, a Valpolicella made in a lighter style is also lovely here, offering a juicy cherry, prune, and cinnamon contrast to the creamy risotto.

### FOR THE SPINACH PESTO

3 cups lightly packed baby spinach leaves (about 2½ ounces)

Finely grated zest of 1 lemon

½ cup extra virgin olive oil

½ teaspoon finely ground sea salt

½ teaspoon finely ground white pepper

### FOR THE RISOTTO

2 tablespoons extra virgin olive oil

2 slices medium white onion, finely chopped to make ⅓ cup

½ teaspoon finely ground sea salt, plus more as needed

½ teaspoon finely ground white pepper, plus more as needed

1¼ cups Arborio or Carnaroli *superfino* rice

⅓ cup dry Italian white wine

⅓ cup roughly chopped spinach leaves

¼ cup finely chopped prosciutto

2 tablespoons cold unsalted butter

2½ ounces Parmigiano Reggiano or Grana Padano, finely grated to make 1 cup

### FOR THE CHICKEN

8 boneless, skin-on chicken breasts

8 paper-thin slices aged Italian prosciutto

Extra virgin olive oil, for brushing and drizzling

Finely ground sea salt and white pepper

**MAKE THE SPINACH PESTO:** In the work bowl of a food processor, combine the spinach, lemon zest, olive oil, salt, and pepper. Pulse until pureed. Transfer to a bowl and refrigerate until ready to use.

**MAKE THE RISOTTO:** In a medium heavy-gauge saucepan or pot over medium heat, bring 4½ cups water to a boil. Reduce the heat to maintain a slow simmer.

In a medium heavy-gauge sauté pan or skillet at least 3 inches deep (with lid handy), combine the olive oil and onion. Cook over low heat until the onion is tender and translucent but not browned. It's okay to add 2 tablespoons water to help the onion soften without browning, just be sure the water has evaporated before moving to the next step. Add the salt and pepper. Add the rice and stir for 2 minutes, until the kernels are well coated. Pour in the white wine and simmer until the wine has evaporated. Ladle ½ cup of the simmering water into the rice and stir continuously until the water has reduced by two thirds. Add a second ladleful of water and stir again until the water has reduced by two thirds. Repeat until most of the water has been absorbed into the rice, which should take about 14 minutes from the time you begin adding the water to the rice. At this point, the rice should be tender, but not mushy, with a creamy consistency. (You may have as much as a cup of water left unused.)

Remove the risotto from the heat. Stir in the spinach pesto. Cover for 2 minutes. Remove the lid and stir in the spinach, prosciutto, butter, and cheese until creamy. Cover and reserve.

**MAKE THE CHICKEN:** Preheat the oven to 375°F. Arrange the chicken breasts, skin side down, on a work surface. Each breast has two lobes. If the breasts are exceptionally large: Separate the breasts into two pieces where the two lobes are joined. Using a sharp knife, slice each breast lobe across the grain, horizontally through the center of the lobe, cutting almost all the way through and folding the top flap back. Place one slice of prosciutto on the bottom half of each lobe. If the breasts are small: Leave the lobes attached. Place one slice of prosciutto on one lobe, leaving the other lobe alongside.

Spoon 2 tablespoons of the risotto over the top of each prosciutto slice. Cover with the top flap of chicken for the large breasts or second chicken lobe for the small breasts. Using sharp kitchen shears, trim any rough edges to neaten.

Brush a large sheet pan with olive oil. Arrange the filled breasts on the tray. Season lightly with salt and pepper. Roast until the breasts are cooked through and the skin is crisp and golden, 35 to 40 minutes. Remove from the oven and let the breasts rest for 5 minutes before serving. Using a sharp, clean knife, cut each breast into ½-inch-thick slices. Shingle the slices on a plate, drizzle with olive oil, and serve. (If you like, you can thicken the pan juices into a gravy by further reducing them on the stovetop or by whisking in a small amount of flour.)

# Chicken Breasts Stuffed with Spring Pea Pesto and Fresh Mozzarella Risotto

## PETTO DI POLLO RIPIENE CON RISO AI PESTO DI PISELLI E FIOR DI LATTE

Derived from the Neapolitan term *mozzare*, which means "to cut off," mozzarella has been a staple in Italy since the 1500s. Initially limited to cheese made from Italian water buffalo milk, the mozzarella category eventually broadened to include cheese made from fresh cow's milk. Fresh, soft, cow's milk mozzarella stored in brine has really come into its own in recent years. While Italians have long loved this mild cheese, which is best consumed right after it's made, diners outside Italy were more familiar with firm, packaged, low-moisture mozzarella varieties commonly used to make pizza. In this recipe, fresh cow's milk mozzarella is the perfect back-drop in a risotto filling with the bright color and textural "pop" of fresh green peas. If fresh peas are unavailable, best-quality frozen, thawed peas may be substituted. MAKES 8 SERVINGS

**WINE PAIRING:** Verdicchio dei Castelli di Jesi has the lovely taste of fresh peapods and lemon zest. Pair a young, high-acid Verdicchio with this dish to highlight the bright, spring flavors and to keep the palate fresh between bites.

2⅓ cups shelled fresh garden peas (English) or best-quality frozen peas, thawed

**FOR THE PEA PESTO**

Finely grated zest of 1 lemon

½ cup extra virgin olive oil

½ teaspoon finely ground sea salt

½ teaspoon finely ground white pepper

**FOR THE RISOTTO**

2 tablespoons extra virgin olive oil

1 slice medium white or yellow onion, finely chopped to make ¼ cup

½ teaspoon finely ground sea salt, plus more as needed

½ teaspoon finely ground white pepper, plus more as needed

1¼ cups Arborio or Carnaroli *superfino* rice

⅓ cup dry Italian white wine

2 tablespoons cold unsalted butter

10 ounces *fior di latte* (fresh cow's milk mozzarella in liquid; see page 20) drained and chopped to make 1½ cups

**FOR THE CHICKEN**

8 boneless, skin-on chicken breasts

Extra virgin olive oil for brushing and drizzling

Finely ground sea salt and white pepper

In a medium heavy-gauge saucepan or pot over medium heat, bring 4½ cups water to a boil. Reduce the heat to maintain a slow simmer. Place the peas in a mesh strainer; immerse in the simmering water to blanch for 1 minute; transfer to a bowl. Leave the water at a very low simmer.

**MAKE THE PEA PESTO:** Place 2 cups of the blanched peas in the work bowl of a food processor with the lemon zest, olive oil, salt, and pepper. Pulse until pureed into a creamy paste. Transfer to a bowl and refrigerate until ready to use. Reserve the remaining ⅓ cup peas for the risotto.

**MAKE THE RISOTTO:** In a medium heavy-gauge sauté pan or skillet at least 3 inches deep (with lid handy), combine the olive oil and onion over low heat. Cook, stirring frequently, until the onion is soft but not browned. It's okay to add 2 tablespoons water to help the onion soften without browning, just be sure the water has evaporated before moving to the next step. Season with salt and pepper. Add the rice and stir until the kernels are well coated, about 2 minutes. Add the wine and stir until it has completely evaporated. Ladle ½ cup of the simmering water into the rice and stir until reduced by two thirds. Add another ladleful of water and again stir until reduced by two thirds. Repeat until most of the water has been absorbed by the rice. The rice will be tender, but not mushy, with a creamy consistency. (You may have as much as a cup of water left unused.) It should take about 14 minutes from the time you began adding the water to the rice to reach this stage. Remove the risotto from the heat. Stir in the pea pesto and the remaining ⅓ cup blanched peas. Cover for 1 minute. Remove the lid and stir in the butter and cheese until creamy. Cover and set aside.

**MAKE THE CHICKEN:** Preheat the oven to 375°F. Arrange the chicken breasts, skin side down, on a clean work surface. Each breast will have two lobes. If the breasts are exceptionally large: Separate the breasts into two pieces where the two lobes are joined. Using a sharp knife, slice each breast lobe across the grain, horizontally through the center of the lobe, cutting almost all the way through and folding the top flap back. Divide the risotto, spooning it onto the bottom half of each lob. Cover with the top flap of chicken. If the breasts are small: Position each breast with its two lobes side by side. Divide the risotto, spooning it onto just one lobe for each breast. Gently fold the other lobe over the lobe with risotto and completely cover the rice filling. Using sharp kitchen shears, trim and neaten any rough edges.

   Brush a large, rimmed sheet pan with olive oil. Arrange the filled breasts on the tray. Season lightly with salt and pepper. Roast until the breasts are cooked through and the skin is crisp and golden, 30 to 45 minutes. Remove the tray from the oven and let rest for 5 minutes. Using a sharp knife, cut each breast into ½-inch-tick slices. Shingle the slices on a plate, drizzle with olive oil, and serve. (If you like, you can thicken the pan juices into a gravy by further reducing them on the stovetop or by whisking in a small amount of flour.)

# Braised Turkey Rolls with Chestnut Risotto, Pancetta, and Sage

## BRACIOLE DI TACCHINO RIPIENE CON RISO DI CASTAGNE, PANCETTA E SALVIA

I have fond memories of chestnuts. As a child, I remember my father bringing home 25-kilo bags of the nuts to be roasted, cracked, and eaten. As an adult in Italy, my early November visits were rife with chestnut moments. We roasted the nuts over the open fire, in a special long-handled pan, and then tossed them on the table, where we cracked and ate them out of the natural shell. Given their fall seasonality and mild, smooth flavor, it seemed only natural to match them with turkey, risotto, pancetta, and sage in these *braciole*, which taste very much like the best components of a Thanksgiving dinner all rolled into one. If you have any trouble finding whole raw chestnuts, look for them already roasted and sold in glass jars at specialty markets.  MAKES 6 TO 8 SERVINGS

**WINE PAIRING:** With so much rich, savory flavor in this dish, a *riserva* Chianti is the right pick here. The Sangiovese in Chianti provides fountains of sour cherries and dried herbs to make the autumn flavors in the dish blossom, while the bit of extra age required for a *riserva* bottling helps wrangle the sharp edges in the wine, softening the tannins and acid.

**FOR THE RISOTTO**

4½ cups vegetable broth (page 66)

2 tablespoons extra virgin olive oil

2 slices medium white or yellow onion, finely chopped to make ⅓ cup

½ stalk celery, chopped to make ½ cup

Finely ground sea salt and white pepper

1¼ cups Arborio or Carnaroli *superfino* rice

⅓ cup dry Italian white wine

1½ ounces Parmigiano Reggiano or Grana Padano, finely grated to make about ¾ cup

12 chestnuts, cooked and shelled, or use jarred, roughly chopped to make 1⅓ cups

**FOR THE *BRACIOLE* AND VEGETABLES**

12 to 16 slices boneless, skinless turkey breast (2 to 3 ounces each), pounded to a ¼-inch thickness

12 to 16 paper-thin slices pancetta

24 to 32 fresh sage leaves

16 pieces of thin butcher's or baker's twine (2 to 3 feet each; see note, page 204)

3 tablespoons extra virgin olive oil

2 slices medium white or yellow onion, finely chopped to make ⅓ cup

1 small carrot, finely chopped to make ½ cup

½ medium fennel bulb, finely chopped to make ½ cup

⅓ cup dry Italian white wine

1½ cups chicken broth (page 101)

**MAKE THE RISOTTO:** In a medium heavy-gauge saucepan or pot over medium heat, bring the vegetable broth to a boil. Reduce the heat to maintain a slow simmer.

In a medium heavy-gauge sauté pan or skillet at least 3 inches deep (with lid handy), warm the olive oil, onion, and celery over low heat. Cook, stirring frequently, until the onion is soft and translucent but not browned. It's okay to add 2 tablespoons water to help the onion soften without browning, just be sure the water has evaporated before moving to the next step. Season with salt and pepper. Add the rice and stir for 2 minutes, until the kernels are well coated. Pour in the white wine and stir until it has completely evaporated. Ladle ½ cup of the simmering broth into the rice and stir until the broth has reduced by two thirds. Add another ladleful and stir again until the broth has reduced by two thirds. Repeat until most of the broth has been absorbed into the rice, which should take about 14 minutes from the time you begin adding the broth to the rice. At this point, the rice should be tender, but not mushy, with a creamy consistency. (You may have as much as a cup of broth left unused.)

Remove the risotto from the stovetop and cover for 2 minutes. Remove the lid and add the cheese and chestnuts, stirring until creamy. Season with salt and pepper.

**MAKE THE *BRACIOLE* AND VEGETABLES:** Spread out a sheet of parchment paper on a clean work surface. Arrange the turkey slices, with the widest edges facing you, on top of the parchment paper. Place a slice of pancetta and a couple sage leaves on each slice of turkey. Scoop a rounded tablespoonful of risotto onto each slice at the widest end. Carefully tucking and folding, roll toward the narrow end of the slice until you finish with a little bundle. Grab a length of twine in one hand and wrap and spiral the twine around the bundle, holding the bundle with your other hand to ensure the filling is enclosed as much as possible and knotting the loose ends of twine when finished. Repeat with the remaining turkey slices and filling.

Preheat the oven to 350°F. Heat the olive oil in a heavy-gauge oven-safe skillet with lid or large Dutch oven over medium heat. Place the *braciole* in the pan and sear on all sides. Reduce the heat to low and add the onion, carrot, and fennel. Pour in the white wine and reduce the wine by half. Add the chicken broth. Cover the skillet or Dutch oven and roast for 45 minutes. Let cool slightly. Remove the twine from the bundles and discard. Slice each bundle into several circular pieces and fan out on serving plates. Top each with the vegetables and drizzle with the pan juices. (If you like, you can thicken the pan juices into a gravy by further reducing them on the stovetop or by whisking in a small amount of flour.)

# CHAPTER SIX

# RICE DESSERTS

DOLCI

**Meant to softly finish the meal** and encourage lingering a little longer, the Italian dessert course is a lovely thing. I grew up in an Italian family of simple means, so our desserts usually kept the focus on the freshest seasonal ingredients, perfectly flavored on their own. In summer, there might be fragrant melons, peaches, pears, or plums still warm with sun; or maybe fresh figs served with a little Parmigiano cheese. Any cookies or baked treats were lightly spiced and not too sweet. When I visited family in Italy, it was the same—except, of course, on holidays or feast days. Perhaps an echo of the elaborate confections of Roman banquets, and the fanciful Venetian creations of the Renaissance, Italy's most famous desserts are linked with holidays. Sicily's cannoli were originally a Carnevale treat. Siena's *panforte* ("strong bread") started as a Christmas bread made by nuns in medieval times, and St. Joseph's Day has become synonymous with zeppole, Italy's diminutive filled doughnuts. Each of these has its own story and legend and place on the Italian feast table alongside humbler recipes.

But some of Italy's most ancient dessert recipes included rice. Food history scholars tell us that rice was first used for medicinal purposes and then began to appear in dessert preparations. To me, rice pudding seems the perfect melding of the ancient Roman tummy-soothing prescriptions and aromatic spice. While many Italian rice puddings include both sweet spices (cinnamon, vanilla bean, allspice) and savory ones (bay leaf, juniper berries), taste buds outside the country gravitate to the simpler warm rice pudding with plumped raisins and freshly grated nutmeg. I have found that desserts are a good place to showcase some of the lesser-known Italian rices. Rosso Integrale, for example, a very fragrant whole-grain brown rice, lends incomparable texture and flavor to the Rice Pudding with Peach Compote in this chapter. And for the Rice Cream with Cantaloupe, I love using Baldo rice.

This chapter would not be complete without the inclusion of rice treats like those served from sweets shops and street vendors in Italy, such as Strawberry Rice Gelato and rice crepes. These are as addictive as they are easy to make.

**PREVIOUS SPREAD AND OPPOSITE:** No-Bake Sweet Rice "Soufflé" with Raspberry Sauce (see recipe, pages 216–217)

## Wine: Sweets for the Sweet

While you might not drink sweet wines as a dinner pairing, with dessert, they're not only exceptional but necessary. Pairing a wine *without* sweetness with a dessert only serves to highlight the contrasting notes in the wine: bitter tannin and sour acids.

Champagne is a dreadful dessert pairing, coming across more like vinegar than sparkles. Cabernet with chocolate? A horrible idea; each makes the other taste bitter and harsh and ruins the entire experience.

Contrastingly, a sweet (or sweet-*ish* wine) tastes *less* sweet and more interesting when appropriately paired with a well-made dessert. I've taught many wine classes where I've served a very sweet wine by itself, and watched the students screw up their faces and refuse to enjoy it. However, encountering the same wine paired with an appropriate dessert later, they can't believe it's the same wine.

So break out those Brachetto and dust off the Vin Santo—it's time for dessert!

—TORRENCE O'HAIRE

# No-Bake Sweet Rice "Soufflé" with Raspberry Sauce

## NON INFORNARE SOUFFLÉ DOLCE DI RISO CON SALSA DI LAMPONI

Soufflés (savory or sweet) are dramatic. Sometimes the drama of hot-from-the-oven soufflés can turn into tragedy, as they often deflate before your eyes. This refrigerated soufflé will not disenchant: It is made in advance, comes to the table cresting above its soufflé dish (it will not sink), and is garnished with fresh raspberries and served with a fresh raspberry sauce.

MAKES 8 TO 10 SERVINGS • PHOTOGRAPH ON PAGES 212 AND 215

**WINE PAIRING:** This calls for a classic Italian dessert wine: Moscato d'Asti. Be sure to choose something of notable quality, from the DOCG, and not bargain-priced. The nicest ones have a lip-smacking orange flower–flavored fizz and a nice balance of sugar and acid.

### FOR THE RICE AND GELATIN:

3½ cups whole milk

½ cup sugar

½ cup Carnaroli *superfino* rice

Thinly grated zest of 2 lemons

2½ teaspoons (7 grams) or
1 envelope unflavored gelatin

½ cup cool water

### FOR THE CUSTARD:

½ cup whole milk

2 egg yolks

3 tablespoons sugar

1 tablespoon rice flour,
preferably Bob's Red Mill Sweet
White Rice Flour

2 pasteurized egg whites
at room temperature,
or equivalent prepared
pasteurized liquid egg whites
(see note)

1⅔ cups heavy cream

### FOR THE RASPBERRY SAUCE:

8 ounces fresh raspberries

⅔ cup confectioners' sugar

3 tablespoons grappa

8 ounces fresh raspberries for
garnish

**MAKE THE RICE:** In a medium heavy-gauge saucepan or pot, add the milk, sugar, rice, and lemon zest. Bring to a boil over medium heat, stirring frequently. Lower the heat to medium-low to maintain a simmer and cook, stirring frequently, until the rice kernels are soft and tender, about 20 minutes from the time the rice begins to simmer. The mixture will still be loose and a bit liquid.

While the rice is cooking, sprinkle the gelatin over the water and stir to combine. Set the gelatin aside to soften. When the rice is fully cooked, remove it from the heat and stir in the softened gelatin until melted and incorporated into the rice. Remove from the heat and allow it to sit for two minutes. Transfer the mixture to a very large stainless steel bowl.

**MAKE THE CUSTARD:** In a medium heavy-gauge saucepan or pot, heat 4 cups water to boiling. In a stainless steel bowl, or smaller pot that can rest snugly on the top of the pot of boiling water, without touching the water, whisk the milk, egg yolks, one tablespoon of the sugar, and the rice flour until smooth. Place the bowl or pot over the simmering water and whisk the mixture until it thickens into a custard, about 2 minutes. Transfer the custard to the cooked rice-gelatin mixture. Stir well. Prepare an ice-water bath in your sink and set the bowl in it.

In a medium bowl, or the bowl of a stand mixer, whip the egg whites with the remaining 2 tablespoons sugar into stiff peaks. In a second bowl, whip the heavy cream.

Carefully fold the whipped eggs whites and whipped cream into the rice-custard mixture while the bowl sits in the ice-water bath. Allow to cool for an additional 10 minutes.

Using heavy brown or white uncoated butcher paper, cut a strip long enough to wrap around the outside of an 8½-inch-diameter, 3¼-inch-deep soufflé dish. Tape the collar securely around the upper lip of the dish. (Note: Tape won't stick to parchment paper.) Fill the dish with the rice soufflé mixture, piling it as high as the collar will allow. Refrigerate overnight, or for at least 8 hours. (Any excess can be chilled in a bowl.)

**MAKE THE RASPBERRY SAUCE:** Puree the raspberries, the confectioner's sugar, and the grappa in a blender. Strain through a very fine-mesh sieve into a container. Cover and refrigerate.

When ready to serve the soufflé, remove the paper collar. Decorate the top with the fresh raspberries. Place the raspberry sauce in a small pitcher or serving bowl. Spoon the soufflé into individual bowls and drizzle with the sauce.

**NOTE:** Since the egg whites used in this dessert are uncooked, choose food-safe pasteurized eggs or pasteurized liquid egg whites sold in cartons.

# Rice Fritters with Apples

**FRITTELLE DI RISO CON LE MELE**

Sweet fried morsels sold from street vendors—including those made with rice—are common throughout Italy. I first enjoyed fritters like these when I was a young culinary student. I like this rice flour batter for its lightness and delicate texture. Cooking the "dough" before adding fresh eggs to smooth the batter removes any "raw" flavor or chalky/graininess, making this one of the tastiest gluten-free sweet recipes I've encountered. **MAKES 96 FRITTERS; SERVES 8 TO 10**

**WINE PAIRING:** A demi-sec Prosecco has enough sweetness for this dessert and enough acid for the fried-food factor, bubbles to scrub the palate clean between bites, and best of all? A fresh-apple flavor profile. Zonin makes an affordable, tasty demi-sec—try that one.

6 Granny Smith apples, peeled, cored, and cut into sixteen ⅛-inch slices each

Juice of 2 lemons

1½ cups (2½ sticks) unsalted butter

¼ teaspoon finely ground sea salt

½ cup sugar

4 cups sweet rice flour (see page 22)

16 large eggs

4 to 5 cups high-smoke-point oil, for frying (safflower, rice bran, soybean, or canola)

**FOR THE CINNAMON-SUGAR GARNISH**

½ cup sugar

2 tablespoons ground cinnamon

In a glass or other nonreactive bowl, combine the apple slices, lemon juice, and 3 cups water, or enough to cover the apples. Soak for at least 1 hour or up to 3 hours.

In a medium heavy-gauge saucepan or pot, melt the butter over medium heat. Stir in the salt, sugar, and 4 cups water and heat to boiling. Remove the pot from the stovetop and stir in the rice flour. Return the pan to the stovetop and continue to stir over medium heat for 2 minutes. The mixture will ball up and take on the consistency of stiff mashed potatoes.

Place the dough in the work bowl of a stand mixer fitted with a balloon whip; add the eggs, one at a time, and mix at medium speed until all the eggs are incorporated and the batter is thick and smooth.

To make the fritters, pour the oil into a small deep fryer or another heavy-gauge pot, ensuring that the oil reaches no higher than 3 inches from the top of the pot. Preheat the oil to 350°F.

Remove the apple slices from the lemon water and pat them dry with paper toweling. Fully immerse each apple slice, one at a time, into the batter. Working in batches to avoid crowding the pot, drop three or four battered apple slices into the oil. Fry until puffed and golden, about 3 minutes per batch. Transfer the fritters to paper toweling to drain.

**MAKE THE GARNISH:** In a small bowl, whisk together the sugar and cinnamon; sprinkle the cinnamon-sugar over the hot fritters. Serve immediately.

# Rice Crespelle with Almonds and Organic Honey

**CRESPELLE DI RISO AL MANDORLE E MIELE BIOLOGICA**

These are addictive: You've been warned. Called *crespelle* in Italy, these gluten-free crepes are delicious for breakfast, brunch, or dessert. In fact, the batter can be swapped in to make a beautiful gluten-free version of your favorite crepe or blintz recipes. The batter is smooth and light and the finished crepes have just the right bit of chew and texture. In Italy, people like to top these with honey and almonds, but they're just as good buttered and sugared into beautiful stacks, or folded around a slathering of Nutella.  MAKES 12 *CRESPELLE*; SERVES 6 TO 8

**WINE PAIRING:** Two choices here: For honey and almond crêpes, head to Friuli for a Verduzzo Dolce—a semi-sweet wine made from the indigenous Verduzzo grape with soft flavors of peach, toasted almond, and honey. For Nutella crêpes: Marsala is absolutely delicious, with its rich flavors of raisin, coffee, walnut, and orange peel.

3 large eggs

4 tablespoons (½ stick) unsalted butter, melted

2 cups whole milk

Finely ground sea salt

2 cups sweet rice flour (see page 22)

**OPTIONAL TOPPINGS**

½ cup melted butter and sugar for sprinkling

1 cup Nutella

1 cup sliced almonds, toasted

1 cup organic honey

Confectioners' sugar, as needed

In a medium mixing bowl, whisk together the eggs, 2 tablespoons of the melted butter, the milk, and salt. Gradually whisk in the rice flour to make a smooth batter.

Place a crepe pan or small nonstick skillet over medium heat. Drizzle a bit of melted butter into the pan. Gently ladle just under ⅓ cup of the batter onto the pan. Tilt and turn the pan until the bottom of the pan has a thin, even coating of the batter. Cook the *crespelle* until lightly golden and lacy at the edges. Flip to finish cooking. Transfer to a serving platter and cover loosely with a sheet of foil to keep warm. Repeat until all the batter has been used.

Here you can play a bit with toppings. Simply drizzle *crespelles* with melted butter and sprinkle with sugar, or spread them with Nutella. Or, combine nuts and honey in a stainless-steel bowl and heat over a double boiler. (Alternatively, combine the nuts and honey in a microwave-safe bowl and warm for 30 seconds to make a topping). For a fancy look, dust *crespelle* with confectioners' sugar before serving.

# Rice Pudding with Peaches

### BUDINO DI RISO CON COMPOSTA DI PESCHE

The sweet-sour (*agrodolce*) combination of vinegar with fruit and sugar is an Italian classic. The mascarpone-enriched custard and the inclusion of both sweet and savory spices in the rice are, too. Because the traditional recipe for this beautiful dolce is almost baroque, with challenging preparation steps and methods, I simplified it considerably. The one thing that could not change was the rice: *Superfino* Rosso Integrale is a very aromatic fragrant whole-grain brown rice that is milled in such a way as to leave a part of its husk intact. When cooked it has an incomparable texture and flavor. You can source this rice, and Italian white wine vinegar, online or from purveyors of specialty Italian food products. MAKES 8 SERVINGS

**WINE PAIRING:** A Moscato Dolce from the Piedmont, with its balanced acid and sugar and a boatload of perfumy peach notes, is a great way to show off this peachy dessert.

### FOR THE RICE PUDDING

¼ cup plus 1 tablespoon granulated sugar

1 cup plus 2 tablespoons Rosso Integrale *superfino* rice

½ vanilla bean, seeds scraped, pod included

½ teaspoon ground allspice

1 bay leaf, preferably fresh

### FOR THE PEACH COMPOTE

1 cup granulated sugar

½ cup freshly squeezed orange juice

¼ cup Italian white wine vinegar

Finely grated zest of 1 lemon

6 ripe peaches, halved and pitted (see notes)

### FOR THE CUSTARD

3 egg yolks, beaten

3 tablespoons sugar

2 tablespoons dry Italian white wine

4 ounces mascarpone cheese (½ cup)

### FOR FINISHING

1 envelope unflavored granulated gelatin (2½ teaspoons), softened in ½ cup cool water

3 pasteurized egg whites, or equivalent of pasteurized liquid egg-white product, at room temperature (see notes)

1 tablespoon granulated sugar

¼ cup confectioners' sugar

1 teaspoon vanilla extract

**MAKE THE RICE FOR THE PUDDING:** In a medium heavy-gauge saucepan or pot, combine 4¼ cups water, the granulated sugar, rice, vanilla bean seeds and pod, allspice, and bay leaf. Heat to boiling over medium heat, stirring frequently. Lower the heat, cover the pot, and simmer until the rice is cooked through and tender, about 55 minutes. If too much liquid remains, remove the lid and cook, stirring, until the rice is the texture of thick soup. Remove the pot from the heat. Cover to keep hot and set aside.

**MAKE THE PEACH COMPOTE:** While the rice is cooking, in another medium heavy-gauge saucepan or pot, combine the granulated sugar, orange juice, vinegar, and lemon zest. Heat

to boiling, stirring until the sugar dissolves. Add the peach halves, lower the heat, and simmer, turning once, until the peaches are tender, about 10 minutes. Remove from the heat. Using a slotted spoon, transfer the peach halves to a large dish, reserving the poaching liquid. When cool enough to handle, remove and discard the skins. Return the peeled peach halves to the poaching liquid; transfer to a nonreactive container with a lid, and refrigerate.

**MAKE THE CUSTARD:** In a small saucepan or pot, heat 3 cups water to boiling over medium heat; reduce the heat to maintain a gentle simmer. In a medium stainless-steel bowl, whisk the egg yolks with 2 tablespoons of the sugar and the wine until smooth. Place the bowl over the pot of simmering water. It should fit snugly but the water should not touch the bottom of the bowl. Whisk constantly until the mixture resembles thick cream. Do not overcook or the eggs will curdle. Transfer the bowl of custard to your work surface; whisk in the mascarpone until the custard is smooth and creamy. Set aside.

**FINISH THE PUDDING:** Remove and discard the vanilla bean pod and bay leaf from the hot rice. Add the softened gelatin, stirring until it is completely dissolved in the rice, about 2 minutes. Fold in the reserved custard-mascarpone mixture. Transfer the rice custard to a large bowl and set aside.

In the work bowl of a stand mixer fitted with a whisk attachment, combine the egg whites with the sugars, and the vanilla extract. Whip until firm peaks form. Set the meringue aside.

Prepare an ice-water bath in the sink. Place the bowl with the rice custard into the ice-water bath and stir until cooled to room temperature. Gently fold in the meringue. Return the bowl to the ice-water bath for an additional 30 minutes to completely chill the custard. Transfer the pudding to a lidded container, or individual ramekins, and refrigerate.

To serve, top the pudding with the peach halves and drizzle with some of the poaching syrup.

**NOTES:**

• To halve the peaches, cut down to the pit lengthwise using a sharp knife. Twist the halves in opposite directions. The peach should separate into two halves, with the pit left in one of them. If the peaches are not fully ripe and the pits don't come out easily, gently cut them away with the tip of a sharp knife.

• When using egg whites that will not be cooked in a recipe, it is necessary to use pasteurized food-safe egg whites. These are available whole or as a liquid. To get full volume, be sure pasteurized egg whites are at room temperature before whipping.

# Sweet Rice Tart with Rum-Rosemary Apricots

## TORTA DI RISO DOLCE CON ALBICOCCHE RUM-ROSMARINO

Renaissance in its leanings, this winter-warming baked dessert is enriched with almonds, coconut, apricot, rosemary, and rum, and topped with apricots poached in rosemary syrup.

**MAKES 8 SERVINGS**

**WINE PAIRING:** Sicily makes a delicious style of wine called Passito, usually from Moscato d'Alexandria grapes. Made by slowly drying the grapes in the hot Sicilian air, Passito-style wines are rich and intense, with deep apricot notes and an earthy, floral complexity, like a field in summer. Perfect here.

**FOR THE RUM-MARINATED APRICOTS**

1 cup dried apricots, chopped

¼ cup dark rum

**FOR THE RICE**

4½ cups whole milk

½ vanilla bean, seeds scraped, pod included

1¼ cups Carnaroli *superfino* rice

**FOR THE ALMOND–COCONUT MACAROON** *CONDIMENTI*

4 large eggs

½ cup sugar

½ cup thinly sliced almonds, toasted

4 store-bought coconut macaroons, finely chopped to make ⅔ cup, or ⅔ cup sweetened shredded coconut, firmly packed

¼ teaspoon finely ground sea salt

**FOR ASSEMBLY**

Butter, for greasing

**FOR THE POACHED APRICOTS IN ROSEMARY SYRUP**

1 cup sugar

3 sprigs rosemary, needles only, to make 3 tablespoons

16 dried apricots, cut in half lengthwise

½ cup dark rum

**MAKE THE RUM-MARINATED APRICOTS:** In a small nonreactive bowl, combine the chopped apricots and the rum. Cover and microwave for 1 minute; set aside.

**MAKE THE RICE:** In a medium heavy-gauge saucepan or pot, combine the milk, vanilla bean seeds and pod, and the rice. Stir once or twice to combine. Bring the milk to a boil over medium heat. Quickly lower the heat to maintain a gentle simmer, stirring occasionally to prevent sticking. Remove and discard any milk protein "skin" that collects on the surface of the cooking liquid. Continue cooking until the rice is soft and creamy and almost all the milk has been absorbed, about 25 minutes. Remove the vanilla-bean pod. Cool the rice to room temperature, stirring occasionally.

**MAKE THE ALMOND–COCONUT MACAROON** *CONDIMENTI***:** In the work bowl of a stand mixer fitted with the whisk attachment, whisk the eggs and sugar until light and lemon colored. Whisk in the toasted almonds, chopped macaroons, and salt, beating on low speed until

completely incorporated. Pat the rum-marinated apricots dry with a paper towel; reserve the rum. Stir these into the egg-nut mixture. Add the cooled rice; mix at low speed for 1 minute to incorporate.

**ASSEMBLE AND BAKE THE TART:** Preheat the oven to 350°F. Grease the inside of a 9-inch springform pan with a removeable bottom with butter or nonstick cooking spray. Line the bottom of the pan with parchment paper cut to fit. Wrap the bottom of the pan with foil. Fill the pan with the rice pudding mixture, smoothing the top with a spatula. Set on a sheet pan. Bake until a cake tester or toothpick inserted in the center of the tart comes out clean, 40 to 55 minutes. Remove from the oven to a cooling rack.

**MAKE THE POACHED APRICOTS IN ROSEMARY SYRUP:** In a small heavy-gauge saucepan or pot over medium heat, combine 1½ cups water, the sugar, and the rosemary. Stir occasionally until the sugar dissolves. Add the halved apricots and the ½ cup rum. Reduce the heat to simmer gently, uncovered, for 30 minutes. Remove the pan from heat; stir in the rum reserved from marinating the chopped apricots. Cover the pot and set aside for 15 minutes.

Using a slotted spoon, transfer the poached apricot halves from the rosemary syrup to a plate lined with paper towels. Allow to drain. Brush the top of the baked tart with a small amount of the rosemary syrup. Arrange the drained apricot halves on top of the baked tart. Let cool for 1 hour.

To serve, unmold the tart by carefully running a thin spatula around the edge of the pan. Release the latch on the springform mold and remove the ring. Using a broad spatula, loosen the tart bottom (beneath the parchment paper) and carefully slide the tart onto a cake plate or platter. Slice into 8 portions and serve.

# Caramel Rice Pudding with Cantaloupe

### BUDINO DI RISO AL CARAMELLO CON MELONE

With the flavor of Mexican flan and texture of a nice pumpkin pie filling, this caramel rice pudding made with Baldo rice is a treat. MAKES 12 SERVINGS

**WINE PAIRING:** Passito di Pantelleria is a dessert wine made in southern Sicily from raisinated grapes. Its musky, nutty notes will do wonders to interact with the savory and bitter notes in the caramel and melon.

**FOR THE CARAMEL SAUCE**

1¼ cups sugar

¼ cup tepid water

1¼ cups heavy cream

4 large eggs, plus 4 egg yolks

**FOR THE RICE**

⅔ cup heavy cream

½ cup Baldo *superfino* rice

½ vanilla bean, seeds scraped, pod reserved for another use

½ teaspoon finely ground sea salt

8 cups boiling water, or as needed

2 cantaloupe, seeds and rinds removed, sliced

**MAKE THE CARAMEL SAUCE:** Prepare an ice-water bath in your sink. In a medium heavy-gauge saucepan or pot over medium heat, stir the sugar and tepid water until simmering. Cook, stirring, until the mixture is honey colored. Remove from the heat. Let rest for 2 minutes. Being extremely careful not to splash the hot sugar, whisk in the cream, which will bubble up and thicken. Keep whisking to ensure any caramelized sugar clumps dissolve. If necessary, return the pot to very low heat and keep whisking to melt any stubborn clumps. Once the caramel is smooth, transfer the pot to the ice-water bath and let cool. While the caramel cools, whip the eggs and yolks together in the work bowl of a stand mixer fitted with the whisk attachment until tripled in volume, thick, and foamy. Gradually add the cooled caramel to the eggs, whisking to incorporate. Set aside while you make the rice.

**MAKE THE RICE:** In a small heavy-gauge saucepan or pot, combine 1½ cups water, the cream, rice, and vanilla bean seeds. Heat to boiling over medium heat, stirring frequently. Lower the heat to medium-low to maintain a steady simmer and cook, stirring frequently, until the rice is tender and almost all of the liquid has been absorbed, 15 to 17 minutes.

Preheat the oven to 350°F. Transfer the rice mixture to a large stainless-steel bowl and place in the ice-water bath to cool. When cool, gently fold in the caramel sauce.

Spoon the pudding into a 2-quart baking dish or soufflé dish. Cover with aluminum foil. Place a roasting pan on the center rack and put the pudding into the center of the roasting pan. Carefully pour boiling water into the roasting pan until it comes at least 2 inches up the sides of the baking dish. Bake until the pudding is cooked through and a knife inserted in the center comes out almost clean, 75 to 90 minutes. Take the baking dish out of the hot water bath, and set it on a cooling rack. Once cool, refrigerate, covered, overnight. Scoop the pudding into individual serving dishes and garnish with the melon slices.

# Strawberry Rice Cream

## GELATO DI RISO ALLA FRAGOLA

Rice gelato is popular in Italy. Frozen rice bits add a pleasing textural pop to the creamy fresh strawberry custard. Known as *originario* due to its long-time presence in Italy, Balilla has a small, soft, round grain, making it a favorite "stir-in" rice. Balilla rice can be purchased online or from purveyors of specialty Italian food products. MAKES 8 SERVINGS

**WINE PAIRING:** Simple, clean flavors require a simple, clean wine pairing—even in desserts. Pop a bottle of "dry" Prosecco. Simple, acacia-scented, and with a touch of sugar, it is a perfect foil for the ripe strawberries.

### FOR THE STRAWBERRY GELATO

⅓ cup sugar

1 pound strawberries, hulled and quartered

1¼ cups unsweetened rice milk

½ cup heavy cream

⅓ cup sugar

¼ cup balilla *originario* rice

### FOR THE STRAWBERRY COMPOTE

1 pound hulled strawberries, cut in half

⅓ cup sugar

**MAKE THE STRAWBERRY GELATO:** In a medium heavy-gauge saucepan or pot, combine the sugar and the quartered strawberries over medium heat. Partially crush the berries to release their juice. Cook, stirring, until the sugar dissolves. Reduce the heat to maintain a gentle simmer. Simmer, stirring frequently, for 5 minutes. Remove from the heat; transfer to a bowl and let cool to room temperature. Puree one half of the strawberry-sugar mixture, reserving the remainder in a bowl. Prepare an ice-water bath in your sink.

Clean the saucepan used to cook the strawberries and return it to the stovetop. Stir together the rice milk, cream, sugar, and rice over medium heat until the mixture comes to a boil. Immediately lower the heat, add the pureed strawberries, and simmer gently, stirring, until the rice forms a soft and creamy custard. This should take about 16 minutes from the time the rice milk begins to simmer. Remove the custard from the heat; stir in the reserved cooked quartered strawberries.

Place the saucepan in the ice-water bath, stirring to bring the custard to just below room temperature. Transfer the mixture to an ice cream maker and process according to the manufacturer's directions. Store the finished gelato, covered, in the freezer.

**MAKE THE STRAWBERRY COMPOTE:** In a medium heavy-gauge saucepan or pot, combine the halved strawberries and the sugar. Partially crush the berries to release some of their juice. Bring to a boil over medium heat. Immediately reduce the heat to maintain a gentle simmer. Simmer, stirring, for 5 minutes. Cool to room temperature. Refrigerate covered.

Spoon about 2 tablespoons of the chilled strawberry compote into 8 parfait glasses. Top each serving with a scoop of gelato. Serve.

# Chocolate Rice Pudding Cup

## COPPA DI BUDINO CON RISO DOLCE AL CIOCCOLATO

Made with three different chocolates and infused with spices and fresh vanilla bean, this dessert is a creamy chocolate rice dream. Serve it warm or cold. It is very popular at Quartino, where we make chocolate curls for the garnish. If creating the curls proves too challenging, simply grate the chocolate on the largest holes of a four-sided grater. MAKES 8 SERVINGS

**WINE PAIRING:** Chocolate makes a delicious pairing with a special dessert wine from the north: Brachetto d'Acqui, a low-alcohol sparkling wine with plenty of sweetness and acid and a huge raspberry-rose profile.

1 cup heavy cream

¼ cup sugar

⅔ cup Carnaroli *superfino* rice

1 bay leaf, preferably fresh

½ teaspoon ground allspice

½ vanilla bean pod, seeds scraped, pod included

4 ounces semisweet dark couverture or glazing chocolate, melted to make 1 cup

2 ounces semisweet dark baking chocolate, shaved into curls or finely grated (½ cup)

2 ounces white baking chocolate, shaved into curls or finely grated (½ cup)

In a heavy-gauge pot, combine 2 cups water, the cream, sugar, rice, bay leaf, allspice, and vanilla bean seeds and pod. Heat to a boil over medium heat, stirring occasionally. Reduce the heat to maintain a gentle simmer, cover the pot, and cook until the rice is tender, 20 to 22 minutes. Remove from the heat. Discard the vanilla bean pod and bay leaf.

Cool the rice to room temperature. Stir the melted couverture chocolate into the cooked rice. Divide the rice among eight dessert cups. Top each serving with the dark and white chocolates curls.

# Classic Rice Pudding with Raisins and Nutmeg

## BUDINO DI RISO CLASSICO CON UVA PASSA E LA NOCE MOSCATA

While rice puddings are typically served chilled in Italy, this version takes the classic American approach—it's served warm with plumped raisins, vanilla bean, and freshly grated nutmeg. The use of Acquerello Carnaroli rice in a milky egg-custard base ensures that this is the ultimate creamy rice pudding. I like to use freshly grated nutmeg rather than cinnamon because I think nutmeg is more fragrant. If you prefer cinnamon, try finishing the recipe with a sprinkling of Vietnamese cinnamon, which has good potency. MAKES 8 SERVINGS

**WINE PAIRING:** This simply begs for Vin Santo, the sweet wine from Tuscany made from raisins. Vin Santo has a gloriously spicy, perfumed nuttiness to it, but also enough acidity and alcoholic heat to provide counterpoint to the rich, soft pudding.

⅓ cup Thompson seedless raisins

⅓ cup golden raisins

⅓ cup boiling water

1¼ cups Carnaroli *superfino* rice, preferably Acquerello

½ vanilla bean, seeds scraped, pod included

½ teaspoon finely ground sea salt

1¼ cups whole milk

1 teaspoon unsalted butter

½ cup sugar

½ cup heavy cream, half-and-half, or milk (depending on how rich you like it)

2 extra-large eggs

Freshly grated nutmeg for garnish

Put the raisins in a small bowl. Pour the boiling water over the raisins and let them soak while the rice cooks.

In a medium heavy-gauge saucepan or pot, combine 3 cups water, the rice, vanilla bean seeds and pod, and salt. Bring to a boil over medium heat. Reduce the heat to medium-low to maintain a steady simmer and cook, stirring occasionally, for 20 minutes, or until the rice has absorbed the water. Stir in the milk, butter, and sugar and continue to cook, stirring frequently, until the rice mixture is thick and creamy.

Drain the plumped raisins, discarding the soaking liquid. Prepare an ice-water bath in your sink. Stir the drained raisins into the rice and cook for 2 minutes. Reduce the heat to very low. Whisk the cream and eggs together and add to the hot rice, stirring for 2 minutes until thick. Place the saucepan in the ice-water bath, remove the vanilla bean pod, and stir the rice pudding until just warmer than room temperature. Transfer the pudding to one large serving dish or individual dessert cups. Garnish with the nutmeg.

# Conversion Chart

*All conversions are approximate.*

## WEIGHT CONVERSIONS

| U.S. | METRIC |
| --- | --- |
| ½ ounce | 14 g |
| 1 ounce | 28 g |
| 1½ ounces | 43 g |
| 2 ounces | 57 g |
| 2½ ounces | 71 g |
| 3 ounces | 85 g |
| 3½ ounces | 100 g |
| 4 ounces | 113 g |
| 5 ounces | 142 g |
| 6 ounces | 170 g |
| 7 ounces | 200 g |
| 8 ounces | 227 g |
| 9 ounces | 255 g |
| 10 ounces | 284 g |
| 11 ounces | 312 g |
| 12 ounces | 340 g |
| 13 ounces | 368 g |
| 14 ounces | 400 g |
| 15 ounces | 425 g |
| 1 pound | 454 g |

## OVEN TEMPERATURES

| °F | GAS MARK | °C |
| --- | --- | --- |
| 250 | ½ | 120 |
| 275 | 1 | 140 |
| 300 | 2 | 150 |
| 325 | 3 | 165 |
| 350 | 4 | 180 |
| 375 | 5 | 190 |
| 400 | 6 | 200 |
| 425 | 7 | 220 |
| 450 | 8 | 230 |
| 475 | 9 | 240 |
| 500 | 10 | 260 |
| 550 | Broil | 290 |

## LIQUID CONVERSIONS

| U.S. | METRIC |
| --- | --- |
| 1 teaspoon | 5 ml |
| 1 tablespoon | 15 ml |
| 2 tablespoons | 30 ml |
| 3 tablespoons | 45 ml |
| ¼ cup | 60 ml |
| ⅓ cup | 75 ml |
| ⅓ cup plus 1 tablespoon | 90 ml |
| ⅓ cup plus 2 tablespoons | 100 ml |
| ½ cup | 120 ml |
| ⅔ cup | 150 ml |
| ¾ cup | 180 ml |
| ¾ cup plus 2 tablespoons | 200 ml |
| 1 cup | 240 ml |
| 1 cup plus 2 tablespoons | 275 ml |
| 1¼ cups | 300 ml |
| 1⅓ cups | 325 ml |
| 1½ cups | 350 ml |
| 1⅔ cups | 375 ml |
| 1¾ cups | 400 ml |
| 1¾ cups plus 2 tablespoons | 450 ml |
| 2 cups (1 pint) | 475 ml |
| 2½ cups | 600 ml |
| 3 cups | 725 ml |
| 4 cups (1 quart) | 945 ml |
| | (1,000 ml = 1 liter) |

# Index